CAMBRIDGE LIBRARY COLLECTION

Books of enduring scholarly value

History

The books reissued in this series include accounts of historical events and movements by eye-witnesses and contemporaries, as well as landmark studies that assembled significant source materials or developed new historiographical methods. The series includes work in social, political and military history on a wide range of periods and regions, giving modern scholars ready access to influential publications of the past.

The History of the Island of Van Diemen's Land, 1824 - 1835

Van Diemen's Land was the name originally given to the island known today as Tasmania, Australia, and it was settled by the British in 1803 as a penal colony. Before writing this history of the island, the author, Henry Saxelby Melville (1799–1873), a journalist, was imprisoned in 1835 for contempt of court over an article he wrote about an ongoing trial. While experiencing the prison system at first hand, he completed this work, which examines the history of Van Diemen's Land, focusing on the period from 1824 to 1835, and offers harsh criticism of the colonial administration and penal reforms enacted by lieutenant-governor Colonel George Arthur (1784–1854). Melville also includes an essay of his views on the island's system of prison discipline. He initially had the book printed on the island, but later smuggled copies to London where it could be freely published and read.

T0381748

Cambridge University Press has long been a pioneer in the reissuing of out-of-print titles from its own backlist, producing digital reprints of books that are still sought after by scholars and students but could not be reprinted economically using traditional technology. The Cambridge Library Collection extends this activity to a wider range of books which are still of importance to researchers and professionals, either for the source material they contain, or as landmarks in the history of their academic discipline.

Drawing from the world-renowned collections in the Cambridge University Library, and guided by the advice of experts in each subject area, Cambridge University Press is using state-of-the-art scanning machines in its own Printing House to capture the content of each book selected for inclusion. The files are processed to give a consistently clear, crisp image, and the books finished to the high quality standard for which the Press is recognised around the world. The latest print-on-demand technology ensures that the books will remain available indefinitely, and that orders for single or multiple copies can quickly be supplied.

The Cambridge Library Collection will bring back to life books of enduring scholarly value (including out-of-copyright works originally issued by other publishers) across a wide range of disciplines in the humanities and social sciences and in science and technology.

The History
of the Island of
Van Diemen's Land,
1824 -1835

Henry Saxelby Melville

CAMBRIDGE UNIVERSITY PRESS

Cambridge, New York, Melbourne, Madrid, Cape Town,
Singapore, São Paolo, Delhi, Tokyo, Mexico City

Published in the United States of America by Cambridge University Press, New York

www.cambridge.org
Information on this title: www.cambridge.org/9781108039208

© in this compilation Cambridge University Press 2011

This edition first published 1835
This digitally printed version 2011

ISBN 978-1-108-03920-8 Paperback

THE

HISTORY

OF

THE ISLAND

OF

VAN DIEMEN'S LAND,

FROM

THE YEAR 1824 TO 1835 INCLUSIVE.

TO WHICH IS ADDED,

A FEW WORDS ON PRISON DISCIPLINE.

LONDON :

PUBLISHED BY SMITH AND ELDER,

AND PRINTED BY HENRY MELVILLE, HOBART TOWN,
VAN DIEMEN'S LAND.

1835.

VAN DIEMEN'S LAND.

VAN DIEMEN'S LAND,

DURING THE ADMINISTRATION OF THE GOVERNMENT BY LIEUT.-GOVERNOR COLONEL GEORGE ARTHUR.

IT is a difficult and an ungracious task to record events which have occurred during the period individuals yet living have held authority; and the difficulty is encreased in the present instance, by those same individuals still possessing the ruling power. It is intended in the following pages to lay before the public an unbiassed account of the British Settlement of Van Diemen's Land, during the period of His Excellency Colonel George Arthur's administration—and as it is with the artist so is it with the historian—the painter may choose a subject for his pencil which may delight, or he may select another which may make the beholder shudder—it is for him to represent faithfully the subject to which his talent is directed, and so will it be the duty of the writer of the present brief history. He is fully aware that he may give offence; yet does he prefer that which all men ought to do—*truth*; nor shall it, for one instant, be imputed that power influences his pen, or that he is guilty of partiality. No writer has ever yet been exempt from the frailties of authorship, nor does the compiler presume to be more gifted than his fellow-colonists. He boldly disclaims the adoption of any spirit of party feeling, and it is his intention to proceed on the duty he has selected, alike spurning the frowns of power, as he will the applause of men hostile to Colonel Arthur and his Government—with this preface alone, the writer will proceed.

It will be necessary before commencing the intended

history, to offer a summary description of the state of the Colony prior to the time of Colonel Arthur's arrival, and this will be done as briefly as possible.

Van Diemen's Land, from the year 1803 to 1817, had been a penal settlement of the Sister Colony; it was at first a jail, and *nothing but a jail* on a large scale, and for many years no free emigrant was allowed to settle therein. All kinds of communication with the settlement were prohibited, save through the medium of the Government transports. But the continental war of Europe having terminated, the attention of the British people was directed to emigration; and favorable accounts having reached the Mother Country of this penal settlement, the British Government sought to promote emigration hither, and a few emigrants, in consequence of the flattering prospects held out, were tempted to visit this distant island. Partly owing to the favorable statements these first emigrants made of the capabilities of the Colony, but more especially owing to the stimulus held out by the Home Government, in a few years the tide of emigration set full on these shores. As might naturally be expected from the description of British characters who first peopled these deserts, the society, if it can be called society, was of a most vicious description; among the twice convicted felons in a jail, what else could be expected? It is not *every* man that is transported that *is a criminal*, neither does it follow that every convict *must be* a man of evil inclinations, Colonial experience has satisfactorily proved the contrary, were it even doubted, but by far the greater number of the *twice* convicted offenders by whom this settlement was first formed, must have been men of wicked propensities; therefore in a society composed of such materials, it is not to be wondered that crimes of the deepest die should be prevalent. As the population became more numerous, so for a time did crime become more frequent, and for the best of all reasons—that there were no effectual means of curbing vice or of punishing offenders. There was no power in the Island, by which crime could receive its proper reward, and every

man who had committed a serious offence against the
laws, had to be sent to Sydney, and there to be tried by
the judges. The expense, the delay, the difficulty, in
bringing offenders to justice were such, that nine times
out of ten, the law, or the inefficiency of evidence,
allowed the guilty to escape.

Those in command, during this period, were entirely
military, and enforced a military discipline ;* these
rulers, composed of themselves a little nest of social
friends, and never, by any chance, mixed with either
the emancipist or the prisoners they had in charge.†

---

* As a specimen of martial discipline, the following anecdote will
be found descriptive of the times. There were great complaints
made (by parties who had to deliver grain into the Government
stores of a township in the interior) of a certain storekeeper. To obtain
redress by law or by application to the Commandant was out of the
question, and in those times, redress was sought for such offences
by posting the party offending; and at the corner of Collins
and Elizabeth-streets, just opposite the shop of Messrs. Lloyd and
Lonsdale, stood the stump of a majestic gum tree ; it was on this
stump that placards of this description were generally posted. A
respectable free settler was, on this occasion, the person chosen to
administer this act of justice. He had the placard written, and was in
the act of pasting it up, when who should be watching his actions
but the very storekeeper whom he was thus "shewing up." Just at
this critical time, also, the military Commandant came by, and the
storekeeper complained to the officer. A kind of Court Martial sat
there and then, and in a few minutes a sentence of three hundred
lashes was pronounced as a verdict—the flogging was by the drum,
and when about two hundred lashes were inflicted on this free settler,
the Commandant, who was present, was told a vessel was in the
river from England—the military order of flogging was dispensed
with, and the last hundred lashes were got rid of by the flagellator
as fast as possible, and away went the Commandant, the officers,
flagellator and all, to hear—what news from England ?

† In this respect, this Colony was differently situated from that
of Sydney. Emigration to this quarter of the globe, commenced in
1820, and the free settlers, on arriving at Sydney, found a wealthy
and numerous body of Colonists, that had become free by emancipation—these emancipists held great power, and owing to the
absence of free emigrants, held official situations. This was not the
case with Van Diemen's Land ; this Colony being but a secondary
place of punishment, and an establishment only of a few years standing when the first emigrants arrived here, the term emancipist was
scarcely known, so few individuals were there of that class : it con-

As however the population became more dense by the
emigration of vast numbers of respectable settlers, and
as also in subsequent years it was the pleasure of the
British rulers to give the Colony a Court of Judicature
of its own—then did the state of society change. The
settlers of good character had influence over those formerly sunk in vice, and either a reformation took place,
or time, or other more summary efforts of the law, relieved the Island of vice in its most hideous form.

Colonel William Sorell was the predecessor of the
present Governor. He arrived here in 1817, and found
the country a wilderness, with here and there a little
knot of settlers of the description described. On his
landing, a class of marauders were infesting those settlers
who were earning their livelihood by the " sweat of their
brow"—these marauders, or bushrangers, were constantly
committing all kinds and descriptions of crimes, and
even most horrid murders were of common occurrence. The first measure of Colonel Sorell's administration, was to give a death-blow to these public despoilers, and by means of offering large rewards for the
death or capture of the several bands, he soon succeeded
in obtaining tranquility. When this grand end was
attained, Colonel Sorell sought to establish the Colony
on a sure and safe foundation for a flourishing settlement. On his arrival the population amounted to about

sequently followed that the free population were at once selected to
hold most of the official situations, and the difference which has so long
caused strife between the conflicting parties in New South Wales,
was thus happily prevented in Van Diemen's Land ; the emancipist
never formed a distinct class in this Colony, for when the days of
a man's tribulation are over, he ranks, as he ought to do, with the
free population—or of what value is the emancipation ? It might be
here observed, that the term " *emancipist*," is not distinctly understood. A man convicted and sentenced to a certain number of
years transportation, becomes free on the day the term of his sentence
expires, indeed he *then is as free as he was the day before his conviction*. The emancipist, on the contrary, is emancipated from his
bondage, before the time expires to which the law has bound him
prisoner. In modern times, however, the " free by servitude" and
the " emancipist," have been erroneously confounded as one and
the same.

two thousand souls, and dependent on themselves and the
Mother Country alone for every article of food, cloathing, or luxuries.* By his encouraging hand were the
capabilities of the island discovered—under his administration was the first bale of wool, and the first tun of
oil shipped to Great Britain ; and at the close of his Go-
vernorship, when he had resided only seven years in
the Colony, the exports of both the ports of Hobart
Town and Launceston to the Sister Colony and the Isle
of France† were large and valuable.   It is not to be understood that the exports of those days amounted to any
thing like in value to those of late years ; but considering
the age of the Colony, its population, and its limited
number of flocks, it may truly be said, that *in proportion* the exports of 1824 were more than equal to those
of 1834.   It was one of Colonel Sorell's chief efforts to
encourage to the utmost free emigration ; under his recommendation the most favorable prospects were held
out for emigrants to settle in the Colony.   He saw that
free people alone could check the customary depraved
habits of the Colonists, and promote industry and virtue.
He was unremitting in his exertions to encourage the
fisheries, and to introduce the finer description of wools ;
and almost every fresh settler that arrived in the Colony
during the latter period of his Government brought with
him stock of an improved breed.   The rate at which the
superior wools sold in the London market, was sufficient stimulus to the emigrant. As to the whale fishery,
in those times so abundant were the whales, that old settlers
will tell you they recollect the time when it was dangerous
to cross the water to Kangaroo Point, in the winter
months, so numerous were these fish ; but the hand of
man has either destroyed those which frequented the
river, or else driven them elsewhere, for now a whole
season may pass by, and scarcely half a dozen whales
are caught in the Derwent.

---

* A bottle of rum, in these days, passed current in the interior as
one pound currency.
† Live cattle were exported in large quantities to the Mauritius.

Under Colonel Sorell the imports of the Colony were merely necessaries of life; and the exports, the Commissariat expenditure, and the capital of fresh emigrants, entirely paid for every thing—truly the trade was exceedingly confined, but what could be expected from a young Colony? As might be imagined, a market so limited in its supply, fluctuated to an amazing extent: at times certain descriptions of British manufactured goods would sell at far less than their cost price, at other times a most extraordinary profit would be realized— but this is the case in all markets so situated; 'and as the trade of the place encreased according to the population, so did these fluctuations become less frequent, and less sudden. The Commissariat then took wheat into the stores at a certain fixed price of 10s. the bushel, and each settler had a right to turn into the stores so much wheat, according to the number of acres he had in cultivation. The Government were then always purchasers, and rations were allowed to free emigrants for six months after their arrival; rations also were allowed to all Government Officers, and convicts in the employ of the Authorities and settlers.* The circulating medium was a currency, and the specie consisted principally of the ring dollars, which passed current at 5s., and the dump, † at 1s. 3d. The balance of trade was

---

* Magistrates were not then paid salaries, in lieu thereof they received rations for themselves and four convicts, in addition to the other privileges of settlers. Emigrants were allowed rations for themselves and families for six months after their arrival, and, also, rations for the convicts in their employ—each settler was allowed one convict for every hundred acres of land located to him ; but in these times the prisoner population was not at all adequate to the demand for labourers. A further encouragement was given on the landing of every settler—he was allowed to bring ashore, duty free, ten gallons of spirits for himself, and the same quantity for each of his family ; this may be considered as trifling, but it was not so, for these "orders to land" were sold at a high price to the traders and others, for the duties then were almost prohibitory. This system caused much smuggling, and the permit to bring ashore thirty gallons of spirits sold by a reverend divine to a merchant, enabled the latter to land, duty free, three hogsheads of brandy.

† A round piece cut out of the centre of the ring dollar and stamped.

in favor of the Colony, Commissariat bills were only at
a premium of from 15 to 20 per cent., whereas the silver
current had a false value fixed upon it to the extent of
nearly 50 per cent. This balance of trade in favor of the
Colony may be accounted for by the frequent arrival of
wealth brought by the fresh settlers.

The greatest difficulty under which the Colony labored
was that caused by the absence of any judicature nearer
than that of the Sister Colony. In Colonel Sorell's
time all criminals guilty of capital offences, were sent
up to Sydney for trial; and, as before mentioned, the
delay, and the difficulty of proof were such, that in nine
cases out of ten the guilty escaped punishment. The only
court extant in Van Diemen's Land, was that of the
Judge Advocate's, and this was a court instituted to dispose of civil cases where the amount in dispute did not
exceed the sum of £50. This court partook sometimes
of a court of law, and sometimes of a court of equity:
its president was a military man, and from his decision
there was no appeal.* Actions wherein the plaintiff
claimed more than the sum of £50, were the same as
felonies, obliged to be sent for decision to the judges of
New South Wales. It might be imagined that under
these circumstances, where there was no authority in the
island to compel the payment of a sum exceeding £50,
that many cases would be forwarded for trial to Sydney;
but the *ingenuity* of the court allowed plaintiffs and de-
fendants to divide their debts, and when a merchant

---

* A celebrated pleader in Judge Abbott's court, usually took
occasion to make a good case by flattering the vanity of His Honor
the Judge. In some paltry action, when he was employed by the
plaintiff, he began with his usual laudatory flow of language, that
" no Court in Christendom had the power of His Honor's Court—
His Honor's decision was final—his judgments, which the whole
Colony always admired, were decisive—there was no appeal, save
to the Lord Chancellor of England." The Judge Advocate here
interrupted, and said " He did not consider an appeal could be made,
even to the Lord Chancellor." " I stand corrected," rejoined the
pleader, " *there is no appeal* from the wisdom of your judgment,
even to the Lord Chancellor himself !" The plaintiff obtained a
verdict.

sold one thousand pounds worth of goods, he invariably drew *twenty* or more bills of £50 and under on the purchaser, all of which bills might be made subject of separate action in the Judge Advocate's Court.*

Compatible with the resources of the Colony was the Colonial expenditure, and the salaries of those in authority, in proportion to the resources of a young colony. His Honor the Lieutenant Governor Sorell, at first received £500 a year, but this sum was ultimately raised to £800 per annum.† That part of the expenditure paid for by the Colony amounted in 1823 to £24,435, and the Colonial income to £22,064, the deficiency of the money required for the *whole* expenditure being made up by Commissariat drafts upon the British Treasury.

Towards the latter end of Colonel Sorell's administration, the Colonists had in a great degree committed that very general error of young colonies—over trading; but the over trading, if it may so be called, was purely of a colonial description. The occasional scarcity of circulating medium—for then the Commissariat did not bring into the Colony British coin—induced many individuals of known capital to issue promissory notes ; this system spread like a contagious fever, and before long, men almost strangers in the Colony, followed the example. At first the notes were of four dollars—some

---

* Were the reports of the trials of this court to be recorded, they would no doubt entertain the reader. At one time a celebrated advocate, employed as plaintiff's counsel, made out a case so exceedingly satisfactory to His Honor, that a verdict was about to be recorded, when it was found no one was present on the part of the defendant. After some little irregular proceeding, the plaintiff's counsel observed that it was a pity no one appeared for the defence, and rather than the defence of the action should not be heard, if His Honor would allow him, he would act for the defendant also. He did so, and the defendant, according to his own shewing, had the best of it, and, to the astonishment of all present, obtained a verdict without a moment's hesitation. The Judge Advocate often observed, that he was no lawyer himself, and would not be bothered with law.

† Paid by the Home Government.

persons then reduced them to three—these sums were divided by others, and ultimately three-penny and three-halfpenny notes became commonly current. The effect of all this was, that improvements of every kind were carried on with vigour ; high wages were given to work-men, for the masters paid them on the Saturday nights with coin of their own manufacture—it was one uni-versal system of credit. This colonial over trading ultimately had a most injurious effect on a few indivi-duals, for soon after the Bank of Van Diemen's Land was established these currency notes were abolished, and on the settlement of accounts *some were found wanting*.

Under the guidance of this able Governor, Van Die-men's Land had arisen from a wilderness to be a popu-lated settlement—from being but a jail on a large scale, to a British colony, highly valued by the Mother Country as an appendage, and one of the most favored shores for enterprising emigrants. The seeds of industry had been sown on a distant but fruitful soil, and roads, bridges, fences, and improvements of all kinds and des-criptions had within seven years changed the face of the country. Commerce had been established on a firm basis, and the prosperity was such, that the Colonists con-sidered the time had arrived when they ought to be in-dependent of New South Wales. It was in vain Colonel Sorell pointed out their error, in vain that he endea-vored to prove to his friends, the Colonists, (for they were all his friends), that the Colony was not then ripe enough to enjoy such privileges—that with independence would be brought in a host of evils—that a separate Go-vernment would incur an expense which a young colony could not afford—and that the prayer of the Colonists ought to be for a judge and a supreme court of their own, or else that the Sydney judges should visit the Colony twice in every twelve months. But the good advice of the Governor was not heeded—it was useless—all rea-soning was unavailable. The Colonists had thriven beyond what could reasonably be anticipated, and head-strong they went to work to obtain independence. In April, 1824, a public meeting was held for the pur-

pose of petitioning His Majesty on the subject, * and the
address was forwarded in the customary manner—the
result of this address will be seen shortly. Almost co-
eval with the arrival of Colonel Sorell's successor, the
constitution of the Colony underwent an entire change,
by the introduction of the much required supreme court

---

* At a Public Meeting of the Landholders, Merchants, and other
Inhabitants of Van Diemen's Land, holden pursuant to a Requi-
sition, at the Court House in Hobart Town, on Tuesday the 20th
April, 1824.

The Provost Marshall having taken the chair and read the Requisition—

Mr. Meredith rose to open the proceedings of the day, in a
speech elucidatory of the sentiments of the Requisitionists and those
Gentlemen who had concurred with them in the propriety of the
present Meeting; and which, though concise in language, and confined strictly to the tenor of the Requisition, embraced every point
necessary to be adverted to, and was alike respectful to the Supreme
Government at Sydney, and highly complimentary to the talents
and administration of Lieutenant Governor Sorell.

The following Resolutions were then put from the chair, *seriatim*,
and carried unanimously :—

1.—That an Address of thanks be presented to His Majesty, ex-
pressive of our attachment to his person and Government; and ac-
knowledging with gratitude, our high sense of the very valuable and
important institutions extended to us by the Royal Charter.

2.—That the independence of this Colony, evidently contemplated
by his Majesty's Government, is essential to its prosperity; and that
the present circumstances of the Colony suggest the expediency of
supplicating our Gracious Sovereign to extend to us that boon which
he is now empowered to do without the further intervention of the
Legislature.

3.—That a petition be drawn up, humbly praying His Majesty to
elevate Van Diemen's Land into a separate and independent Colony, and that a Committee be appointed, with power to add to
their numbers, for the purpose of framing the said Address and Petition.

4.—That copies of the Address and Petition be sent to agents
fixed on by the Committee, for the purpose of receiving signatures.

5.—That a subscription be opened, for the purpose of defraying
the expences of the proposed measures.

6.—That the Committee do consist of the following Gentlemen,
with power to add to their number:—

Messrs. Kemp	Messrs. Bethune
Meredith	Cartwright
Scott	Kermode

of judicature, for scarcely had the Chief Justice and the
Attorney General landed two months * than Colonel
George Arthur arrived to take the reins of Government.

Colonel Sorell may perhaps be considered one of the
most popular Governors that ever held rule over a British colony.   He was a man of active mind, and shrewd
penetration, affable and gentlemanly in the extreme—
there was a facility of access to his person at all hours,
and his desire to please every individual applicant greatly
added to his popularity—with him there was no auste-
rity, no wish to have favors begged ; on the contrary,
to ask was to have, if it was in Colonel Sorell's power
to grant, and few applicants ever heard him express the
monysyllable " no !"   Whilst thus affable, the dignity of
his person, as well as his general deportment, commanded respect, and no man, ever so intimate, was
known to treat him otherwise than as a Governor.   It
cannot be wondered that such a man should enchain the
good wishes of all classes of society, and the frequent
congratulatory addresses fully shew the feelings of those
over whom he ruled.   In those days there was no " getting up" of fulsome addresses, contrary to the wishes
of the generality of the Colonists, for the whole number
of those in authority, or of those connected with the
Government, scarcely amounted to a score of individuals.
It may be said, and with some justice, that Colonel
Sorell was eased of many very unpleasant duties by the
Colony being a dependency of New South Wales, and

Messrs. Gregson	Messrs. Wood
Anstey	Dawes
Gordon	Paton

JOHN BEAMONT, *Chairman.*

Anthony Fenn Kemp, Esq. was called to the chair, upon the
Provost Marshall quitting it.

Resolved unanimously—

That the thanks of this Meeting be given to John Beamont, Esq.,
for his impartial conduct in the chair.

ANTHONY FENN KEMP.

* His Honor the Chief Justice, John Lewes Pedder, was sworn
into office on the 7th May—he took his seat on the bench on the 10th
—and His Excellency Colonel Arthur arrived on the 12th.

that it was the Governor General who had occasionally to put in force unpopular, yet necessary measures. There are some who say, that had Colonel Sorell been a ruler of this Colony under its independence, he would not have been as popular as he was—it is, however, the intention of the writer to record facts, and not problematical suppositions. A Governor so extremely popular, deservedly received the most grateful tributes any set of men could bestow. On one occasion a piece of plate was presented to him, of the value of £750, the whole of it raised by voluntary contributions, which, considering the youth of the Colony, and the manner in which it was levied, was a present of no mean value. Just previously to the arrival of his successor, a large body of the Colonists held public meetings in Hobart Town and Launceston, in order to frame petitions to His Majesty, that His Honor Colonel Sorell might not be removed from office.*   That a man so esteemed

---

* *At a Public Meeting of the Landholders, Merchants, and Free Inhabitants of Van Diemen's Land, by public advertisement assembled at the Court House, in Hobart Town, the 30th day of Oct.* 1823.

                               JOHN BEAMONT, ESQ.

Resolved unanimously—

1.—That in the present state of this Colony, that union of wisdom and experience which His Honor Lieutenant Governor Sorell has on every occasion so strikingly exhibited, is most essential to our general and individual interests. It becomes therefore of the very utmost importance to us, that in any contemplated changes as to this Colony, Lieutenant Governor Sorell may not be removed from his present government, inasmuch as no successor, whom it may be the pleasure of His Majesty to appoint, can be possibly expected to bestow all that general and individual attention to our wants and wishes, and to be able, satisfactorily and advantageously to encounter any difficulties which may occur, without a considerable lapse of time, and much probable increased inconvenience; while from the steady, calm, decided, and experienced judgment of His Honor Lieutenant Governor Sorell, we have every reason to hope for the most prosperous continuation of his present successful administration.

2.—That a most dutiful Address be presented to His Majesty, grounded upon the preceding resolution, and that a Committee of fifteen Gentlemen be appointed to prepare the same, and to carry

and so popular, should regret leaving a colony which he
had raised from a desert to a habitation for civilized man,

into effect the object of the present Meeting in such manner,
shall appear most proper and expedient.

3.—That the Address, when signed, be forwarded with the least
possible delay, to Edward Barnard, Esq., our Colonial Agent in
London, requesting that gentleman to adopt the necessary measures,
for forthwith submitting it to His Majesty's most gracious consideration, and to use his utmost endeavours to obtain the object of the
same.

4.—That a subscription be forthwith entered into, to defray the
expences which may arise from carrying into effect the present resolutions, and for the purpose of presenting to His Honor Lieutenant
Governor Sorell a piece of plate, in token of our affectionate remembrance of the great obligations we owe him, and that such subscrip-
tions be limited to the sum of two dollars individually.

5.—That H. J. Emmett, Esq., and P. A. Mulgrave, Esq., be
requested to undertake the offices of Treasurers of the subscription
for the counties of Buckingham and Cornwall respectively.

6.—That a copy of these resolutions and of the Address to His
Majesty, be transmitted to His Honor Lieutenant Governor Sorell,
in such manner as by the Committee shall be considered most
respectful to the Lieutenant Governor, and suitable to the occasion.

7.—That the following fifteen Gentlemen do form the Committee,
for the purposes before resolved :—

E. Abbott	S. Hood
T. Anstey	A. W. H. Humphrey
J. Archer	A. F. Kemp
W. A. Bethune	R L. Murray
F. Dawes	H. Ross
H. J. Emmett	G. F. Read
J. Gordon	J. Scott.
T. G. Gregson	

8.-That these resolutions, and a copy of the address to His
Majesy be inserted three times in the Hobart Town and Sydney
Gazetts, and in the Times, New Times, and Courier, and Morning
Chronice, London newspapers.

JOHN BEAMONT, *Provost Marshall, Chairman.*

The Provost Marshall having quitted the chair, and James Gordon, Esq.having been requested to take the same.

Resolved unanimously—

That the thanks of this Meeting be given to John Beamont, Esq.
for the readiness with which he has convened the present Meeting,
and for his able, upright, and impartial conduct in the chair.

JAMES GORDON, *Chairman.*

Another Public Meeting of the Landholders, Merchants, and Free

cannot be wondered at; and his official Address to the
Colonists on his being relieved from the Government,

Inhabitants of the County of Cornwall, Van Diemen's Land, assembled at the Court House, at Launceston, 15th Nov. 1823.
    Resolved unanimously—
    1. That during the period of the administration of the Government
of this Colony by His Honor Lieutenant Governor Sorell, its prosperity has rapidly, and uniformly encreas d, and the progress of
general improvement has been great—beyond example in the
early history of Colonies. That His Honor's able application of the
means confided to him, has effected the security of property, as far
as security was attainable, without a court of criminal jurisdiction
in the Island for the punishment of high offences; has facilitated
communication throughout the Island by the formation of roads and
the construction of bridges ; has encouraged general industry, the
effects of which are manifested in the numerous public and private
buildings and other improvements of a durable nature, that appear
in all parts of the Island, whilst during the time that these many
advantages have been conferred, the expenses to the Mother Country
have been in a progressive state of diminution.
    That the encouragement hence resulting to agriculture is exem-
plified in the cultivation of the soil, to an extent heretofore unheard
of in a colony of equal age and so limited population, while commerce has been proportionably advanced by the constantly encreasing
surplus of agricultural produce.
    That the encrease and improvement of the public schools are alike
honorable to the Government that supplied the means, and to the
zeal and wisdom with which His Honor has pursued the best measures to enlighten the minds and improve the morals of the rising
generation.
    That the firm, though temperate and judicious exercise of His
Honor's authority, has on all occasions ably supported the dignity
of the Crown he represents; while the ready, courteous, and considerate attention uniformly extended by His Honor to the persons
and interests of every class of Colonists entitle him to our highest
respect and most affectionate attachment.
    That, viewing the numerous and important benefits derived from
the administration of the Government by His Honor, and those pros-
pective advantages which his zeal and abilities, aided by his long
experience and local knowledge, would promise us, we should deem
his removal from the Government of the Colony at this time a great
public misfortune ; which opinion is supported by the laudatory tone
of the report of His Majesty's late Commissione , Mr. Bigge,
touching the whole conduct of Lieutenant Governor Sorell.
    2. That our Fellow-Colonists of the county of Buckinghamshire,
having prepared an Address from the Landholder , Merchants, and
Free Inhabitants of Van Diemen's Land, to our Most Gracious

fully shews what his feelings were at the time of his removal.* The Colonists, just before his embarkation,

---

Sovereign, praying " His Majesty's Royal acquiescence to their dutiful solicitation, that His Honor Lieutenant Governor Sorell may not be removed from the administration of this Government," in which wish we fully and earnestly coincide, it is expedient that we should subscribe our names to the said Address.

3. That our said Fellow-Colonists, having by their fourth Resolution at their Public Meeting at Hobart Town, on the 30th day of October, 1823, resolved to raise a subscription for the purpose specified in the said Resolution, we concur in the same.

4. That these Resolutions be inserted three times in the Hobart Town and Sydney Gazette, and in the Times, New Times, Morning Chronicle, and Courier, London newspapers.

JOHN BEAMONT, *Provost Marshall, Chairman.*

The chairman having left the chair, Thomas Archer, Esq., J.P., having been called to it,

Resolved unanimously—

That the thanks be given to our worthy Provost Marshall, John Beamont, Esq., for the readiness with which he has convened the present Meeting, and for his able, and upright, and impartial conduct in the chair.

THOMAS ARCHER, *Chairman.*

* GOVERNMENT AND GENERAL ORDERS.

Government House, Hobart Town, May 14th, 1824.

Seven years expired, last month, since Lieutenant Governor Sorell assumed the charge of the Colony, and the period is now arrived for him to take leave of it in his official character.

To the state of these Settlements, when Lieutenant Governor Sorell succeeded to the command—their progress during his administration, and the system and measures which he has pursued with a view to render the powers that he has exercised, most efficacious, for their welfare and improvement—the recent and general sense of his services, which has been expressed by the Colonists, prohibit an allusion further than this Address upon the conclusion of his official labours indispensibly requires.

Lieutenant Governor Sorell will say then only, from the moment that he took upon him the Government of the Colony, on the 9th of April, 1817, he has endeavoured by a zealous, faithful, and impartial exercise of the authority with which his Majesty was pleased to invest him, to re-establish its order, to improve its condition and resources, and to do justice to all. He retires, conscious of having performed his duty, and with the gratifying reflection that his administration is approved by His Majesty's Government; and that his services have been acknowledged by the unanimous voice of the Colonists.

Few men could hold authority for seven years in a young and en-

presented him with one more mark of their esteem, in the form of a final Address ; * and his successor, as

---

creasing colony, and witness its progress during that period, from little more than a penal appendage to New South Wales, with a population under two thousand, to a free and rising Colony, augmented in number to eleven thousand people, in great part by emigration from the Mother Country, and diffused over a large portion of the Island, without imbibing an anxious interest in its success and prosperity.

That feeling could be stronger in no man's breast than in Lieutenant Governor Sorell's : and in now taking leave of the inhabitants, he requests them to be assured that he carries with him a warm and lasting impression of the respect and attachment which they have manifested towards him ; and it will be his fervent prayer, that under the blessing of Divine Providence, with the great extension of its laws and institutions, and the protection to its commercial resources, which the Colony has received from a beneficent Government and Legislature, and by an energetic use of its natural advantages, Van Diemen's Land may always improve and prosper, and that its inhabitants may be united, independent, and happy.

With these feelings, and with sincere wishes for the happy and prosperous Government of his successor, Lieutenant Governor Sorell bids farewell to the inhabitants of the Colony.

By the command of His Honor the Lieutenant Governor.

H. E. ROBINSON, *Secretary.*

* The Rev. R. Knopwood, M.A., read the following address of thanks upon His Honor quitting the Government of Van Diemen's Land :—

We, the Clergy, Magistrates, Landholders, Merchants, and Inhabitants of Van Diemen's Land, deeply impressed with the manifold advantages which we owe to your wise and energetic administration of the Government of this Island, during the long period of seven years, cannot permit you to leave the Colony without expressing our best thanks and profound gratitude for the unvarying impartiality and rectitude which you have displayed in the exercise of your public functions.

High official characters can seldom exercise power without producing feelings of discontent and annoyance to those subject to their control, and it has rarely fallen to the lot of any Governor to be so cordially esteemed, and so universally respected as yourself.

You have had the pleasing satisfaction to conciliate all ranks of society in the Colony, while at the same time you have secured the approbation of those, whose duty it has been to scrutinize your conduct.

The sense which we entertain of the weighty obligations we owe to your prudent administration, has been so recently avowed, that to recapitulate them here is unnecessary.

Our esteem for you, and anxiety for your welfare, cannot but

soon as he had been installed into office, issued a Government Order, to the effect that " all compliments and
honors paid to his predecessor, whilst Lieutenant Governor
in this Colony, should be continued to be observed during his stay,"—which was but of short duration, for
Colonel Sorell embarked within a month on board the
Guildford, * for England. The Lieutenant Governor,

long survive your retirement from office; our best wishes will accompany you to the land of your nativity.

We beg leave to express our most cordial hope, that your talents may be employed in a way most acceptable to your Sovereign, beneficial to your country, and satisfactory to yourself.

His Honor favored the Committee with the following answer:—

Sir and Gentlemen,—I beg to return to you, and through you,
to the Inhabitants of the Colony my cordial thanks, for the very
kind and affectionate Address, which you have now presented to
me, upon the termination of my official functions amongst you, and
my departure from this Colony.

The great and recent marks of respect and good will which I
have received from the Colonists, have already called forth acknow-
ledgments on my part, which leave me little more than the power
of repetition on this occasion.

If I feel that I have performed my duties as your Lieutenant
Governor for seven years zealously and faithfully, and have spared
no effort in my power to promote the improvement of the Colony;
on the part of the Inhabitants, I have assuredly received all the return which they could offer, or which I could expect or desire at
their hands; and it will not be unpleasing to them to know that
those services, which they have acknowledged as beneficial to them,
have been honored with the gracious approbation of our Sovereign.

Of the future prospects and destiny of the Colony, I cannot but
carry with me a favorable augury. Under the fostering protection of
the Mother Country, the industry and perseverance of the Colonists
will enable them to triumph over the difficulties of a first settlement;
and this Island, so interesting from the numerous emigration which
has been directed to it, for its valuable resources, its salubrious climate, its varied soil and surface, and its picturesque beauties, will,
I trust, progressively advance in moral and physical improvement,
and become to yourselves, and your descendants, an abode respected and valued throughout the world.

That these anticipations may be realized—that all possible prosperity may attend the Colony, will ever be one of my first wishes;
for you may be assured that my interest in its welfare cannot cease.

Permit me, Sir, and Gentlemen, to offer you my best thanks for
your personal attention upon this occasion, and my sincere wishes
for your individual health and happiness.

* The very same vessel he came out in to this Colony.

accompanied by the Chief Justice, the Officers, and Magistrates, " and nearly the whole of the gentlemen of the Colony, repaired to his residence at the appointed hour, and accompanied him to the King's Wharf,"*— the parting scene must have been gratifying to Colonel Sorell; he shook hands with those who happened to be standing nearest to him, and expressed himself to one gentleman, that he was sorry he could not pay the same compliment to all that were present. As Colonel Sorell embarked, every true Colonist felt he was bereaved of a friend as well as a Governor.

It was on the 12th May, 1824,† that Colonel George Arthur arrived, and on the 14th was invested with the responsible trust he has since held for so many years. On his taking the reins of Government into his hands, the Colonists offered him a congratulatory Address :‡

---

* See Hobart Town Gazette.

† GOVERNMENT GENERAL ORDERS.
Government House, Hobart Town, Wednesday, May 12, 1824.
His Majesty has been graciously pleased to appoint Colonel George Arthur to be Lieutenant Governor of Van Diemen's Land, in succession to Lieutenant Governor Sorell.

On Friday next, at one o'clock, His Honor Colonel Arthur's Commission will be read and published with all due form in front of Government House, upon which occasion the detachment of the 3rd Regiment (Buffs), under the command of Major Marley, will parade under arms; and immediately after the reading of his Majesty's Commission, the troops will fire three vollies—a Royal Salute will be fired at the same time from Mulgrave Battery, in honor of the occasion.

After the publication of His Majesty's Commission, His Honor Colonel Arthur will have the usual oaths administered to him at Government House ; and the Clergy, Magistrates, and Officers of the Colony, Civil and Military, are requested to attend, and to witness the ceremony of his receiving charge of the Government.

On His Honor's being sworn in, a salute of seventeen guns to be fired from Mulgrave Battery, in honor of the occasion.

The Artificers and Labourers in the immediate employment of Government at Hobart Town, are to be exempt from work on Friday next.

By command of His Honor the Lieutenant Governor.
W. E. ROBINSON, *Secretary.*

‡ *To His Honor Lieutenant Governor Arthur.*
We, the Clergy, Magistrates, Landholders, and Inhabitants of

To follow a popular predecessor, is at all time hazardous, and any man to succeed Colonel Sorell, as Governor

---

Van Diemen's Land, beg leave to offer Your Honor, as the Representative of our Sovereign, our respectful and cordial congratulations upon the arrival of yourself and family, after a voyage of un-
usual length, peril, and disasters; and upon your assumption of the
Government of this Island.

Impressed with the most lively and grateful sense of the important accession of privileges so dear to us as Britons, which this
Colony has received from recent Legislative Enactments, establishing
Courts of Civil and Criminal Judicature, we cannot but anticipate
in Your Honor's Administration the most beneficial results to our
general interests.

Our loyalty and gratitude will, we feel, be best evinced by
respect to Your Honor, and by deference to your authority ; and
we beg to assure Your Honor, that it will be no less our inclination
than our duty, to manifest our respect and attachment to your Person
and Government, on all occasions.

We earnestly hope, that Your Honor's Administration of the
affairs of this rapidly extending Colony, will ever be a source of
satisfaction to yourself, and conducive to the best interests of all
classes of the community.

To which His Honor was pleased to return the following
reply :—

Gentlemen—I beg you will accept the expression of my best
thanks for the very gratifying Address which you have done me
the honor to present.   Equally impressed with the important privileges you have derived from the recent Legislative Enactments,
which have established Courts of Civil and Criminal Jurisdiction in
Van Diemen's Land, I can alike anticipate with yourselves the
most beneficial results.

I am highly gratified at the confidence with which you express
that my Administration will prove advantageous to your general interests ; because, as I enter upon the Government of the Island
with a conviction that little can be done by the Executive Authority
alone, I receive it as a pledge, that I shall in every measure of improvement be strengthened by your cordial co-operation.   It is to
your exertions, and still more to your example, that I mainly con-
fide, under Divine Providence, for any effectual reformation in the
moral character of a very large class in this community—a measure
most essential to the security of your personal property and domestic
peace ; and consequently involving your best interests and happiness.

Looking therefore, anxiously to you ; both collectively and personally, for support, I can sincerely assure you, that whilst it will
be my duty to maintain the just rights of the Crown, it will be my
most earnest desire to exercise the power and authority with which

of a Colony, was certain to be placed in a situation
any thing but enviable. From the landing of Colonel
Arthur, it was evident that he did not seek popularity
in the Colony—he apparently, from the very first, considered the settlement in the same light as did Governors
of provinces of former days. Those in power in the
Mother Country, had appointed him to rule, and to
them, and to them only, did he conceive himself answer-
able for his conduct. The Colonists, in his eyes, were
only regarded so far as they might be made instrumental
in furthering British interests and British patronage;
and no man could have done his duty to his employers
more effectually. It is not intended to advert to the
situation in which Colonel Arthur was placed, prior to
his arriving as Governor of the Colony, for the writer
is only recording events which have occurred in Van
Diemen's Land; but, nevertheless, it ought to be mentioned, that Colonel Arthur had before been a ruler of
a British settlement, in America—and that at Honduras
he made himself any thing but popular with the Colonists. His Honor, from the very commencement, shewed
that he had been brought up in a good school, but it
was a military school, and the most inefficient men that
can be chosen, as Governors, are military tacticians—
accustomed to command, and to subservient submission,
they think that to remonstrate against measures which
may perhaps be impolitic, is to oppose, and to oppose is
to merit destruction.

Colonel Arthur, on his arrival, was Lieutenant Colonel
of the York Chasseurs, but by a Government General
Order of the Commander-in-Chief, it appears he was
placed on the Staff, so long as he should remain in the
Colony.*

---

our most Gracious Sovereign has been pleased to invest me, for the
general prosperity of the community at large."

*GOVERNMENT AND GENERAL ORDERS.
Brigade Major's Office, Sydney, May 12, 1824.
His Royal Highness the Commander-in-Chief, with the sanction
of His Majesty, has been pleased to appoint Lieutenant Colonel
George Arthur, on the half-pay of the York Chasseurs, and who

The first public measures of His Honor, was that of
nominating his nephew, J. Montagu, Esq., Captain of
the 40th regiment, as Colonial Secretary, and to draw
around him a circle of advisers, from whom he gained
that insight into the resources and capabilities of the
Colony, which afterwards formed the ground-work of
his system of administration. As the Colony had advanced too rapidly under his predecessor, it became apparent that the system of encouragement formerly held out,
must, to a certain degree, be changed; but it was no
pleasant task to curb a popular system, although founded
upon unsound principles, and the change caused discontent, and party feeling soon became manifest. Colonel
Sorell, himself, was of opinion that the state of affairs
were not in an healthy condition, and probably had he
remained a little longer in office, he would have himself
witnessed the effect of the over trading, before alluded
to, for just previous to the arrival of his successor, he
had been heard to express himself, that whoever might
succeed him, would not, *at first*, have an enviable situation. Another great cause of Colonel Arthur commencing his Government in an unpopular manner, was
caused by the mode of life of himself and his predecessor
differing so widely—persons who had been in the daily
habit of visiting his predecessor, were scarcely noticed
by him, and two or three individuals who were unpopular and ignorant of the real state of the Colony,
were selected as advisers. In spite, however, of the
difficulties under which he commenced his labours, he
displayed all the qualifications of an able and experienced
diplomatist—and though difficulties surrounded him on
all sides, Colonel Arthur overcame them by degrees,
and with the masterly hand of an experienced tactician,

---

has been appointed Lieutenant Governor of Van Diemen's Land,
to serve as Colonel upon the Staff in this territory. All reports of a
military nature from the troops serving in Van Diemen's Land, will
hereafter be addressed to Colonel Arthur.

By command of His Excellency, Major General Sir Thomas
Brisbane, K. C. B.

J. Ovens, *Major of Brigade.*

shortly succeeded in placing himself firmly in the seat of Government.

The first few years were not conspicuous for any marked feature—there did not appear any fixed system of Government, differing from that of his predecessors. Colonel Arthur seemed as if he felt himself scarcely firm enough seated to commence operations on different principles.

During the first year of his Administration, he re-modelled the Prison Discipline System, existing in the Colony. Formerly too great a laxity had prevailed among the prisoner population : the prisoners hitherto had scarcely been subject to any restraint whatever : various Government Orders were therefore issued relative to the cloathing, to the labour, and to the general guidance of the assigned servants, and the prisoners in Government employ. These orders had the most salutary effect ; and with the rapid introduction of free emigrants, the task of separating the convict from the free became more easily accomplished, and a system of penal coercion more readily put into operation. The Police of the Island also, underwent considerable improvements ; but yet it was lamentably inefficient, nor was it for several years afterwards placed on a proper footing. By the introduction of the Supreme Courts of Judicature, Colonel Arthur had placed under his Government the most desired boon that could be accorded to the Colony, which thus became virtually independent : but no sooner had the Court commenced operations, than a series of evils occurred. The Colonists, it would appear, had hitherto been deprived of the means of annoying each other by expensive law proceedings, and immediately means were at command, a whole string of civil actions and criminal informations were instituted, as if the disputants themselves were anxious to discover *the hidden mysteries of the law*—among other proceedings before the Court, was a criminal information instituted by a public writer against some dozen leading merchants and settlers in the Colony. The writer alluded to had boldly opposed * the almost

---

* Mr. R. L. Murray.

general wish of the Colonists, as respected the application to His Majesty for independence. It was in answer
to one of his published letters, that a string of violent
resolutions were drawn up, and signed by the same dozen
individuals, against whom the proceedings were instituted. The law of the case was fairly discussed, and
after a trial of considerable interest, the whole of the
gentlemen were found guilty of the libel—of course the
prosecutor never prayed that judgment might be given—
so there the matter ended,

In this year the aborigines of the Island began to
annoy the settlers to a degree that required some active
measures of the Government to allay the outraged feelings of this ill-fated race of human beings. These
poor bewildered creatures had been treated *worse* than
were any of the American tribes by the Spaniards.
Easy, quiet, good-natured, and well-disposed towards
the white population, they could no longer brook the
treatment they received from the invaders of their country. Their hunting grounds were taken from them, and
they themselves were driven like trespassers from the
favorite spots for which their ancestors had bled, and
had claimed by conquest. The various tribes which
formerly were at war with each other, about this time
seemed to forget their private differences, and their great
aim was to protect themselves from slaughter, and to
be revenged ! The stock-keepers may be considered as
the destroyers of nearly the whole of the aborigines—
the proper, the legitimate owners of the soil : these
miscreants so imposed upon their docility, that at length
they thought little or nothing of destroying the men for the
sake of carrying to their huts the females of the tribes ;
and, if it were possible in a work like this to record but
a tithe of the murders committed on these poor harmless creatures, it would make the reader's blood run cold
at the bare recital. * In self-defence were these poor

* One case may suffice. A *respectable* young gentleman, who
was out kangaroo hunting, in jumping over a dead tree, observed
a black native crouched by the stem, as if to hide himself.
The huntsman observing the white of the eye of the native, was

harmless creatures driven to desperate means, their fine kangaroo grounds were taken from them, and thus were they in want of their customary food ; and when every other means of obtaining a livelihood was debarred to them, *necessity* compelled them to seek food of their despoilers.   Colonel Arthur pitied them—he no doubt was made fully acquainted with the aggressions of the *civilized* portion of the population; and much to his credit he caused a General Government Order * to be issued,

---

induced to examine the prostrate being, and finding it only to be a native, he placed the muzzle of his piece to his breast and shot him dead on the spot. Hundreds of similar cases might be adduced.

* PROCLAMATION.

By Colonel George Arthur, Lieutenant Governor of Van Diemen's Land, and its Dependencies, &c. &c.

Whereas it has been represented to His Honor the Lieutenant Governor, that several Settlers and others are in the habit of maliciously and wantonly firing at, injuring, and destroying the defenceless Natives and Aborigines of this Island ;—and whereas, it has been commanded by His Majesty's Government, and strictly enjoined by His Excellency the Governor-in-Chief, that the Natives of this Colony and its Dependencies shall be considered as under British Government and protection.

These instructions renders it no less the duty than it is the disposition of His Honor the Lieutenant Governor, to support and encourage all measures which may tend to conciliate and civilize the Natives of this Island ; and to forbid and prevent, and when perpetrated, to punish any ill-treatment towards them.   The Natives of this Island being under the protection of the same laws which protect the Settlers, every violation of those laws, in the persons or property of the Natives, shall be visited with the same punishment as though committed on the person or property of any Settler.   His Honor the Lieutenant Governor therefore declares thus publicly his determination, that if, after the promulgation of this Proclamation, any person or persons shall be charged with firing at, killing, or committing any act of outrage or aggression on the Native People, they shall be prosecuted for the same before the Supreme Court. All Magistrates and Peace Officers, and others His Majesty's subjects in this Colony are hereby strictly required to observe and enforce the provisions of this Proclamation, and to make them known, more especially to Stock-keepers in their several districts, enjoining them not only to avoid all aggression, but to exercise the utmost forbearance towards the Aborigines, treating them on all occasions with the utmost kindness and compassion.

Given under my hand at Government House, Hobart Town,

commanding that the aborigines should be protected, and that outrages against these much injured people should be punished as if perpetrated against the white population; unfortunately the order could not have the effect anticipated by the Lieutenant Governor, for the evil was too far rooted, and it was "*war to the knife.*" Whenever an aborigine could waylay an enemy, he sacrificed him, and the aborigine was invariably destroyed by the settler, whenever an opportunity occurred. A Sydney native, named Musquito, became, about this time, a most daring leader of a hostile tribe; the history of this man is curious.   He was transported from New Holland, and was employed in this Colony as a stock-keeper, from which situation he was taken to assist in capturing the bushrangers.   The knowledge the aborigines of New South Wales and Van Diemen's Land have of the bush—their extraordinary method of tracing the tracks of man, even over barren rocks, were found to be of great utility, and Musquito was instrumental in bringing to justice many of the most notorious of the marauders; but no sooner was this accomplished, than the prisoner population insulted and jeered him for the services he had rendered the Colony.   Such a life to such a wild creature, was insufferable; he took to the bush, and became a chief of a tribe he formed himself, and which consisted of the worst description of the aborigines.   In this state he would, in all probability, have led a quiet life, but the stock-keepers and other evil-disposed persons, frequently attempted to carry away his "*gins,*" * and often his life was in imminent danger; desperate conflicts frequently ensued, and for a time Musquito was fortunate. Thus hunted about, every white man he saw was an enemy, and revenge was taken when opportunity offered.   Many deeds of terror are laid to

---

this Twenty-third Day of June, One Thousand Eight Hundred and Twenty-four.

GEORGE ARTHUR.

By His Excellency's command,

JOHN MONTAGU, *Secretary.*

* *Gin*—the aboriginal name for wife.

D

Musquito's charge, which it is impossible for him to
have committed, but, doubtlessly, several lives were
sacrificed by him.   One of the most serious accusations
made against the aborigines of this Island, is their mode
of warfare; it is urged that they made no distinction of
persons—that those individuals who treated them with
kindness, suffered by their revenge equally as did their
enemies ; but is not this accounted for when the white
population made no difference with them ?   Whether
the man standing before the loaded musket of the settler,
was one of peaceable disposition, or a warrior, mattered
not—each and every one was massacreed when opportunity offered.[1] This murderous warfare, in the course
of a few years destroyed thousands of the aborigines,
whilst only a few score of the European population were
sacrificed.   Many good traits could be recorded of the
peaceable nature of this race of human beings, which are
now almost extinct, * but little could be urged in favor
of the conduct of the settlers towards them.

Colonel Arthur had scarcely been in office one
month before fresh cause of alarm pervaded the
whole body of Colonists ; and in addition to the
" Guerilla" war with the aborigines, bushrangers threatened even more disastrous consequences.   The Police
was extremely imperfect, and the military in the Island
only consisted of a few detachments, the greater part of
which were stationed in Hobart Town and Launceston.
Active measures to stop the threatened evil seemed out

* Perhaps, taken collectively, the sable Natives of this Colony
are the most peaceable creatures in the universe. Certainly so taken
they have never committed any acts of cruelty, or even resisted the
whites, unless when insufferably goaded by provocation.   The
only tribe who have done any mischief were corrupted by Musquito,
a Sydney black, who with much and perverted cunning, taught
them a portion of his own villainy, and incited them after a time to
join in his delinquencies.—*Hobart Town Gazette*, 1824.

The many recent unfortunate deaths of stockmen, afford the
sad example of the imprudence of maltreating the Natives, who
have always been considered the most harmless race of people in the
world ; and have consequently never been known to shew their revenge until within these last few months.—*Ibid.*

of the question, and it appeared to be left to chance to procure a remedy. The system of bushranging which Colonel Sorell so successfully eradicated, now broke out with all its horrors; fourteen prisoners escaping from Macquarie Harbour, by degrees organized themselves into a strong party. The system of torture carried on at that settlement, was such, that death was sought as a relief by many of the unfortunate individuals whose offences against the laws had rendered their removal from society necessary. There are many cases on record, where prisoners confined in that horrid place, have committed murder, expressly to be brought up to Hobart Town—there to be executed; and there are numerous instances where parties of a few determined men have resolved on escape, and owing to the barrenness of the soil in that part of the Island—which produces nothing eatable for man—these men have ultimately destroyed each other, for food. One of the most extraordinary cases of this description is, that of the notorious Pearce,*

---

* The Revd. Mr. Conolly, who attended this unfortunate man, administering to him the consolations of religion, addressed the crowd assembled around the scaffold, a few minutes before the fatal drop was let fall, in words to the following effect:—

He commenced by stating that Pearce, standing on the awful entrance into eternity on which he was placed, was desirous to make the most public acknowledgment of his guilt, in order to humble himself as much as possible in the sight of God and man; that to prevent any embarrassment which might attend Pearce in personally expressing himself, he had requested and directed him to say, that he committed the murder under the following circumstances:—

Having been arrested here after his escape from Macquarie Harbour, Pearce was sent back to that settlement, where the deceased, (Cox), and he worked together in the same gang. Cox constantly entreated him to run away with him from that settlement, which he refused to do for a length of time. Cox having procured fish hooks, a knife, and some burnt rag for tinder, he at last agreed to go with him; to which he was most powerfully induced by the apprehension of corporal punishment for the loss of a shirt that had been stolen from him. For the first and second day they strayed through the forest; on the third made the beach, and travelled towards Port Dalrymple, until the fifth, when they arrived at King's River. They remained for three or four days in an adjoining wood, to avoid soldiers, who were in pursuit of them, and were all the time, from the period they started, without a morsel to eat. Overcome by famine,

who confessed, just prior to his execution, that many
victims had fallen by his hands, to satisfy the cravings
of hunger.

No sooner had the fourteen runaways landed on the

Pearce determined to take Cox's life, which he effected by the stroke
of an axe while Cox was sleeping. Soon after the soldiers had de-
parted, Pearce occupied the place they had been in, where he remained a day and a night, living on the mutiliated remains of Cox;
he returned to the settlement, made signal, and was taken up by the
pilot, who conveyed him to Macquarie Harbour, where he disclosed
to the. Commandant what he had done, being weary of life, and
willing to die for the misfortunes and atrocities into which he had
fallen.

The Revd. Gentleman then proceeded to state that he believed it
was in the recollection of every one present, that eight men had
made their escape last year from Macquarie Harbour. All these,
except Pearce, who was of the party, soon perished or were destroyed by the hands of their companions.

To set the public right respecting their fate, Pearce is desirous to
state that this party, consisting of himself, Matthew Travers, Bob
Greenhill, Bill Cornelius, Alexander Dalton, John Matthews, and
two more, named Bodnam, and Brown, escaped from Macquarie
Harbour in two boats, taking with them what provision the coal
miners had, which afforded each man about two ounces of food per
day for a week. Afterwards they lived eight or nine days on the
tops of tea tree, which they boiled in tin pots to extract the juice.
Having ascended a hill in sight of Macquarie Harbour, they struck
a light, and made two fires, Cornelius, Brown, and Dalton placed
themselves at one fire, the rest of the party at the other; those three
separated privately from the party, on account of Greenhill having
already said that lots must be cast for some one to be put to death,
to save the whole from perishing. Pearce does not know personally
what became of Cornelius, Brown, and Dalton; he heard that
Cornelius and Brown had reached Macquarie Harbour, where they
soon died, and that Dalton perished on his return to that settlement.
After their departure, the party, then consisting of five men, lived
two or three days on wild berries, and their kangaroo jackets, which
they roasted. At length they arrived at Gordon's River, where it
was agreed that while Matthews and Pearce collected fire wood,
Greenhill and Jones should kill Bodnam, which they accordingly
did. It was insisted upon that every one should partake of Bodnam's
remains, lest in the event of their ultimate success to obtain their
liberty, any of them might consider himself innocent of his death,
and give evidence against the rest. After a day or two they all
swam across the river except Travers, whom they dragged across by
means of a pole, to which he tied himself. Having spent some days
in distress and famine, it was proposed to Pearce by Greenhill and

shores of the river Derwent, than they were assisted by
their friends, and their number considerably augmented
by individuals, who were ready to take to the bush, and
by others whom they forcibly compelled to join their
band.   These bushrangers had adherents in Hobart
Town, to whom it is generally believed they disposed of
their ill-gotten plunder, and in exchange were supplied
with every necessary required for a roaming life.   These
men were a terror to all the Colonists—no settler could
be secure, for one moment, from their depredations.
One day they would be committing outrages near Launceston, and in an astonishing short space of time would
be striking terror to the inhabitants in the vicinity of
Hobart Town—and the most atrocious crimes were committed by them.   The Colonists called loudly upon the
Governor to interfere, to adopt vigorous means by which
this scourge might be destroyed ; he replied that it was
the duty of the Colonists, individually, to protect themselves from these desperate men.*   The Government

---

Travers, that Matthews should be killed, to which he agreed. Travers
and Pearce held him while Greenhill killed him with an axe. Living
on the remains of the deceased, which they were hardly able to
taste, they spent three or four days through weakness, without advancing beyond five or six miles, Travers being scarcely able to
move from lameness and swelling of his feet. Greenhill and Pearce
agreed to kill Travers, which Greenhill did while Pearce collected
fire-wood. Having lived some time on the remains of Travers, they
were for some days without anything to eat, their wants were dreadful, each strove to catch the other off his guard and kill him,
Pearce succeeded in finding Greenhill asleep—took his life, and lived
on him for four days. He was afterwards for three days without any
sustenance, fell in at last with the Derwent River, and found some
small pieces of opossums, &c., at a place where the natives had
lately made fires.   More desirous to die than to live, he called out
as loudly as he could, expecting the natives would hear him, and
come and put an end to his existence.   Having fallen in with some
bushrangers, with whom he was taken, Pearce was sent back to
Macquarie Harbour, from whence he escaped with Cox, as has
been already stated, for whose death he is now about to suffer.—
Hobart Town Gazette.
* GOVERNMENT AND GENERAL ORDERS.
Government House, Hobart Town, August 27, 1824.
The Lieutenant Governor feels it necessary to announce that the

refused its aid, and a body of volunteers organized themselves in the interior, in order to check the outrages—
but without the assistance of the Government it was
childless to imagine any beneficial effect would arise.
Occasionally skirmishing parties would capture two or
three runaway prisoners, *supposed* to belong to the chief
band of bushrangers under command of Brady and
M'Cabe, and in order to check their outrages, frequent
executions of such captured criminals took place—yet
did this have no effect. The Government appeared to
look on in silent wonder at the outrageous proceedings
of this little band, and instead of offering rewards—instead of active and decisive measures being adopted to
procure peace and good order, nothing effectual was
attempted, and the war between the bushrangers and
the settlers continued, and the loss of life became frequent on the part of the Colonists. The audacity with
which these men acted, is most astonishing ; not content
with ransacking and putting at defiance the whole of
the country, they made frequent excursions into Hobart
Town : and their leaders have been known to be ca-
rousing there, for days and days together, as if to mock
the energies of the Government and the Colonists, to
capture them.

---

party of prisoners who escaped from Macquarie Harbour, have
again passed into the interior. His Honor begs in the most earnest
manner to call upon all settlers in their respective districts, to enter
with encreased zeal and determination into measures for the apprehension of these robbers. To the most common understanding,
not laboring under the miserable depression of personal danger,
means will be presented, after a robbery has been committed, of
tracing the movements of the depredators; and it must be understood to be the positive duty of every settler to spread the information immediately, and to adopt the most prompt and energetic steps
for closely pursuing these miscreants until they are fairly hunted down.

All Crown servants are to be immediately assembled by their masters, and apprized that the Government expects every man should
give all possible information, and that a pardon is offered to any
prisoner who may give such intelligence as may lead to the apprehension of these bushrangers.

By command of His Honor the Lieutenant Governor,

JOHN MONTAGU, *Secretary.*

It was in October of this year, that a defalcation was discovered in the accounts of the naval officer, Mr. E. F. Bromley; an enquiry was instituted to discover to what extent the deficiency had amounted, and the board of enquiry returned that the sum was £8,269.   A Mr. W. H. Hamilton, was appointed as naval officer, in lieu of the individual whose accounts had become embarrassed.

Colonel Arthur had scarcely been in office six months, before the Press became obnoxious to his Government, and the proprietor of the Official Gazette of the Colony, the only Journal then published, was, the following year, prosecuted for an imaginary libel on His Honor the Lieutenant Governor; but it would be more proper to notice these proceedings in a future page.

It was in the month of December, of this year, that two aborigines were brought to trial before the Supreme Court, charged with murder.   One was Musquito, the Sydney native already noticed,* the other was an aborigine of this Colony, nick-named "Black Jack."   The former had been made acquainted with English manners, but not with English laws.   He had been accustomed to frequent the outskirts of Sydney, and in his intercourse with the whites, had contrived to pick up some score or two of English sentences, which formed all his vocabulary.   Black Jack was even more ignorant; this man scarcely knew half a dozen English words, and the whole of these were most horrid oaths, picked up from the bushrangers and stock-keepers, with whom he had, in former times, had occasional intercourse ; these men were placed at the bar, to be tried for their

---

* Musquito was captured by an aborigine named Teague, and a man named Gotfried Hanskey, near Grindstone Bay.   He climbed up a tree, and was shot by Teague in the groin.   He travelled in great misery from thence to Hobart Town, and was a long time under the care of Dr. Scott, previous to his trial.   Teague was reared from a child in the family of Dr. Luttrell.   Colonel Arthur promised him a whale boat and several other rewards for this service ; but poor Teague never got his boat—the disappointment affected him most seriously, and he fretted himself to death in consequence.   He died at Mr. Hobbs's stock hut.—*From an old settler.*

lives. It has already been shewn under what circumstances Musquito had made war against the Colonists;
and the reader can imagine the awful situation in which
the legitimate prisoner of war, "Black Jack," was
placed, when he appeared at the dock of an English
court of law to be tried for his life. On the one side
was the learned Attorney General, pressing, as in duty
bound, the conviction of the offenders against laws
brought by the invaders to the country; and on the
bench sat a Judge to administer impartially these laws,
which neither Musquito nor Black Jack comprehended.
" Convict" witnesses were brought forward, whose evidence was taken and believed, because it was sworn to;
and yet these poor, perhaps guilty creatures of the crime
imputed to them, (which in them was no crime, but
retaliation), were called upon for their defence!—what
mockery ! The wretched prisoners were not aware of one
tittle of evidence adduced against them, were totally
ignorant of having committed crime, and knew not why
or wherefore they were placed at the criminal's dock in
the Court House, and so many eyes fixed upon them.
Both these aborigines underwent the ordeal of trial
twice on one day, and without counsel, * Musquito

* Musquito and Black Jack, (the first a native of New
South Wales, the latter born on the Island), were placed at the
bar, and arraigned as principals in the second degree, for aiding and
abetting in the wilful murder of William Hollyoak, at Grindstone
Bay, on the 15th November, 1823. Plea—Not Guilty.
    The Attorney General described the facts, and called John Rad-
ford, who deposed as follows:—
    I am, and for six years have been a stock-keeper on the run of
Mr. Silas Gatehouse, at Grindstone Bay. I had a fellow servant
named Mammoa, who was a native of Otaheite; I knew the deceased, he was a servant to Mr. George Meredith, at Swan Port,
and came to our hut in November twelve months: he said he was
returning home from the Colonial Hospital, where he had been an
invalid, and begged permission to remain a day or two, as he was
not very able to go further. He came on a Wednesday, between
the 10th and 15th, and remained until the following Saturday. The
morning after he came, a party of the natives arrived, with the prisoners at the bar. Their number was about 65, some of them had
spears, and sticks about two feet long; but some of the spears,
which were wooden ones, might be six, and others twelve feet long.

was found guilty of the first offence, of aiding and abetting in the wilful murder of William Hollyoak and Black

I asked Musquito whither he was going, and he said to Oyster Bay.
He then begged for some provisions, and I told him to follow me
into the hut, where he should have some bread and meat. After he
had eaten some, I inquired how many natives were with him, he
answered he could not tell. I then asked if they would kill any of
the sheep ; he said no. Soon afterwards he retired for that night.
On the following morning he again came to the hut, and brought
two or three women : some of the blacks were on the opposite side
of the creek. He asked for, and had some breakfast with me. He
lingered with the party about the plains until 2 or 3 o'clock, and
then went away to hunt. In the evening he returned, and I gave
him some supper ; this was Friday night. In the hut there hung a
small fowling-piece, and a musket, the one by the bed, and the
other over it. Musquito handled the musket. On Saturday morning
early the blacks were in the sheep yard, sitting round a fire at their
breakfast; this was about half-past five o'clock. At six they came
to the hut, with the prisoners at the bar, over the creek, on the other
side of which they had been at their diversions, some of them still
remained there near the stock-yard, which approaches to within 10
yards of the hut. The natives who were playing might be 150
yards from the hut, I walked out to look at them, after Mammoa,
and left the deceased in the hut, but he came out after me. At this
time Musquito was on the other side of the creek with a number of
blacks, who were armed, but he had no spear. The weapons he
had were a waddy, and a stick shaped like the axe of a tomahawk,
I had desired the deceased to bring the guns, should he leave the
hut before my return, but he did not. Musquito then called Mammoa to the other side of the creek, and he went over. He first,
however, asked if the blacks would spear him, and Musquito said
"no." They talked to Mammoa for a few minutes, then took up their
spears, and walked towards the hut. I got to it first, the guns had
been taken away; when I returned, Hollyoak was walking behind
me, and I asked him if he had put away the guns, he said " no,"
I made the same enquiry of Mammoa, and received the same reply.
At this moment he and Musquito were at the other side of the creek,
coming towards the hut : when they came opposite they got over,
the other natives were by the hut door, so that now the whole body
of the natives was assembled. I stood with the deceased two or
three yards off. I had three kangaroo dogs, and a sheep dog, the
deceased had one dog, they were tied to a stump. I saw Musquito
untie them, and take them into the sheep yard. I heard Mammoa
beg of him not to take them, but he made no answer. The natives
stood with their spears raised, and their points directed to the deceased and me. I told him the best thing we could do was to run
away, and that otherwise we should be killed. We accordingly did
run, when one of the blacks threw a spear which pierced my side.

E

Jack not guilty ; both the prisoners were acquitted on
the second trial of aiding and abetting in the wilful
murder of Mammoa, an Otaheitean.   A month or two
afterwards Black Jack was again tried, charged with
the murder of Patrick Macarthy, a stock-keeper at

I at first ran 200 or 300 yards, but the deceased could not keep up
with me, he called out for me to return, and pull a spear out of his
back, I did so. The wound was 3 or 4 inches deep. Some of the
natives armed with spears, were pursuing us, there might be from
30 to 40. I again ran away, and the deceased after me. I received
another spear in the back of my thigh : at this moment the blacks
were within 30 yards of me. The deceased exclaimed " Jack,
don't leave." I made no answer, but continued running till I heard
him cry, " Oh, my God ! the black fellows have got me," he was
then about 200 yards behind me. I looked back, the natives were
close to him, I saw 5 or 6 spears sticking in him, (some in his side,
and others in different parts of his body.) He was throwing some
rotten sticks at the blacks, who appeared to be standing quiet. After
looking at them a few minutes, I re-commenced my flight, and
some of them still pursued me ; eventually, however, I was lucky
enough to escape. When ten days from the time had elapsed, I ven-
tured back to the hut, and four days after my return I found the
body of the deceased, quite dead, covered with sticks, and more
than half consumed by vermin. There were some spears broken in
it. I am quite positive as to the persons of Musquito and Black
Jack. I can swear that no provocation was given to the natives, or
any violence shewn by me, or to my knowledge by the deceased.

   Cross-examined by the Court.—When the dogs were untied by
Musquito, I was deterred from interfering by the whole body, who
raised their spears with the points directed to me. I knew Black
Jack very well by his figure, and because his lips are much thinner
than those of the natives in general. He had gone into the hut several
times, and I saw him in it on the Saturday morning, three quarters
of an hour before the body of the blacks came to it. On being
spoken to, he answered me in English perfectly well. I never heard
the prisoner called " Black Jack," I call him Black Jack from his
colour.

   Cross-examined by Doctor Hood, (one of the Jury).—There
were some women with the natives, but neither the deceased nor
myself had offered any offence, or wanted to take any liberties.

   Verdict—Musquito guilty—Black Jack not guilty.

   The same prisoners were then arraigned, as principals in the second degree, for aiding and abetting in the wilful murder of Mammoa, the before-named Otaheitean.

   His Honor the Chief Justice summed up, and the Jury, after
retiring a few minutes, pronounced an acquittal.—*Hobart Town Gazette*, 1824.

Sorell Plains—he was found guilty, and with Musquito*
and six bushrangers, was executed on the 24th February.
The trial and execution of these men is looked upon by
many, as a most extraordinary precedent.

Nothing else of any importance occurred during the
year 1824. The Colony was in a most frightful state,
and but little prospects of any immediate relief.

The year 1825 was ushered in with troubles, and
from the first of January to the thirty-first of December,

---

* Musquito, in conversation with Mr. Bisdee, the jailor, and some
other persons, after his sentence, said, "Hanging no good for black
fellow."

Mr. Bisdee.—"Why not as good for black fellow as for white
fellow, if he kills a man?"

Musquito.—"Very good for white fellow, for *he* used to it."

He evidently meant that *his* execution was useless as an example
to the savages: although executions were useful amongst the white
people, who from custom understood the reason of men being
thus punished as examples for others.

Musquito, after he had been charged with murder, and a reward
had been promised for his apprehension, acted in a friendly manner
on more than one occasion to persons who had been kind to him
when he was in the habit of visiting the settlers' houses on peaceable
terms. One person, who fell into his power in a defenceless condition, in a remote place, was recognized by him as a former bene-
factor, and treated with great kindness by him and his tribe. This
person advised him to accompany him to Hobart Town, and make
peace with the Governor; but Musquito declined, giving the following explanation of the outrages laid to his charge:—"I stop
wit white fellow, learn to like blanket, clothes, bakky, rum, bread,
all same white fellow: white fellow give'd' me. By and by Gubernor send me catch bushranger—promise me plenty clothes, and
send me back Sydney, my own country: I catch him, Gubernor
tell too much a lie, never send me. I knockit about camp, prisoner
no liket me then, givet me nothing, call me b——y hangman nose.
I knock one fellow down, give waddie, constable take me, I then
walk away in bush. I get along wid mob, go all about beg some
give it bread, blanket: some take't away my "*gin* :" that make a
fight: mob rob the hut: some one tell Gubernor: all white fellow
want catch me, shoot me, 'pose he see. I want all same white
fellow he never give, mob make a rush, stock-keeper shoot plenty,
mob spear some. Dat de way me no come all same your house.
Never like see Gubernor any more. White fellow soon kill all black
fellow. You good fellow, mob no kill you."

It is but justice to add, that it was under Colonel Sorell's administration Musquito was sent to track the bushrangers.

the Colonists had little else to think of. Among the most distressing, were the depredations committed by the bushrangers and the aborigines. The Lieutenant Governor made a tour of inspection through the Colony; he visited most of the settlements, and made a short stay at Launceston, during which period he laid the foundation stone of St. John's church,* Launceston, was just then shewing symptoms of a flourishing port.†

During this year, a great number of emigrants arrived, and among the number, Alfred Stephen, Esq., and family, ‡ who came out to this Colony with the appointment of Solicitor General, to which office he was installed on the 27th April. At the commencement of this year, several other important appointments took place. Dudley Fereday, Esq. was nominated as the first Sheriff of the Island, and Joseph Hone, Esq. as the first Commissioner of the Court of Requests, a Court which commenced operations on the 5th May, in which claims to the amount of £10 might be decided by the Commissioner, without appeal to any superior court : and the Rev. W. Bedford, then Assistant Colonial Chaplain, was appointed to the situation of Superintendent of Public Schools, *vice* Mr. Mulgrave, who had resigned.

Another penal settlement was this year fixed upon. It had been found that Macquarie Harbour was illadapted for the purpose intended. The bleak climate, the sterility of the soil, and the great delay, difficulty, and danger there was in navigating vessels to the port, induced the Government, a few years afterwards, to abandon it altogether. Considering the great expense of this settlement to the British Government, it is a matter of regret that the expenditure thus incurred

---

* Twenty-eighth of January.

† Launceston contains 209 buildings of various sorts, and 800 inhabitants; amongst the former are 123 houses, 16 skillings, and 33 unfinished dwellings, 15 stores, 18 stables, and 4 workshops ; whilst of the latter, 279 are free, 306 are prisoners in Government employ, 146 are assigned, or hold tickets, 30 are females, and 39 are in gaol.—*Hobart Town Gazette*, 1825.

‡ By the *Cumberland*, 22nd January. This vessel was captured by pirates, on her homeward passage.

was not appropriated to some Colonial improvements which might ultimately have been paid for by the Colony. At the time of the compilation of these pages, not one single human being resides at Macquarie Harbour, or within one hundred miles thereof. The second penal settlement chosen was that of Maria Island; it was selected as a place of secondary punishment for educated convicts and others, whose crimes were not of such a grade as to require transportation to Macquarie Harbour. Its approximation to the river Derwent—its climate and fertile soil, and yet its sufficient distance from the main shore, (so as to cut off all chance of escape for the prisoners,) held out hopes that it would be a well-chosen spot. This settlement was therefore formed in March, and Peter Murdoch, Esq. was appointed as the Commandant.

The Hobart Town merchants, about this time, felt great apprehensions that the Government intended to remove the common wharf, from the present Old Jetty, to the Rev. R. Knopwood's Point. Great expenditure had then been incurred in buildings, by various merchants at the Old Jetty, and it was considered that should the legalized wharf be removed, that a great private loss would be sustained. The merchants, therefore, drew up an appeal to His Honor Colonel Arthur, praying that no such alteration should be sanctioned. His Honor, in reply, said he did not contemplate any such removal, "the survey of Sullivan's Cove, which had created the alarm, was solely connected with an application made to erect certain machinery, in or near the water's edge."*

A further cause of alarm was given to the inhabitants of Hobart Town, by the supposition that the authorities intended to remove the seat of Government to Brighton, that township being more centrically situated. New Norfolk was also strongly recommended by some interested individuals, as a proper site, but a strong protest was entered against such a change, which had the de-

---

* Hobart Town Gazette.

sired effect, for the project was abandoned altogether.
The erection of a splendid Government House was also
in contemplation, but abandoned; various spots were
fixed upon, and in the Government Domain the remains
of a foundation are still visible.

The first of the annual Sorell dinners, was held on the
7th of April of this year. A large number of the most
respectable settlers in the Colony attended, and the Colonists in no measured terms, expressed their satisfaction towards the administration of this able Governor.
It must have been gratifying to Colonel Sorell to have
heard of these annual festivals, held by the Colonists in
remembrance of him; and when years passed by, and
this same festival was repeated, it betokened that Colonel Sorell was still cherished in the memory of those
whom he had governed. This gratitude, on the part of
the Colonists, might serve as an instructive lesson for
future Governors, whose aim may be—" popularity."

Commerce this year was flourishing, and gradually
extending itself: large quantities of fat sheep were exported to Sydney, and the profit obtained in this trade,
induced still further shipments to be made for several
succeeding years. Wheat also was shipped to the Sister
Colony in large quantities, and the state of commercial
affairs was highly satisfactory for a settlement of only two
and twenty years standing. Some articles, which in
those days were luxuries, but which the Colonists of
modern times consider as necessaries of life, were yet
sold at exorbitant prices—among others, common teas
realized by the chest, from £30 to £40.

The township of New Norfolk, at this period, received
very great encouragement from the Government; the
church was considerably enlarged, and several houses
erected,* also, Richmond and other townships, shewed
evident symptoms of improvement.

Hitherto, in all transactions with the Government, the
dollar had been paid and re-issued at 4s. sterling; but an

---

* During the spring of this year a species of whale called a
" fin back" was caught close by the Falls, at New Norfolk.

order now appeared, by command of the Governor-in-chief, that dollars should be received in liquidation of sums due and payable to the Colonial Government, at the rate of four shillings and four pence. *

During this winter the rations that were formerly given to all fresh settlers for six months after their arrival, were reduced to four months.   This was the first check given to the emigrants—hitherto every encouragement, every possible inducement had been held out —the emigrant was promised land to cultivate, and food, till such times as he was enabled to supply himself from his own resources; but it would appear the British Government repented of its liberality, and was now anxious to check that great stimulus to emigration which had been formerly so advantageous.

His Honor the Lieutenant Governor was of opinion that every encouragement ought to be given to agriculture, and a society of that description, founded under Colonel Sorell, received his patronage.   At a dinner given by the society, His Honor and his friends attended.†

---

* GOVERNMENT PUBLIC NOTICE.
Colonial Secretary's Office, June 29th, 1825.

His Excellency the Governor is pleased to direct, that in the payment from the Colonial funds of New South Wales and its Dependencies, of all civil salaries and allowances of sterling rate, which shall become due for the period subsequent to the commencement of the ensuing quarter on the 1st of July next, the Spanish dollar shall be valued at four shillings and four pence, instead of four shillings, as heretofore, the former rate being that at which, according to the Government Notification of the 24th of April last, the said coin is received in liquidation of sums due and payable in sterling money, on account of the Colonial revenue.

All claims for salaries and allowances for any period, anterior to the 30th instant, inclusively, are requested to be presented and settled as soon as convenient, after this date.

By command of His Excellency the Governor,
R. GOULBURN, *Colonial Secretary.*

† The Agricultural Society of Van Diemen's Land had their annual dinner at the Ship Inn, Collins-street, on Friday last.   The chair was filled by James Gordon, Esq., J.P., and amongst the guests were His Honor the Lieutenant Governor, His Honor Chief Justice Pedder, and Captain Montagu.   The feast was sumptuous, and after the cloth was removed, certain resolutions relative to the

Every inducement was held out by this society for the improvement of the soil, and of stock, and valuable importations were made of the very finest description of woolled sheep by several of its members.

At the commencement of this year a second journal appeared, entitled the *Tasmanian, or Launceston Advertiser*—this paper for a time was published at the northern part of the Island, but subsequent events induced its publication in Hobart Town, and for several years afterwards, the town of Launceston had no journal of its own. The Public Press of the Colony underwent considerable improvements, and the public writers assumed a boldness of language, that seemed to excite apprehension on the part of some of those in authority. It was at this time that the letters, signed "COLONIST," made their appearance; which letters were written with a firmness of purpose, that would have done credit to any Journal in Europe. It is presumed that the spirit of opposition which had characterized the official organ of the Government, induced Colonel Arthur to remove the Government printing from the possession of its conductor; for Messrs. Ross and Howe were appointed Government Printers, and forthwith commenced publishing another *Hobart Town Gazette*. It cannot be expected, that those in authority would employ as servants, men who were constantly opposed to their measures, nor can it be wondered that Colonel Arthur should select Government Printers of his own choice. No one can doubt the propriety of taking the printing from Mr. A. Bent; but when Messrs. Ross and Howe commenced publishing the *Hobart Town Gazette*, the property in this title had been Mr. Bent's for upwards of ten years. It is impossible to reconcile this piracy with that justice which might have been expected from impartial authorities. But the depriving Mr. Bent of the Government printing and support, was not all that oc-

---

subjects for which the premiums will be given at the next annual exhibition, were carried nem. con. We are happy to add that the meeting continued until a late hour, enjoying uninterrupted festivity. —*Hobart Town Gazette.*

curred to him during the year ; for in July he was twice
tried criminally for libel upon his Honor Colonel Arthur.
The imputed libels were of an extraordinary description,
and, as before noticed, had been published in the official
Gazette. In reading the reports of these trials, it would
appear as if the libels were of a wholesale description ;
and the unmeaning nonsense of one, upon which he was
found guilty, would be, according to the opinion of modern
law and common sense, not libellous, but a parcel of unmeaning trash. However, Mr. Bent was tried twice
before a military jury, and, as was anticipated by all
the Colonists, found guilty—for the first offence he
suffered three months, and again for the last did he
suffer a similar term of imprisonment. Mr. Bent, finding
it impossible to oppose those whom the Government supported in the piracy of his title to the Gazette, was at
length compelled to change the name of his journal,
and the *Hobart Town Gazette*, of ten years standing, was
continued under the title of the " *Colonial Times.*"

It was towards the summer of this year that Mr.
Solicitor General Stephen made his celebrated attack upon
His Majesty's Attorney General, J. T. Gellibrand, Esq.
The Solicitor General first commenced proceedings by
making a motion in the Supreme Court, to have the
Attorney General " struck off the rolls," for what he alleged improper conduct as a member of the legal profession. The charges imputed were generally, that on
several occasions he advised the attornies of one party
how to proceed, at the same time he was employed as
counsel for the opposite side—that he held general retainers, and yet advised attornies how to proceed against
his own clients.

Few events have caused more general public excitement, than did these proceedings : it was not the open
manner in which accusations were made before the Supreme Court, which excited the public mind—it was the
secret investigations which were carried on, that made the
Colonists compare them to inquisitorial examinations.
His Honor the Chief Justice would in the morning sit on
the judgment seat in the Supreme Court, there to hear

F

public accusations made against the second law officer of that Court; and in the evening he was present at a board of enquiry, a secret tribunal, assembled at his own private dwelling, where the private transactions and the familiar conversations were made subjects of accusations. All kinds of petty scandal were exaggerated to a frightful extent—spies were employed to collect any information that might tend to culpate the Attorney General, and the sanctity of the family circle around the fire-side, was not exempt from intrusion—men were known to be watching whom he went to visit—and men were stationed under windows, or to listen at the crevices of doors, to collect fresh matter for renewed charges. These were indeed unpleasant times! Paper war was at its highest zenith: the most popular writers denounced this secret tribunal, but it continued its operations, * and the result may be imagined, J. T. Gellibrand was the following year suspended from office, and Joseph Hone, Esq., appointed *pro tempore.* †

---

* *The Inquisition.*—This most odious and illegal tribunal has received a sudden check. On Wednesday, in consequence of some remarks made. by the *quasi* Commissioners, the Attorney General bluntly told them in words which we do not wish to repeat, that he should no longer be present at their proceedings. The gentlemen finding themselves posed, have accordingly determined upon coming to a close; and we believe, that they will settle their little odds and ends this day, and make their report to-morrow. We shall feel it our duty to submit to our readers, the observations respecting the introduction into a British Colony of a tribunal, unknown to the British law, and which has been applied to the most illegal purposes, and threatens the most dangerous consequences to every individual, from the highest to the lowest, in the whole Colony.— *Colonial Times.*

† From the fact that Mr. Gellibrand was ultimately suspended from office, the reader will conclude that the charges laid against him were proved, and were of such a nature as to cause his removal from an office of such responsibility. Not willing that anything should appear in this work prejudicial to any individual, the author requests the reader will peruse the following opinion : it will prove that to say the least, a difference of opinion existed among the profession, as to the irregularity of the proceedings complained of by the Solicitor General :—

" I am of opinion that if the order of suspension complained of, had remained unconfirmed, and the authorities at home had waited

Connected with this unconstitutional enquiry, was the affair usually denominated " the deed-be-done" business.

until an opportunity could be offered to Mr. Gellibrand of making his defence, he would during such interval have had a right of appeal, under the 22 Geo. iii, c., 75, s. 2, to His Majesty in Council. In this case, according to the words of the statute, the proceedings in such appeal would be exactly like those in any other appeal from judgments pronounced in the Colonial Courts, which depend on the particular laws and local usages of the Colony; of these therefore, I am not at present prepared to advise ; nor is it material to consider them, in the existing and most unfortunate position of affairs, because I understand that the suspension of the Governor has been followed by an actual removal of Mr. Gellibrand from his office by the authorities in England, and that another person has been appointed to succeed him—against this exercise of the undoubted prerogative of the Crown, to dismiss its own officers, there cannot, I fear, be any appeal as matter of right ; and this was fully felt in the case of Mr. Serjeant Rough, the late President of the Court of Civil and Criminal Justice in Demerara, which in all its legal bearings is strictly analogous to the present, but, as in that case, a hearing before the Privy Council was granted as matter of favor, so I have very little doubt, on a petition to His Majesty in Council, such hearing would be granted to Mr. Gellibrand, in whose case it would unquestionably be a *mere act of tardy justice.* I think it, however, very improbable that even if Mr. Gellibrand should succeed in fully convincing the Privy Council of the falsehood of the charges on which he was suspended, it would be thought politic to restore him to the office of Attorney General, at least while the other authorities of the Colony remain unchanged, but, in such a case, he would have an equitable claim for compensation, the practical value of which must depend on other circumstances than the mere justice of his cause.

" In Mr. Gellibrand's case, I am clearly of opinion, on an attentive perusal of all the documents, that the charges have been grounded in mistake or malice, pursued with entire inattention to the rights of the accused, and decided in prejudice and anger. The charges respecting professional practice are too absurd to stand for a moment, when submitted to any man who understands business in England ; and who knows not only that a Barrister may, but that in many cases he must, by the law of Retainers, act for one party with a knowledge of the case of the other. On this ground Mr. Gellibrand has nothing to dread. It is certainly to be regretted, that ill-treated as Mr. Gellibrand was by the Commissioners, he did not remain and make his own defence, as by so doing he could have reduced his whole case into a compact and authentic form. It is also equally to be regretted that Mr. Johnson is not furnished with an authentic report of the proceedings on the motion made against Mr. Gellibrand in Court, an l which terminated in his favor.

Temple, October 11, 1835.   (Signed) J. R. T\LFOURD."

It appears from documentary evidence before the writer, that Mr. Gellibrand was not the only obnoxious officer belonging to the Government, but that H. W. Humphreys, esq. the Principal Superintendent of Police, had also enemies among those, "basking in the sunshine of power." The attacks were made on both these gentlemen simultaneously; but Major Honor's share in the transaction gaining publicity, all proceedings against the latter gentleman of course fell to the ground. It is no doubt cruel to tear open old wounds, and to advert to personal animosities which did exist, and which time may have seared, but nevertheless it is the duty of an historian to record public facts. The letter addressed by Major Honor * to the Superintendent of Police, warned him

---

* SIR,—I have lately received a most extraordinary letter from Capt. Montagu, in which, amongst other matters, I am threatened with a criminal prosecution, but for which I am left ignorant, except that my letter, relative to Ann Pope, and some private letters which I addressed to His Excellency, the subject of which were, certain abuses stated to have taken place in your office, are to form the ground work. These private letters which are thus to be handed over to the Attorney General, His Excellency pledged his honor to me, should never be produced, and that my name should never be brought into question relative to them, as His Excellency knew well that they contained information procured in the first instance, at the request of Mr. Thomas, no doubt with the knowledge and sanction of His Excellency, and in the last instance at His Excellency's own particular request ; thus, Sir, being placed as a criminal for trial, on these letters so procured, the faith I now see I foolishly relied upon, broken—no less than my total ruin and destruction meditated, branded under the official cloak of office with epithets not fit to be used to the meanest individual, your destruction aimed at through my prosecution. * * *

I must tell you that I have been employed, months back, to collect information to be laid before the Governor, and even during the investigation, to collect evidence against Mr. Gellibrand, and which shall appear in the proper time and place; in consequence of this intercourse, the subject of the abuses in the police, became the subject of conversation, and Mr. Thomas furnished the memorandum. (Copy of which I enclose) as the grounds of the letter I was to write to the Governor, and in which I was to procure information to be relied upon. I accordingly wrote a letter, and headed it " private," on receipt of which, His Excellency sent for me almost immediately— the informant required two free pardons, (if he proved what he stated) and His Excellency argued on the danger of giving them before the

of the dangerous situation in which he had been placed, and his popularity alone may be said to have saved him from utter ruin. It is beyond dispute, that "free pardons were to be placed in the hands of Major Honor, and left blank, as to the parties' names, provided *certain evidence could be procured ;*" and it is also notorious that one of the principal movers in the charges made, and to be made, against the Attorney General and the Principal Superintendent of Police, wrote the following note to Major Honor, relative to these proceedings :—

"MY DEAR MAJOR.—You may depend on me—I will ask no names or questions, but will perform what you promise, provided *the deed be done !*—Your's, J. T."

The "deed-to-be-done" was the getting up evidence

---

matter was prosecuted to conviction, lest it might be said they were given to procure evidence ; he pledged his honour to do so when the affair was finally finished, according to the statement made : and requested of me to make some better terms.

I applied again to the informant, who refused to trust His Excellency's promises, but expressed his satisfaction if the pardons were left blank with me, to be delivered in twelve months, if he proved his statement. The Governor sent for me again, and still requested to make better terms, which as I could not do, I neither wrote or called, intending not to give myself any more trouble about it. * * *

I stated exactly what was stated to me, and which implicated His Excellency also : if any public money was embezzled or misapplied, and that the Governor consented that the pay of the individual should be stopped to make it good, you were no more to blame than him —and if blame was imputable, he was equally implicated with you. You will see, Sir, that it has been endeavoured to make a tool of me, and when it was found that I could not stand forward to be an accuser—taking the whole responsibility on myself, those who should have protected and saved me, are the very persons who now, in this ungenerous and most unjustifiable manner, wish to sacrifice me to their own ends.—I have the honor to be, &c.,

R. HONOR.

To the Hon. H. W. HUMPHREY, ESQ.
Principal Superintendent of Police.

Copy of a memorandum referred to in the foregoing, private and confidential :—

GOVERNMENT ABUSES IN THE POLICE OFFICE.—No person can get any document from the Office without bribery—every thing is paid for—B—d pocketted the license money, £100 currrency, has kept it twelve montns—and Mr. Humphrey knows that he is now in arrears for the fees due to the Crown for a large amount.

which might lead to conviction, and for which two free pardons were named as the price. It was these secret assassin-like proceedings, that made people dissatisfied and disgusted with men in power, who could so conduct themselves—but years have since passed by—much is forgiven, and still more forgotten, and few of the modern settlers have ever heard of Major Honor, and the disgraceful transactions in which he was mixed up—may similar proceedings never again outrage the feelings of the Colonists, or tarnish the history of Van Diemen's Land.

Bushranging during this year was rapidly on the increase. At times, one or two of the desperadoes were captured and executed, but all endeavours to bring the Colony into a state of tranquility, seemed unavailable. The notorious Plumb was one of the most daring, and his apprehension and execution, for a short period, seemed to check the outrages of his companions. The Government, finding the Colonists were unable of themselves to bring these outlaws to justice, issued a Government Order, offering rewards. * The bush-

---

* GOVERNMENT AND GENERAL ORDERS.

Government House, April 14th, 1825.

It has occasioned the Lieutenant Governor much concern, that the continued outrages of the two prisoners M'Cabe and Brady, have led to the untimely death of another settler.

His Honor has directed that a reward of twenty-five guineas shall be given for the apprehension of either of these men, and that any prisoner, giving such information as may directly lead to their apprehension, shall receive a Ticket-of-Leave, and that any prisoner apprehending and securing either of them, in addition to the above reward, shall receive a Conditional Pardon.

The Magistrates are very pressingly desired to circulate this Order, and to direct the Constables to visit all huts of Stock-keepers, Shepherds, and others, in their respective districts ; notifying the rewards offered, and cautioning such persons against receiving, harbouring, or supporting these men, who are charged with the commission of murder. Fifty acres of land, free from restrictions, will be given to the Chief Constable, in whose district either M'Cabe or Brady are taken, provided it shall be certified by the Magistrate of the district, that he has zealously exerted himself in the promulgation of this Order, and in the adoption of the measures for giving it effect.

The Magistrates will see the importance of conveying timely in-

rangers had then been committing their depredations nearly twelve months—these rewards however, were insufficient; these desperate men had means whereby they could elude all the endeavours made to apprehend them. In fine, the pecuniary rewards were doubled, and any information given by a prisoner, by which a capture could be made, was to be recompensed by a conditional pardon; and should a prisoner of the Crown apprehend either of the leaders, Brady or M'Cabe, he was to have a free pardon, as also a free passage to England; yet were these offers also for a time insufficient, and the bushrangers continued their depredations in a systematical manner. Towards the latter end of the year, the people of Hobart Town again intimated their willingness to do the duty of the military in the town, and thus allow the military to proceed into the interior, and at length His Honor accepted the offer.* The whole disposable

formation of the movements of M'Cabe and Brady; and they will consider themselves fully authorised to incur any reasonable expense in so doing.

By command of His Honor the Lieutenant Governor,
JOHN MONTAGU, *Secretary.*

* The inhabitants in Hobart Town having most handsomely volunteered to undertake, as Special Constables, the protection of the town, the Lieutenant Governor feels the most perfect confidence in their prudence and courage, and accepts their services as a means of enabling him to despatch a greater number of troops into the interior.

His Honor anticipates that this sacrifice of personal comfort on the part of the residents in Hobart Town, will at once operate as a stimulus throughout the Colony; and that every free inhabitant in the country will heartily co-operate with the military, in assisting the civil powers in the apprehension of the gang of bushrangers, headed by Brady. Every district is now occupied with troops, so that none feel unprotected; and if all will unite in circulating information of the movements of this banditti, it is quite impossible that they can long escape the hands of justice. To this most material point His Honor anxiously calls the attention of the whole community, and more especially of the Magistrates and District Constables, and begs, as they value the security and protection of each other, that they will no longer be so negligent in giving information.

It seems to have been the successful policy of the bushrangers to threaten with violence any persons whom they plunder, if they stir within a certain number of hours to occasion alarm. The Lieutenant Governor begs that this threat may be despised; and although he would desire every master of a family to remember the conduct

force of the Colony, both civil and military, was then
sent in pursuit of Brady and his gang ; and although
the chief of the band could not be apprehended, yet
M‘Cabe, his most desperate companion, fell into the
hands of justice, and suffered for his numerous crimes.
The public journals were filled with the repeated outrages of these men *—and Brady was every where.

---

of Mr. George Taylor, and like him determine to resist, yet if any
should unavoidably be surprised, he begs them not to hesitate in
spreading the alarm the instant the robbers have withdrawn, and if
possible, watching at the same time the direction they take.—*Extract
from the Government Regulations.*

* We regret to be obliged to announce that the hopes we expressed in our last, of the apprehension of the banditti, have not
been justified by the event, they have passed the Derwent ; how is
yet not accurately known. That there are wretches base enough
to cherish and foster these unhappy men, is however, certain. That
such may meet the fate they deserve, is our hearty wish. The mischief they do is incalculable, they are the worst of criminals, because every offence which the banditti commit, is in a certain degree to be attributed to their aid, without which their associates
could not have so long evaded justice. It appears that about three
weeks ago they passed the river. The first place where they made
their appearance, was upon the farm of Mr. Silas Gatehouse, near
Oyster Bay, they met Mr. Den, (Mr. G.'s) overseer, in the fields,
near the house, and taking him with them, kept him for six days and
nights their prisoner. It is but justice to them to say that they
treated him with civility, and as they boast of being furnished with
the Hobart Town newspapers, they will see that this forbearance
from adding violence to their other crimes is not overlooked. Their
treatment to the females at the different houses they have robbed,
has also been remarkable, in every individual instance, (notwithstanding the numerous reports to the contrary) for propriety, if such
a term can be applied to any of their lawless acts. Brady declared
in one instance, that if any of the gang should dare to offer insult to
a female, that he would blow his brains out. We are happy to
state this, because the most injurious reports have been circulated,
calculated to create misery in families, without the smallest foundation in fact. The last accounts of these men were from the neighbourhood of Bagdad, where they were seen on Sunday evening last,
as to which we forbear stating any particulars at present, and we
are glad of the opportunity of readily complying with the communication with which we were favoured from a high official quarter :
not more from the report which we feel it our duty to shew invariably to such, than that we completely concur with the views therein
expressed.—*Colonial Times.*

The daring of the bushrangers was so great, that at one
time they made themselves masters of the jail at Pittwater, and arrested several free settlers and the military.*

---

* On Friday evening last, about dusk, Brady, Bird, Dunn,
Murphy, and four others, made their appearance at the house of
Mr. Robert Bethune, at Pitt-water. They made himself, his overseer, and all his servants prisoners, and took possession of his house
and premises—remained there the whole of the night and the next
day, on the evening of which, about eight o'clock, Mr. Walter Bethune and Mr. Bunster arrived there on horseback. The weather
was extremely rainy. On their arrival at the door, a man presented himself, who called out, as if to servants, to take Mr. Bethune's horse, and who turned out to be Brady. These gentlemen
were, however, treated with the utmost civility. Dinner was provided for them, and every attention paid them. About ten o'clock,
Brady announced to them his intention of proceeding to liberate
the prisoners in the jail at Sorell Town, and accordingly tying the
Mr. Bethune's together, and all their other captives, eighteen in
number, two by two, they were forced to accompany them to that
town, where they arrived just as Mr. Gunn's party of soldiers were
cleaning their firelocks, having been out the whole of the day in
pursuit of the very men, who now taking them by surprise seized all
their arms, and locked them into a cell of the gaol. At this moment
Mr. Long the Gaoler escaped from his residence immediately adjoining, and ran to Mr. Gunn at Dr. Garrett's, to communicate the
intelligence. Mr. Gunn immediately took up his double-barrelled
piece, and was proceeding towards the gaol, when he was met by
two of the banditti. He raised his gun, but at that moment received
the entire contents of one of theirs' in his right arm, which tore it
to pieces above the elbow. Several shots were fired at this moment,
one of which grazed Dr. Garrett, and another slightly wounded
Mr. Gunn in the breast, Mr. Glover had a little before gone to the
gaol, armed with a double-barrelled gun, and was captured, his
gun taken from him, and broken to pieces, and himself confined
with the other gentlemen who had fallen into their hands. Nothing
more of them is accurately known, the prisoners did not quit the
gaol, but remained there quietly ! On the bushrangers departing
they put up a stick with a great coat and hat upon it, to imitate a
sentinel at the gaol door, in order to gain as much time as possible—
they were perfectly open and unreserved in their communications.
In answer to the enquiries from Mr. Bethune, as to how they crossed
the river, they stated that they had a boat of their own with six oars,
with which they could cross at any time. One circumstance is
certain, that none of these men were at Bagdad at the time spoken
of lately, and therefore some other robbber must have personated
Brady, upon that extraordinary and mysterious occasion. He had

On the 24th of November, General Darling touched at this Port, on his way to take the charge of the Government of New South Wales. He arrived here on board the merchant ship the *Catherine Stewart Forbes,* and on his landing, the usual military honors were paid him by the troops—his stay was but of short duration. He brought with him the reply of the Home Government to the address of the Colonists for independence. The British Government had listened to the prayer, and from this time the Colony became independent of New South Wales.*

heard of it, and that the Lieutenant Governor had been informed that he had offered to surrender with his party, at which he expressed extreme indignation. They stated, that they had a farm in the mountains, were they had quantities of sheep, cattle, and horses, to which they could retreat when necessary. We believe this is an accurate relation of what occurred on this extraordinary occasion. No possible blame can attach to the military, who had just arrived after a fatiguing day, in very rainy weather, and who were in the act of cleaning their arms when the banditi captured them. We lament to state that Mr. Gunn's arm has been amputated, but it is some consolation to know that he is doing well. We have no doubt that his gallantry and his sufferings will not be overlooked in the proper quarter, and that this gentlemen, disabled as he is, and lost by this unhapppy event to the honorable profession to which he promised to be an ornament, will be liberally provided for. They took one man with them, but made him intoxicated, and then left him.— *Colonial Times.*

 * *By His Excellency Lieutenant General Ralph Darling, com-*
     commanding His Majesty's Forces, Captain General and
     and Governor-in-chief of the Island of Van Diemen's Land.

The King having thought fit to constitute and erect the Island of Van Diemen's Land into a separate Colony, independent of the Government of New South Wales; and His Majesty having further been pleased to appoint Lieutenant Governor General Ralph Darling to be the first Governor thereof, His Excellency takes the earliest opportunity to notify the same.

The Governor, in offering his congratulations to the Inhabitants on the event which he has now had the pleasure to announce, begs to assure them, that he not only participates in their feelings on the satisfactory evidence which it affords of the growing importance of this interesting and valuable settlement, and though circumstances do not permit of his continuing to administer the Government, His Excellency has the satisfaction to think that in the discharge of his duties in the Sister Colony as Governor-in-Chief, he shall find fre-

With this seperation, came many of the evils which Colonel Sorell had pointed out. The Government being wholly distinct from that of New South Wales, it became necessary to model numerous departments, which before were unnecessary. The Charter appointed two Councils—the Executive and the Legislative. The former much resembling the Privy Council at home, the members of which, are the advisers of the Governor on all occasions. The Legislative Council, as its title signifies, is for the purpose of enacting laws for the Colony; the members of both are nominated by the Crown, or, rather, by the Lieutenant Governor, for on the death or suspension of the members, the Governor appoints, and as the official dignity is entirely honorary, the Home Government invariably approves of the nomination. That a Council so formed, should prove unsatisfactory to the Colonists, cannot be wondered. The Legislative Council, which most strangers would believe to be a Representative Body of the free Colonists—a little Colonial House of Commons—has proved to be worse than nothing, as far as the interests of the Colonists are concerned. The great power the Lieutenant Governor has had

quent opportunities of co-operating with the Local Administration, (the conduct of which affords the most gratifying testimony of the zeal and ability of His Honor the Lieutenant Governor), in seconding His Majesty's paternal exertions for the prosperity of this infant Colony; and the Inhabitants may depend on His Excellency's earnest desire to contribute to this important object, and to promote their welfare by every means in his power.

His Majesty, in consequence of the separation of this Colony from the Government of New South Wales, has been pleased to issue a warrant, bearing date the seventeenth day of July last, constituting a Legislative Council for this Government, and His Excellency is pleased further to notify, that His Majesty has also appointed an Executive Council, the members of which, respectively, are as follow, viz.—

EXECUTIVE COUNCIL.—The Lieutenant Governor, The Chief Justice, The Colonial Secretary, A. W. H. Humphrey, Esq., Jocelyn Thomas, Esq.

Dated at Government House, Hobart Town, this third day of December, One Thousand Eight Hundred and Twenty-five, in the sixth year of His Majesty's reign.

RALPH DARLING.

in the nomination of fresh members, has ultimately reduced the Assembly of fifteen to be little more than a circle of his relations and friends; and members. whom the people imagined studied their interests, became obnoxious, and their suspension and ultimate removal followed—the proceedings of this Council, will require further notice in this work. On the independence of the Colony being declared, the designation of "His Honor," by which the Lieutenant Governor had hitherto been addressed, was changed to the appellation of "His Excellency," a term which is invariably given, where the party has no immediate superior.

Little else of importance occurred during this year; the Colonists assembled on one occasion, and drew up an address to the Governor, in which they regretted that the press was subjected to persecution—that they were happy that they enjoyed the Freedom of the Press, and hoped to enjoy the still greater liberty of Trial by Jury.*

The condemnations and executions of this year, were truly awful. At one time, seventy-one human beings received sentence; twenty-five were sentenced death.†

---

* We have witnessed with sincere regret that prosecutions for libel have been instituted against one of the two journals published in this town, and we hear that other prosecutions are in progress against the other journal. We assure your Excellency we heartily lament to witness these occurrences, because, independent of the natural abhorrence which Englishmen naturally feel against personal vituperation and slander, we cannot but feel much regret in observing that the official organ of the Government has become exposed to such prosecutions. We refrain from noticing the abuse it so liberally bestows on the whole community, for we are convinced that your Excellency must have seen upon a late occasion, that the most respectable part of it have shewn their attachment and loyalty to the Government.—*Extract from an Address to His Excellency Colonel Arthur.*

† One of the most lamentable sights which can be exhibited in any country, took place this morning, in the placing at the bar of the Criminal Court, seventy-one human beings, to receive their sentences, for crimes of every degree of turpitude, committed in a country where the population is so comparatively small, and where the inducements to crime are so few.—Of these unhappy men, twenty-five received sentence of death! many of whom will most probably suffer this awful doom.—*Supreme Court, December 20.*

During this year, also, executions took place at the penal settlement of Macquarie Harbour.

The commencement of the year 1826 brought no relief to the Colonists. Bushranging continued with all its horrors.* It now became absolutely necessary, that

---

* " On the night of the 5th the bushrangers set fire, and burnt down the stock-yard, with all the wheat belonging to Mr. Abraham Walker, and Commissary Walker, opposite Mr. Thomas Archer's. The extent of the damage is not yet ascertained. The bushrangers were seen between the Punt and Mr. Gibson's stock-yard, and on the 6th they sent word to Mr. Massey, on the South Esk, Benlomond, that they would hang him and burn his wheat. A great fire was seen in the direction of the house, but it is to be hoped they have not executed their threat. The bushrangers have Mr. Dry's two white carriage horses with them. They shot Thomas Kenton dead at the Punt, on the South Esk; they called him out of the house, and deliberately shot him. Two runaways were last week sent into Launceston gaol, from Pressnell's, where they were taken; one of them broke our of gaol, and was met by the bushrangers, who asked him to join them, and on his refusal, they shot him dead. Brady now wears Colonel Balfour's cap, which was knocked off at Dry's. When the bushrangers were going down the Tamar, they captured Captain White, of the *Duke of York*, in his boat, Captain Smith, late of the *Brutus*, who was with him,· being well dressed, was mistaken for Colonel Balfour. They knocked him down ; but, discovering their mistake, they apologized. They then made Captain White go down upon his knees, and were going to shoot him, but Captain Smith interfered, and saved his life, on representing to them the misery it would inflict upon his wife and children. During the night, Captains Smith and White were allowed to depart, and they made the best of their way to Launceston, where they gave the necessary information ; but unfortunately, it was too late, the bushrangers having crossed the river, and proceeded to commit the dreadful enormities before stated."—*Colonial Times.*

EXTRACT OF ANOTHER LETTER.—" Watson, who was employed by Brady and his gang as a carrier, says, that on their route, they got into such a thick scrub, that they could not extricate their horses, although they took the saddles off, and of course there left them. The first day after their arrival, Brady went out at dusk to a high hill, to look for the *Glory*, but not returning till morning on the third day, Guilders made his escape, (to give information, which he did, to Colonel Balfour), while Goodwin was on sentry ; for this he was brought to a Court Martial, shot dead, and flung out of their prize boat into the Tamar. They then sailed three times round the *Glory*, Brady advising them to take her—he went to the stern of the boat, and said, 'decide among yourselves, let not my voice avail you anything;' they then said, as the wind was foul. they would

the rewards offered for the apprehension of these men should exceed those that could be given by the banditti for their preservation. The desperate band headed by Brady, had been twenty-one months carrying terror and desolation in their progress, from one end of the island to the other, when a Proclamation was at length issued, offering a reward of one hundred guineas, or three hundred acres of land, free of all restrictions; or a free pardon, and passage to England, to any prisoner giving information whereby any one of the twelve principal desperadoes might be taken. Almost immediately after the publication of this Proclamation, the total extinction of the bushrangers ensued. The military, aided by a portion of the prisoner population, scoured the country; the different parties were fell in with, and deadly skirmishes took place, in which generally the bushrangers were worsted. As their bands became more divided, so did their capture become more easily accomplished—one by one they fell into the hands of those in pursuit of them—and in about a month after the high rewards were offered, not a single bushranger remained at large. During, one week in the month of May, twelve of the

---

not take her. They then landed, and sent Watson into Launceston to say, that they would that night rob Mr. Dry, and would go to the gaol in Launceston, take out Jeffries, torture him, and then shoot him. It was treated with derision! A man who escaped from Mr. Dry's came into Launceston at 10 o'clock, P.M., to say that the banditti were there. Colonel Balfour instantly started with one serjeant, ten soldiers, and some volunteers. They surrounded the house just as they had packed up their booty, when a brisk fire commenced; the bushrangers were forced out of the house into the back yard, and kept firing into the house; it was quite dark, and the banditti were thought to have gone, when Colonel Balfour proceeded with half the soldiers, to defend the town, (rendered the more necessary, as a part of the banditti, under Bird and Dunn, had been previously despatched by Brady to attack Launceston.) On his going away, the banditti went up to Mr. Wedge's hut, (adjoining one of the out buildings), and began to plunder; when the soldiers, with Dr. Priest, proposed to charge. The bushrangers heard it, and fired a volley, by which Dr. Priest's horse was shot dead, and himself shot in the knee. The soldiers, not above five in number, with some volunteers, fired and charged, but owing to the darkness the banditti escaped."—*Colonial Times.*

most notorious offenders suffered death.   Amongst the
most enterprising of those engaged in capturing them,
may be named Colonel Balfour, of the 40th Regiment, to
whom the inhabitants of Launceston offered public testimony of their high esteem towards him, upon his retirement as Commandant of that settlement, to which
appointment he was succeeded by Major Abbott, who
had then just returned from England.   In affirming that
the bushrangers were entirely destroyed at this period,
it should be explained that a few petty robbers for some
time after committed paltry depradations, but on such a
trifling scale, that with the capture of Brady, bushranging for years after may be said to have been extinct.
A great stand was also made about this time against the
wholesale system of sheep and cattle robberies, which,
to this period had been carried on with effrontery, to an
extent almost incredible—the determined measures, however, enforced by the Government, had the effect, if not
wholly of abolishing these nefarious practices, at least
of giving the system a very salutary check.

The aborigines continued their warfare with determination and effect; scarcely a week passed over without
robberies being committed by them; and many stock-
keepers and others met untimely deaths by means of
these poor deluded creatures.   A public writer, of this
year, recommended that the whole of the aborigines should
" for their own safety, be sent to the main, or else to
King's Island, as otherwise they would all be hunted
down like wild beasts and destroyed;" he also declared
that there were only two hostile tribes, that of Oyster
Bay and the Shannon ; and from the localities where the
depredations were most common, there appears to be
some truth in the assertion.   The war, however, became
more general, and it is much to be feared that other
tribes were attacked by the white population—perhaps
through ignorance—which ultimalely caused no discri-
mination to be shewn by either party.   It was in May,
of this year, that two aborigines of this Colony were
tried in the Supreme Court, for the murder of Thomas
Colley, a stock-keeper—this *farce* occupied two days.

The Attorney General for the time being, was of course
the prosecutor : but much difference of opinion having
arisen as to the propriety, and even the legality of the
trial and execution of Musquito and Black Jack, the
Court appeared to be more considerate towards these
poor ignorant creatures ; for not only did the Chief
Justice appoint counsel for them, but also, an interpreter
was employed on the occasion.*   Few events have tar-

---

* By reference to our report of the proceedings of the Supreme
Court, it will be seen that the two Aborigines, named Jack and
Dick, have been tried and found guilty of murder. We very much
question the policy, to say the least, of this proceeding. Let us
look a little at the facts. These unhappy men, removed it is universally admitted, but by a very slight shade from the brute creation,
are subjected to all the forms of our criminal laws, and are further
subjected by the verdict to receive the punishment which Englishmen, for whom these laws were made, would suffer in a like case.
We are aware of the legal dogma, that all persons on English land
become subjected to English laws.—Good!   But as far as these poor
wretches are concerned, it is not quite clear, that as relates to them
it is English ground. It is true that formal possession has been
taken of this country by the hoisting of the English flag, and by
other mummeries of the same description. But what do these poor
creatures know of this, and even if this position is accurately and
closely investigated, is it quite clear that it will bear the enquiry.
Let us look at it a little. A British force arrives here, and takes
formal possession of the country. If that force had been opposed by
the natives, and streams of blood had flowed on both sides, we
should have been then supposed to have acquired possession by the
right of conquest ; and of course these poor blacks would then
have been subjected to all the consequences which, on reference to
Vattel, Grotius, and other writers, on international law, might appear to attach. What would then have been the result?   Why
that, instead of their being subjected to our law, we, the invaders
would have been subjected to theirs ! It is wholly out of the argument to refer their state, and that they are little better "*feræ na-
turæ.*"-that they have no laws ! that very doctrine itself says
abundance against the system now adopted as to them ; because, if
indeed they are so degraded in the scale of humanity, surely it would
almost be as just to subject any other description of wild animal to
the operation of the British law ! But the argument itself, in another
point of view, is wholly untenable. The plain and only fact to be
enquired into, according to the writers we have referred to, would be,
how did we obtain possession of the land. For we repeat, if by conquest, the conquerors became subject to the territorial laws of the
conquered. Their inhumanity—their being wholly unappropriate to

nished the history of any Colony more than the manner
in which the *civilized* portions of society conducted themselves towards their fellow-creatures—the less gifted
blacks of these wild woods ; and it is distressing that
these pages must record, for years to come, conduct disgraceful on the part of the Colonists, as also impolitic
on the part of those in authority.   On the occasion of
the trial of " Jack" and " Dick"—convict stock-keepers
gave testimony against them, and a Military Jury of
seven, pronounced a verdict of guilty.   Let it not be

---

the circumstances and habits of the former, is wholly out of the argument.   Two instances will suffice.   What was the defence of the
ever lamented Sir Thomas Picton, when he was tried in the Court
of King's Bench, for torturing a Spanish girl in Trinidada?   That it
was a conquered country, and the law of torture being that of the
country, which alone could be acted upon, it was justifiable.
Again.   The Cape of Good Hope ; the execrable and detestable fiscal
proceedings lately adopted in that Colony upon British subjects,
were justified under the Dutch law, which being that of the land,
alone prevailed.   It is foreign to the purpose to answer these remarks by a sneer as to any law of these wretched savages.   The only
question is,—is the position we have taken, the accurate one, and
we defy its refutation!   Let us look at the present invasion of Ava !
the inhabitants of which country we contend, are two-fold less civilized than the Tasmanian Aborigines, because their habits and practices are ten-fold more detestable.   Their idol worship, their human
sacrifices, their infanticides their worse than Molochian abominations,
will bear no comparison as to civilization, with the simple and comparatively harmless habits of these poor miserable creatures. And will it
be contended that the British law would be for one moment even talked
of in reference to such a subject, if such occurred at Rangoon?   Our
limits prevent our continuing this subject !   But we have said enough
to set the great " Moralists" we possess, at work.   We trust the
" Devi s' standard bloody battle men," will not let their enthusiasm sleep on this occasion.   To be sure, we have seen that pro-
motion followed fast thereon.   And such is an amazing sedative.
But we hope that there are those here who will use their influence
to prevent these poor creatures becoming victims to a breach of law
which they understand not, and their responsibility to which is
questionable, by the very highest authority.   As example, their
execution will be worse than useless.   For to whom will such be
made—not to the aboriginal tribes, because none of them will be
present to witness it, and their scattered habits of life, prevent even
the possibility of their hearing of it.   We trust those in authority
will not consider these observations, either facetious or unworthy remark.   Humanity alone dictates them—*Colonial Times.*

H

inferred the reference to the Military Jury is intended to impute to these gentlemen, anything but the most honorable conduct: as men upon their oaths, bound to decide according to the evidence given, they in all probability could not come to a different conclusion; but it should be remembered that these military officers had, in all probability, been themselves stationed at out-posts, where the natives may have been committing depredations—nay, they may even have assisted in repelling them by force, and were no doubt accustomed to look upon them, (as was common in those times), as mere beasts, to hunt which, was a sport almost as common as that of kangarooing. The two unfortunate aborigines, "Jack," and "Dick," were executed with four malefactors; and from a publication of that time, it would appear that, "after the elder of the aborigines, named 'Dick,' had received the sacrament, (who had never since his confinement, been able to walk, suffering under a loathsome cutaneous disease, which almost covered his body), he screamed out most bitterly, apparently fully sensible of his impending fate; and notwithstanding he could climb up the ladder to the platform, he refused, when he was carried up by the executioner. Being placed on the platform, he would not stand up along with the rest of the unhappy sufferers: he was therefore placed upon a stool, which dropped with him. when the awful moment arrived which plunged them all into eternity. His partner in crime, an interesting youth, seemed quite unmoved at his awful situation," until just before his execution, "the poor lad then became sensible of his destiny, and prayed most fervently for the forgiveness of his sins."* Thus finished this second legal outrage on these bewildered people.

---

* During the period he has been confined in gaol, if any one spoke to him in a friendly manner, he would laugh and appear as cheerful as if he were with his sable brethren in the woods. He declared his innocence, both before and after trial. The old black died very hard; and the cord slipped from the younger up to the elbow, he reached up his hand to his neck, and bled profusely from the nose.—*Colonial Times.*

It would appear from a Government Notice,* issued
on the very day on which the execution of these unfortunate men took place, that the conduct of the Government required some vindication. The Colonists foresaw
that, if the execution would have any influence whatever
on the native tribes, it would be that of engendering
revenge. These natives could not be expected to comprehend that the lives of their companions had been
sacrificed to the outraged laws, when they knew not what
laws meant, and were totally ignorant of the customs of
their invaders. Strange as it may appear, His Excellency the Lieutenant Governor " *hoped*" that this
example might tend, " not only to prevent the commission of similar atrocities by the aborigines, but to induce
towards them, the observance of a conciliatory line of
conduct, rather than harsh or violent treatment." The

---

* GOVERNMENT NOTICE.

Colonial Secretary's Office, September 13, 1826.

In the number of the unhappy men, upon whom the extreme
sentence of the law has this morning been carried into execution,
were the two natives who murdered the stock-keeper of Mr. Hart, at
Great Swan Port, and the Lieutenant Governor would hope that
this example may tend not only to prevent the commission of similar
atrocities by the aborigines, but to induce towards them the observance of a conciliatory line of conduct, rather than harsh or violent
treatment, the latter being but too likely to produce measures of retaliation, which have their issue in crime and death. His Excellency is particularly desirous, that Magistrates and Settlers generally, shall impress on the minds of their servants, the necessity for
preserving a good understanding with this ignorant race, which is
alike dictated by humanity and self-interest ; for although it may at
present be found difficult, and perhaps impracticable, to improve
their moral condition, forbearance and kindness may do much towards lessening aggression on their part, and rendering them comparatively harmless.

Whilst, therefore, a manifestly wanton and direct violation of the
common law of mankind, such as was perpetrated by the two individuals who suffered this day, will assuredly be visited with the
same punishment, the Lieutenant Governor is determined to protect
the aborigines of the Colony from injury or annoyance : and on
offenders in this respect, the severest penalties which the law may
prescribe, will be inflicted without the slightest interposition of
mercy.—By command of His Excellency,

W. H. HAMILTON.

execution of these men, in the opinion of the considerate Colonists, appeared *a strange method of conciliation!* Supposing it possible that the whole of the tribes could have been made acquainted with the manner in which these two aborigines met their death—would not the reasoning of such men point out to them, that it was a deliberate murder? To have fallen by a musket ball, in the heat of a conflict with the whites, would, in the eyes of such men, have been considered as one of the chances of war, which all were subject to—but why they were taken and deliberately put to death on a scaffold, must have been beyond their comprehension—they could not account for such conduct. It is to be regretted that these men suffered—if example had been required, how much more advisable would it have been to have commenced by the trial and execution of some of the whole-sale murderers of the aborigines—the first perpetrators of crime; but *not one single individual was ever brought to a Court of Justice, for offences committed against these harmless creatures.**

The Van Diemen's Land Company, incorporated by

* From the earliest period of the Colony, there had always been more or less communication, between the Aborigines, or the original inhabitants, and their European visitors—it may be said, invaders. Perhaps of all creatures that wear the human form, these natives may justly be placed in the very lowest scale of barbarism. Their complexion is quite black, their hair woolly—their features flat and disagreeable—they go perfectly naked—live wholly in the woods, having no huts, or other dwellings, unless the occasional placing of a little bark across a few upright sticks may be so termed—and although they are known to have distinct tribes, each with its chief or leader, they do not appear to have any rites or ceremonies, religious or otherwise, but live in a state of brute nature. In all these respects they are infinitely inferior to the Aborigines of New South Wales. Very soon after the Colony was first settled by the English, an unfortunate affair took place between a party of the 102d regiment, then quartered here, and some of the natives, which ended in the use of fire-arms, and by which some of the latter were severely wounded. To say that this was the origin of the ill-blood that has ever since subsisted at times between the two parties, would perhaps be hazarding too much; but it may be fairly asserted, that until a very late day, too much of the spirit that gave rise to this wanton outrage has been continued towards them with impunity—

an Act of the British Parliament, became subject of much uneasiness to the Colonists, who were fearful

---

their women having been forcibly taken away by stock-keepers and others, and treated with every species of indignity. Still, in most parts of the country, there was usually a shew of friendly intercourse between the English and the natives; the latter coming fearlessly into the settled districts, and being often entertained with bread, and other articles of common use. Things went on this way for many years; but about 1814 the natives began to be troublesome, and to exercise at times their dexterity with spears and waddies, to the injury of the settlers and their servants; and from that period to the present, aggressions of this sort have been often repeated. It was only about the year 1826 or 7, however, that the evil began to assume a serious character. The friendly visits that had been common on the part of the blacks, particularly in the winter, had been for some time discontinued; accounts were constantly reaching head-quarters of some atrocity or other, committed on the person of whatever unhappy straggler was so unfortunate as to fall in with them. They were doubtless incited to much of this hostility by the manner in which their women were treated by persons who, living in remote corners of the Colony, fancied they were beyond the reach of control or punishment; but it may still more perhaps, be attributed to the instigation of an aborigine of New South Wales, who was known to be the immediate cause or instrument of several murders, and who, having been taken in 1824, was tried, convicted, and afterwards executed.

Subsequently, numerous bodies of the blacks still made their appearance in the winter, even in the streets of Hobart Town, with no unfriendly disposition; and it must be granted, that upon these occasions every thing on the part of Colonel Arthur was attempted towards improving their condition, that humanity could dictate; but it was useless. Their savage state made them insensible to all that was endeavoured for their good; and the whole result of this, and other similar efforts, has been to give them such a taste of civil life, as to stimulate a desire of possessing themselves of sugar, blankets, and other articles in use with the settlers, that were previously unknown to them, and to procure which they have since constantly committed cruel robberies.

They have frequently shewn themselves endowed with great quickness of perception, or an acuteness in the senses, not unfrequently bestowed by Providence, where such gifts are needed to supply other deficiencies. Their language is not clearly known, although it is now better understood than formerly; but it may be observed that they sound the letter R, with a rough deep emphasis, particularly when excited by anger or otherwise, and that upon these occasions also, they use the word werr, werr, very vehemently. Their usual food is kangaroo, opossums, or any other native animal

that the large capital, and great influence possessed at
home, by some of its shareholders, would ultimately be

---

they can catch. They broil the flesh, or rather, just warm it on the
coals, and then devour it with greediness. They likewise eat a root
which they sometimes find in the earth, and which is not in taste
altogether unlike a yam. They never kindle large fires, lest their
haunts might be tracked, and generally where provisions and water
are easily attainable. They are so extremely dexterous in the use of
the spear, as seldom to miss a mark, even at a considerable distance;
and in managing their waddies also, they display great skill and
prowess. When they fight among themselves, the chief weapon is
the waddy, which they flourish in the air for some time, with boisterous threats and gestures, and then fall to in good earnest. It has
been said that their skulls are thicker than those of Europeans—
they had need be so, to receive the blows that are inflicted on these
occasions, as they sometimes appear heavy enough to fell an ox.

They are said to be extremely fond of their children, and to treat
their women kindly; the latter however, are compelled to do all the
drudgery of the party, as is usual with savages. In their natural
disposition, they have the character of being fierce, treacherous,
and revengeful. There scarcely appears however, grounds for im-
puting to the natives of Van Diemen's Land, a superhuman share of
these, or of other bad qualities, or on the other hand, a less proportion
of some of the better properties of our nature, than belong to others
of their species, if they were capable of being developed by circumstances. It should be remembered, that these Aborigines exhibit man as nature has made him; unwrought upon by civilization
—unpolished by the influence of the arts and sciences—unformed,
unmoulded, into anything like shape of mind. In this riot of wild-
ness, favourable in its very existence to the display of our worst at-
tributes, and to the concealment of our better ones, how have they
been treated? Worse than dogs, or even beasts of prey—hunted
from place to place—shot—their families torn from them—the mother snatched from her children, to become the victim of the lust and
cruelty of their civilized Christian neighbours! Every allowance
should therefore be made for them, if, smarting under such treatment, they have adopted, and have shewn, an indiscriminate abhorrence of those, at whose hands they have seldom received good,
but very frequently much and aggravated evil.

So far as means have been presented of judging of their numbers,
they are very inconsiderable; probably not exceeeding a couple of
thousand in the whole Island, and of these the greatest proportion
by far, are males. What is the cause of this departure from the
usual rule of nature, does not seem explained. Some have supposed that many of the female children are suffered to perish in in-
fancy, not being thought by their mothers worth the trouble of
rearing. Whatever it may be, the fact seems that there are at least

of an injurious tendency to the Colony; but time has
shewn that the Colonists benefited therefrom—that great
expenditure has taken place in the Colony, and that the
breed of horses and cattle has been considerably improved by the means of this Company.   Whether or no
the result has been favorable to the shareholders, is *not
the question*—it is another affair, with respect to which,
the writer will not presume to offer one single word.

Emigrants arrived in great numbers during this year,
and after the total destruction of the bushrangers, the
settlers had fewer troubles, and could employ themselves
on their farms with greater security. The exports continued on the increase ; and were it not for the frequent
depredations of the natives, the Colony might have been
considered in a flourishing and happy condition—prosperous it was beyond doubt!   The Sterling Money Act
received the sanction of the Legislative Council in September, the great object of which was, to do away with
the currency, and establish a sterling circulation ; the
dollar by this law became sterling at 4s. 4d., instead of
as formerly 5s. currency : and promissory notes negotiable
or transferrable, under the sum of 20s., were prohibited.
Several markets were established in the interior, and
two or three race-courses were marked out.   The regulations put in force relative to the prisoner population,
were highly advantageous to the Colony, and creditable
to the authorities who enforced them. Towards the latter
end of the year, John Burnett, Esq. arrived, appointed
from home as Colonial Secretary ; and Mr. Frankland
succeeded Mr. E. Dumaresq as Surveyor General.

The prosecutions against the press were carried on with
redoubled vigour. Mr. Bent, whilst suffering incarceration

six times as many males as females—some say, even more. They
are perpetually engaged in conflicts between rival tribes, and we
are told that they are frequently attended by fatal issues.   The
settlers know by experience, that some of these tribes are infinitely
more savage and mischievous than others : more skilled in the art of
war, more treacherous, and more difficult to be wrought upon by
anything save unrelenting severity.—*General History of the Colony
for* 1832, *as published in the Van Diemen's Land Almanack.*

in jail, underwent a third prosecution for libel against His Excellency the Lieutenant Governor : a Military Jury found him guilty, and he was sentenced to an additional three months imprisonment, and a fine of £100.

During the year 1827, the prospects of the Colony appeared still more flattering, and far beyond what might have been anticipated by the most sanguine. Nothing of very material consequence occurred during this period, either as regarded the Colonists, or their adopted land.   In March a public meeting was convened by the Sheriff, and was most numerously attended by the respectable portion of the Colonists.   The purport of the meeting was to frame an Address to His Majesty and both Houses of Parliament, for Trial by Jury, and a House of Assembly.* The 'Independence' had been the

---

* The humble Petition of the Gentry, Merchants, Landholders, Housekeepers, and other free Inhabitants of His Majesty's Colony of Van Diemen's Land, in Public Meeting, assembled by the Sheriff :—Most humbly sheweth,—

That your Petitioners beg leave to approach your Honorable House, to express their feelings of unshaken loyalty to His Majesty's Government, and attachment to your Honorable House, in which feelings, though so far separated from the Mother Country, they are not surpassed by any class of Subjects in any part of His Majesty's dominions.

That your Petitioners are desirous of conveying to your Honorable House, their expressions of unfeigned gratitude, for the introduction into this Colony of the privileges which have been conferred, under the Act passed in the fourth year of His Majesty's reign, intituled, " An Act to provide, until the 1st day of July, 1827, and until the end of the next Session of Parliament, for the better Administration of Justice in New South Wales and Van Diemen's Land, and for the more effectual Government thereof, and for other purposes relating thereto," under which Act the Inhabitants of this Colony have enjoyed greater protection in their persons and property, by the erection of the Supreme Court of Judicature, and the partial introduction of Trial by Jury.

That your Petitioners beg most respectfully to impress upon your Honorable House, that your Petitioners are British Subjects, and that they have been accustomed to enjoy all the rights and privileges of the British Constitution, and whilst your Petitioners express their gratitude for the creation of the means by which these privileges have been partially enjoyed, they cannot refrain from conveying to your Honorable House, their most ardent desire for

means of engrafting on the Colony an expensive form
of Government, and which, as a dependency, was quite
unnecessary.　It became apparent also, that the governed had no voice whatever in the administration of
affairs, or in the distribution of money levied on them—
that those in authority possessed power far exceeding

---

the perfect introduction of Trial by Jury, and a participation through
their own representatives, in making those laws and enactments
which may be necessary for the future Government of the Colony,
or the protection and expenditure of its Revenue; and although
your Honorable House did not consider when the Act was passed,
to grant a Legislative Assembly, or a Trial by Jury, your Petitioners now cherish the hope, that the time is arrived, when your
Petitioners are not only fit to enjoy such benefits, but that your
Honorable House will be pleased to grant them.

That your Petitioners beg to remind your Honorable House, that
the Colony of Van Diemen's Land was not acquired by conquest,
and that it is, with the Sister Colony of New South Wales unlike
any other of His Majesty's Plantations, inasmuch as it is a British
Colony, entirely peopled by Britons, and governed by British laws
alone.

That although the Juries in the Criminal Court, composed of
seven British Officers, and though two Magistrates as Assessors in
the Civil Court, may have acted in every instance with integrity,
yet your Petitioners, admiring the British Constitution, cannot consider themselves secure or happy under any institutions, which may
be offered as a substitute for them, which are not only the pride and
the birth-right, but the safe-guard of every Briton—Trial by Jury,
and Legislation by Representation.

These, the earnest wishes and desires of your humble Petitioners,
they submit to your Honorable House, in full confidence that their
importance and necessity will obtain that share of consideration,
from your Honorable House, which they merit, and from the experience which your Petitioners have had of the paternal regard
and solicitude of your Honorable House for the prosperity and happiness of His Majesty's subjects, your Petitioners entertain the confident hope, that your Honorable House will not withhold from this
Colony of Van Diemen's Land blessings so dear and valuable.—
And your Petitioners will ever pray, &c.

A Committee, composed of W. Gellibrand, E. Lord, A. F. Kemp,
W. A. Bethune, S. Hood, and D. Lord, Esquires, and also Dudley
Fereday, Esq., the Sheriff of the Colony, were appointed to
wait upon His Excellency the Lieutenant Governor, with the
Petition, for the purpose of its being forwarded to the Secretary of
State, to be presented to His Majesty; and soliciting His Excel-
lency's high influence in support of the same.

that which the public weal pointed out as desirable. The Chief Ruler, as already mentioned, had *virtually* the nomination of all the members of the Legislative Council; and the Colonists were thus shut out from any semblance of representation in an Assembly purporting to be of their own—the Colonists had no means whereby they might oppose measures likely to be prejudicial to society. If, however, the want of a representation in the Council, was a source of regret on the part of the emigrants and settlers, the deprival of the boasted liberty of Englishmen, 'Trial by a Jury of their Peers,' was the cause of various and repeated complaints. These two most important subjects, have in subsequent years been the means of repeatedly collecting the Colonists together at public meetings; but those in authority, unwilling to yield up the power which had been bestowed upon them by British interests, have prevented those blessings being granted by the British Government. On the occasion of the Petition of 1827, a difference arose between the Chief Authority and the gentlemen appointed to present the Address to the Governor, for transmission to the Secretary of State. It appears, that on the Deputation waiting upon His Excellency at the hour fixed, these gentlemen were not admitted; and this, perhaps unintentional insult, was the cause of a letter being sent to His Excellency, on the part of the Deputation, which was anything but flattering to the Governor.* An explanation followed. It appears, that when

---

* *Hobart Town, March 19, 1827.*

SIR,—I am directed by the gentlemen, appointed as a deputation at the Public Meeting, held on Tuesday last, of the Gentry, Merchants, Landholders, and free Inhabitants of this Colony, to Petition His Majesty and the two Houses of Parliament for Trial by Jury and Legislation by Representation—to acquaint your Excellency, that having waited upon your Excellency at Government-house, at the hour fixed according to appointment, to receive the Address to His Majesty for transmission to England; and being informed that your Excellency was engaged, we desire to inform your Excellency, that we are under the necessity, from the respect due to the public, to acquaint your Excellency that we shall not give

the Deputation attended at the hour appointed, His
Excellency was engaged with a private individual, and
that after the gentlemen were kept waiting some
short time, a household servant told them the Governor
was busy, and would not be able to see them for an
hour. This want of *etiquette* gave rise to a still stronger
feeling of dissatisfaction. The Deputation addressed a
letter to the Right Honorable Lord Bathurst, the then
Secretary for the Colonies, in which the manner in which
that body of Representatives had been treated, was
severely commented upon. William Gellibrand, Esq.,
one of the oldest magistrates of the Colony, on account
of the share he had in the correspondence, became obnoxious to the Chief Ruler, and early in the following
year, a notice appeared in the *Gazette*, announcing that
His Excellency had been pleased to dispense with his services. From the result of the complaints made by the
Deputation of the People to the Secretary of State, the

---

your Excellency any further trouble upon this occasion.—I have
the honor to be, your Excellency's most obedient servant,
                                        W. GELLIBRAND.
To His Excellency George Arthur, Esq. Lieutenant Governor of
the Island of Van Diemen's Land, &c. &c. &c.

Colonial Secretary's Office, March 19, 1827.

SIR,—I am directed to acknowledge the receipt of your communication addressed to the Lieutenant Governor, and to acquaint you
that Mr. Curr, (the agent for the Van Diemen's Land Company),
was engaged with His Excellency on pressing business, from 12 until
within a few minutes of 2 o'clock.

Seeing the hour for receiving the Deputation had nearly arrived,
the Lieutenant Governor requested his Private Secretary to make an
immediate intimation to the Sheriff, that he would beg, if it was not
inconvenient, to postpone receiving the deputation for an hour.
Having stated these facts, I am only to express the Lieutenant Governor's regret, that such a temper should have been manifested on
this occasion, as your letter bespeaks, as it may tend to injure the
cause you must be supposed willing to promote. I have the honor
to be, Sir, your obedient servant,
                                        J. BURNETT.

To W. Gellibrand, Esq., J.P., Hobart Town.

Several other letters were addressed to His Excellency by the gentlemen of the Deputation, more fully explaining the reasons why they
considered themselves slighted.

Colonists discovered that the Home Rulers were determined to support, to their utmost, the dignity of the Representative of Majesty, and that little might be expected from complaints forwarded to such a quarter.

In this year, the Island was divided into certain districts, and police magistrates, with a salary of £400 per annum, appointed to six of the most populous settlements; this was an excellent piece of policy, and the most beneficial results have followed. Hitherto, all magistrates had been allowed certain petty indulgences, such as rations, clothing, &c., but now a regular police establishment was formed, the nomination to the magistracy became only honorary. A few mounted policemen served materially to aid the interior stipendiary magistrates in the execution of their duty. By the establish ment of this police, the mischievous and bad characters became better known, and were subject to a control which hitherto had been impossible—for as the magistrates of former times were numerous, and not directly responsible for the tranquillity of their districts, it was oftentimes no one's duty to act or to interfere, and thus crime frequently remained unpunished.

The commerce of the Island was on the increase; wheat was exported, in very large quantities, to New South Wales and the Mauritius; indeed, so great was the glut at the former place, that the price fell to 4s. per bushel, and the Sydney people called upon their Government to put a duty of two, or more shillings, per bushel, on all wheat imported from this Colony—of course this suggestion was not complied with.

The exports of live sheep were very considerable, and realized a very great profit to those connected with this trade. The whale fishery* also, proved favorable to those engaged in the speculation; and the wool was improving, both in price and quality. It will scarcely be credited, that during this and subsequent years, meat was so abundant in town, that none but the very best

---

* A whale, taken by Mr. G. Meredith, at Oyster Bay, the blubber of which was quite blood red, and the oil, which was of very good quality, assumed the same color.

joints were saleable at any price : sheeps' heads, and the skins with wool on, as also bullocks' heads, hides, and feet, were not valued, and were cast on one side by the butchers—in modern times, however, these are valuable considerations, and reckoned by the butchers as the profit. This trifling circumstance is instanced, for two reason, firstly, to shew how little pretensions the Colonists had to economy ; and secondly, that the Colonial reader may contrast the abundance of *former*, to the scarcity of *modern* times.

The East India Company's cruiser, the *Researche*, Captain Dillon, put into this port in April, to refresh— this vessel was on her voyage to Bai, in search of information relative to the loss of the French discovery ship, *La Boussole*, and the unfortunate Count de la Perouse. Whilst here, Dr. Tytler prosecuted the Captain criminally, for illegal imprisonment and assault during the voyage from Calcutta. The Jury found a verdict of guilty, and the Court sentenced this navigator to an imprisonment of two months, and a fine of £50, besides finding large securities to keep the peace.   It is not necessary to advert to the full particulars of this transaction ; but it may be stated, that the whole affair excited a good deal of surprise ; and it was the wonder of many, that it took such a serious termination.   However, at the intercession of the prosecutor, and several influential gentlemen, Captain Dillon was liberated from jail, and allowed to proceed on the interesting expedition.

The attacks on the Liberty of the Press were continued with unabated determination, Mr. Bent was again prosecuted criminally, for libel on His Excellency, and found guilty by a Military Jury, but was not brought up for judgment. The enemies of the Press, however, resolved on what they considered an effectual means of destroying it.   In New South Wales, a stamp duty of 4d. had been imposed upon all newspapers ; but this tax was scarcely put in force before it was abolished—not so in this Colony, for an Act was passed by the Legislative Council, rendering it necessary to have a license, to publish and print any periodical in the shape of a newspaper, and also this very same Act enforced the payment of a stamp duty. The *Colonial Times*, the oldest Journal in the Colony, in consequence of this Act, was published without any political or other information, save that furnished by advertisements. That Journal of the 19th of October, appeared in deep mourning, and the place usually occupied with political and other matter, was left blank. By an advertisement it was explained, that the proprietor of that Journal had neither a stamp nor a license, and that the Colonists declared generally, that they would " *not allow a stamped paper to enter their houses.*" A few days afterwards a *license* was applied for, but the Authorities refused granting one for the *Colonial Times*. In the month of October the official *Gazette* ceased to be a newspaper, and the *Courier* was established—the *Gazette* from this time became the official organ of the Government, and the *Courier* may be termed a *demi*-official, for this Journal, being printed and published by the Government Gazette Printer, the latter was permitted to insert (for years afterwards) all the official notifications in his private Journal, which enabled him to have an influence much complained of by other newspaper proprietors, as well as by the public generally. An Address was forwarded to His Excellency the Lieutenant Governor in November, most respectably signed by the leading Colonists, praying His Excellency " to repeal the Act of Council, subjecting the Free Press to a license," and calling upon the Government to suspend the operation of the stamp duty on newspapers, until the sentiments of the British Government could be made known. The reply to this Address from His Excellency was a negative, but he promised to send the Petition to the Secretary of State.

Sandy Bay races were instituted this year, the course was on the beach, where, for some years, an annual race was held. A bridge across the Derwent, at the Falls, New Norfolk, was in contemplation, by which the northern division of the Island might be connected with the southern, but to this day, no bridge, save the undertaking at Bridgewater, has been commenced across the

Derwent. The Van Diemen's Land Bank encreased the capital of that establishment to £30,000—a large quantity of specie arrived for the Commissariat, and pecuniary affairs were highly favourable for so young a Colony. The natives still committed depredations in the distant stations, but with this exception, the tranquillity of the interior was undisturbed. Executions, which had so profusely taken place during the preceding years, were not now necessary.* Norfolk Island was appointed as a penal settlement for the reception of transported felons from this Colony, but in very few instances have any transportations taken place to that settlement, which is considered more particularly appropriated to the twice convicted of New South Wales.

In the year 1828, the Colony shewed evident signs of having overcome many of the difficulties certain to attend the establishment of a Colony. At this period, this British settlement had been formed twenty five years; but its rise and progress, as a Colony of any standing, cannot be dated previously to the year 1820, when the effects of the wise and popular administration of Colonel Sorell first began to be felt. The improvements carried on in all parts of the Colony, just previously to 1828, and the two or three subsequent years, were truly astonishing; but the enterprise and perserverance of the Colonists cannot be appreciated but by those who have witnessed the settlement; and the rapidity with which the Colony has advanced, since the last twelve years, is this day a matter of astonishment to every person who visits these shores.

During this year the Clerical Establishment particularly occupied the attention of the Government. Van Diemen's Land constitutes a part of the Archdeaconry of the Sister Colony, and both belong to the diocese of Calcutta. That these two important Colonies should be without a primate, is much to be regretted; for as to

---

* It appears that from the 13th April, 1823, to the 19th July, 1824, only *four* persons were executed, and that from the last period to the 30th December, 1826, *seventy-six* had been executed in Hobart Town, and nearly *thirty* at Launceston.—*Colonial Times.*

the head of the church stationed at Calcutta, having
that due and proper control over the pastors of the flocks,
which would be advisable, the distance and the difficulty
of communication are effectual preventatives.   As regards both these Colonies, they have been miserably
neglected in their clerical affairs : it is true occasional
visits have been paid by the Archdeacon, but they have
been limited, and the Clergy may be considered as without any Head or Chief.   In this year were appointed
several lecturers and catechists, and an Orphan School
for male and female children, was established.   This
latter institution is perhaps the very best ever undertaken in the Colony.   From the circumstances under
which the settlement has been populated, it must be
apparent that many children would have been left completely destitute, were it not for this public institution.
A great majority of the emigrants who have settled
here have—save those living at their own table—no other
family connection or social tie in the Colony ; and the
death of a parent in such cases, has often merged the
offspring into a wretched state of poverty and misery—
in such cases this institution has given relief.   But if
such an establishment is desirable for the free portion of
our society, how much more necessary is it for the
offsprings of the prisoner population ?   In this Orphan
School are to be found the children of the once wealthy
settler—the children of the most desperate prisoner of
the Crown—and the offspring of the aborigine, all
collected together, and educated, and taken care of,
with a praiseworthy attention.

The revenue of the Island, from the year 1824, had
been gradually increasing ; but the expenditure had also
increased in proportion, and at this period the civil expenditure may be reckoned at more than the Colonial
income.   Various measures of finance were therefore
resorted to, which soon gave a considerable surplus at
the end of each year.   Previously to the passing of the
Act of Parliament for the Administration of this Colony
and New South Wales, in which the power of imposing
duties is vested with the Legislative Council, Colonel

Arthur issued a proclamation, by which various imposts were established.* The chief source of revenue was obtained from a duty on imported spirits and tobacco. There were other means by which the revenue was considerably augmented, such as by the selling licenses to manufacture spirits in the Colony, as also for licenses to sell spirituous liquors, &c. Crown lands were also rented, and quit-rents imposed on land which was then being located. Other trifling means of increasing the revenue were likewise resorted to, such as the demand made on each settler, in the shape of one guinea, for clothes, for every assigned servant he had transferred to him—in all, these taxes and duties brought in a revenue of between fifty and sixty thousand pounds.

The merchants and traders addressed His Excellency, pointing out the injury likely to be sustained to the commercial interests by the imposition of such duties—those exacted in the Sister Colony, were pointed out as being less than those now attempted to be enforced. This Address was not favorably received, and had no effect in reducing the grievances of which the petitioners complained.

The Legislative Council passed several Acts of Council, which, if they were not what might have been wished for, were at all events, on the whole, advantageous to the Colony. The Licensing Act was perhaps the most complained of, several of its clauses were exceedingly harrassing in their enforcement, and quite unnecessary; but this Act has since been repealed. The duty imposed by the Government on spirits manufactured in the Colony, was also injurious, inasmuch as it encouraged the Foreigner in preference to the Colonist—but this has been the stumbling-block of our rulers, and future years will prove this assertion. In December the Liberty of the Press was again granted to the Colony, and the enemies thereof found their endeavours to

---

* Duties from 1st March, on Colonial spirits, 3s. 6d. per gallon ; British spirits, 7s. 6d., foreign, 10s.; tobacco, 1s. 6d. per lb.; teas, and foreign wines, 15s. per cent. ad valorem.

K

destroy it unavailable. Sir George Murray, the then Secretary of State for the Colonies, communicated to the Chief Authority, that the Liberty of the Press should not be interfered with* and a Newspaper Act was expressly sent out, to be passed by the Council. For more than six years no legal proceedings were instituted against the publishers of newspapers, on the part of the Government, and this undoubtedly aided in furthering the general interests of society, by abolishing, to a degree, political prejudice.

His Excellency made several excursions into the interior, and in many instances granted, in the name of His Majesty, additional locations of 1,000 acres and upwards, to individuals who had deserved encouragement by agricultural enterprise, His Excellency observing, that he "was well assured His Majesty was always desirous that the character of a plain, worthy, good, and upright farmer, should receive due encouragement and reward."

About this time a plan of a new harbour was projected by the Civil Engineer and Surveyor General, for the approval of the Home Government, the expense was estimated at £80,000—this plan was subsequently approved of, and was commenced a few years afterwards, at the Revd. Robert Knopwood's Point—this new wharf, the Colonial reader well knows has been injurious to the interests of some, whilst it has been highly advantageous to others.

Two Banking Establishments were formed this year, one in Hobart Town, called the Derwent, and the other at Launceston, called the Cornwall Bank. When these establishments first started, many of the Government Officers were anxious to become shareholders, and the

---

* PROCLAMATION.—Whereas His Majesty hath been pleased, through the Right Honorable Sir George Murray, one of His Majesty's Principal Secretaries of State, to signify to me His Majesty's disallowance of the Act of this Island, entitled "An Act to regulate the Printing and Publishing of Newspapers, and for the prevention of blasphemous and seditious Libels," I, the said Lieutenant Governor, do therefore by this Proclamation, notify and publish the said disallowance accordingly.

Derwent Bank was selected by several holding official situations ; but His Excellency directed, and very properly so, all Government Officers to withdraw themselves therefrom, as proprietors. The stimulus to commerce given by the establishment of these Banks, can be easily imagined. A very extensive Lumber Yard was at this period erected, for what purpose few individuals, save those connected with the Government, can form the least idea. The Military Barracks were also erected, and a new Burial Ground marked out, which, however, was not ultimately sanctioned. The population of the Colony at this period may be reckoned at 20,000 souls, and the Colonists were possessed of about 500,000 sheep, and 80,000 head of cattle.

The natives became exceedingly troublesome, and many persons were frequently speared by them. Their depredations became so frequent that the authorities knew not in which way to proceed towards them. If, however, the white population suffered from the frequent attacks of these misguided creatures, they themselves in return were massacred without mercy. At this period it was common for parties of the *civilized* portion of society to scour the bush, and falling in with the tracks of the natives, during the night to follow them to their place of encampment, where they were slaughtered in cool blood. The aborigines were a particularly timid race of beings, and never moved during the dark. They appear to have had some superstitious feelings, and they imagined an evil spirit stalked abroad at night. This spirit they called " *Debble*," " *Debble*," and a whole mob might be frightened and separated at night time, by crying out the name of their supposed fiend. It might not be amiss to mention an act of cruelty perpetrated towards these creatures, as a specimen of the conduct too frequently evinced towards them. A mob of some score or so of natives, men, women, and children, had been discovered by their fires, and a whole parcel of the Colonists armed themselves, and proceeded to the spot. These advanced unperceived, and were close to the natives, when the dogs gave the alarm ; the natives jumped up in a mo-

ment, and then was the signal for slaughter given, fire-
arms were discharged, and those poor wretches who
could not hide themselves from the light thrown on their
persons by their own fires, were destroyed. The writer
recollects the description of one of these scenes, as given
by an eye-witness. "One man," said the informant,
"was shot, he sprang up, turned round like a whipping-
top, and fell dead ;—the party then went up to the
fires, found a great number of waddies and spears, and
an infant sprawling on the ground, which one of the
party pitched into one of the fires." It cannot be wondered that the aborigines should have such a deadly
hatred against people who could treat them thus!

It was in April, and after many suggestions were
offered and not adopted, to secure the natives, that the
celebrated ' Demarkation Proclamation,'* received the

---

* PROCLAMATION.—Whereas, at and since the primary settlement of this Colony, various acts of aggression, violence, and
cruelty, have been, from different causes, committed on the Aboriginal Inhabitants of the Island by subjects of His Majesty.

And Whereas, for the preventing and punishing such sanguinary
and wicked practices, it was, by a certain General Order, made by
Colonel David Collins, then Lieutenant Governor of this Island and
its dependencies, at Government House, Hobart Town, on the 29th
day of January, 1810, declared, "That any person whosoever,
who should offer violence to a Native, or should, in cold blood,
murder, or cause any of them to be murdered, should, on proof
being made of the same, be dealt with, and proceeded against, as if
such violence had been offered, or murder committed, on a civilized
person." And, it was also, by a certain Proclamation, made and
issued by me, as such Lieutenant Governor, as aforesaid, at Government House, Hobart Town, on the 29th of June, 1824,—after
reciting the command of His Majesty's Government, and the in-
junction of His Excellency the Governor-in-Chief, that the Natives
of this Colony and its dependencies, should be considered as under
British Government and protection, declared, that every violation of
the laws, in the persons or property of the Natives, should be visited with the same punishment, as if committed on the person or
property of any settler : and all Magistrates and Peace Officers,
and others, His Majesty's subjects in this Colony, were thereby
strictly required to observe and enforce the provisions of that Proclamation. And Whereas, the Aborigines did not only defend themselves, and retaliate on the offenders; but did also, subsequently to
the Order and Proclamation aforesaid, and notwithstanding the re-

sanction of His Excellency the Lieutenant Governor. It is said the Proclamation itself was drawn out by the At-

---

cital, declarations, and requisitions mentioned, perpetrate frequent unprovoked outrages on the persons and property of the settlers in this Island, and their servants being British subjects; and did indulge in the repeated commission of wanton and barbarous murders, and other crimes; for the repression of which, as also for the prevention of further offences by either of the said parties, instructions, directions, and injunctions, were promulgated for general information, and for the especial guidance of the Civil Authorities, and the Military Forces, by the Government Notices of the 29th of November, 1826, and 29th of November, 1827, respectively.

And Whereas, those several measures have proved ineffectual to their objects; and the persons employed in the interior of this Island, as shepherds and stock-keepers, or on the coast, as sealers, do still, as is represented, occasionally attack and injure the Aboriginal Natives without any authority; and the Aborigines have, during a considerable period of time, evinced, and are daily evincing, a growing spirit of hatred, outrage, and enmity against the subjects of His Majesty, resident in this Colony, and are putting in practice modes of hostility, indicating gradual though slow advances in art, system, and method, and utterly inconsistent with the peaceable pursuits of civilized society, the most necessary arts of human subsistence, or the secure enjoyment of human life.

And whereas, on the one hand, the security and safety of all who have entrusted themselves to this country on the faith of British protection, are imperatively required by the plainest principle of justice; and on the other hand, humanity and natural equity, equally enforce the duty of protecting and civilizing the Aboriginal Inhabitants.

And whereas, the Aborigines wander over extensive tracts of country without cultivating, or permanently occupying any portion of it, making continual predatory incursions on its settled districts, a state of living, alike hostile to the safety of the settlers and to the amelioration of their own habits, character, and condition.

And, whereas, for the purpose of protecting all classes and orders of persons in this Island, and its dependencies;—of bringing to an end, and preventing the criminal and iniquitous practices hereinbefore described, by whomsoever committed; or preserving, instructing, and civilizing the Aborigines—and of leading them to habits of labour, industry, and settled life;—it is expedient, by a Legislative Enactment, of a permanent nature, to regulate and restrict the intercourse between the white and colored inhabitants of this Colony; and to allot and assign certain specified tracts of land to the latter, for their exclusive benefit, and continued occupation.

And whereas, with a view to the attainment of those ends, a negotiation with certain chiefs of aboriginal tribes has been planned;

torney General, whose aberration of mind ultimately caused his removal from office. The proclamation was

---

but some prompt and temporary measure is instantly called for, not merely to arrest the march, but entirely cut off the causes and occasions of plunder and crime, and to save the further waste of property and blood ; and it is therefore become indispensably necessary to bring about a temporary separation of the coloured from the British population of this territory, and that therefore the coloured inhabitants should be induced by peaceful means to depart, or should otherwise be expelled by force from all the settled districts therein.

Now, therefore, I, the Lieutenant Governor aforesaid, in pursuance an l in exercise of the powers and authorities in me vested in this behalf, do hereby notify, that for the purpose of effecting the separation required, a line of military posts will be forthwith stationed and established along the confines of the settled districts, within which the aborigines shall not and may not until further order made, penetrate, in any manner, or for any purpose, save as hereinafter specially permitted. And I do hereby strictly command, and order all aborigines immediately to retire, and depart from, and for no reason, or on no pretence, save as hereafter provided, to re-enter such settled districts, or any portions of land cultivated, and occupied by any person whomsoever, under the authority of His Majesty's Government, on pain of forcible expulsion therefrom, and such consequences as may be necessarily attendant on it.

And I do hereby direct and require all magistrates and other persons by them authorized and deputed to conform themselves to the· directions and instructions of this my Proclamation, in effecting the retirement or expulsion of the aborigines from the settled districts of this territory. And I do further authorize and command all other persons whomsoever, His Majesty's civil subjects in this Colony, to obey the directions of the civil, and to aid and assist the military power (to whom special orders adapted to situations and circumstances will be given) in furtherance of the provisions thereof, and to resort to whatever means, a severe and inevitable necessity may dictate and require, for carrying the same into execution ; subject, however, to the following rules, instructions, restrictions, and conditions :—

1st.—Lands, the property of the Crown, and unlocated or adjoining remote and scattered stock-huts, are not to be deemed settled districts, or portions of land cultivated or occupied, within the meaning of this Proclamation.

2nd.—All practicable methods are to be employed for communicating and making known the provisions of this Proclamation to the aborigines, and they are to be persuaded to retire beyond the prescribed limits, if that be possible.

3rd.—On failure of the expedient last mentioned, capture of their persons, without force, is to be attempted, and if effected, the prisoners are to be treated with the utmost humanity and compassion.

promulgated, and a greater piece of absurdity can scarcely be imagined. The document set out by stating, that great cruelty had been committed on the aboriginal inhabitants of the Colony, and after alluding to certain Government Orders, which declared that offences committed against these blacks should be punished in a similar way as if committed against the white population—and that the aborigines did not only defend themselves, but subsequent to those Government Orders, perpetrate frequent unprovoked outrages on the settlers, by committing wanton murders, although it was represented stock-keepers and such like, attacked these aborigines—it became necessary to allot certain specified tracts of land to the aborigines, for their exclusive benefit, &c. After this, the proclamation stated, that military posts were stationed, and certain imaginary lines determined, beyond which all the natives were ordered to retire, under pain of forcible expulsion. One of the most extraordinary parts of this most extraordinary Proclamation is that which allows the respective leaders of the tribes, if provided with a passport under Colonel

---

4th.—Whenever force cannot be avoided, it is to be resorted to, and employed with the greatest caution and forbearance.

5th.—Nothing herein contained, shall authorize, or be taken to authorize, any settler or settlers, stock-keeper or stock-keepers, sealer or sealers, to make use of force (except for necessary self-defence) against any aboriginal, without the presence and direction of a magistrate, military officer, or other person of respectability named and deputed to this service by a magistrate ; of which class, a numerous body will be appointed in each district.—And any unauthorized act of aggression or violence, committed on the person or property of an aboriginal, shall be punished as herein-before declared : And all aborigines are hereby invited and exhorted to inform and complain to some constituted authority, of any such misconduct or ill-treatment, in order to its coercion and punishment.

6th.—Nothing herein contained shall prevent the aborigines from travelling annually, (according to their custom), until their habits shall have been rendered more regular and settled, through the cultivated or occupied parts of the Island to the sea coast, in quest of shell-fish for sustenance, on condition of their respective leaders being provided with a general passport under my hand and seal, arrangements for which, form a part of the intended negotiation.

GEORGE ARTHUR.

Arthur's hand or seal, to conduct their several tribes to
the sea coast, at their usual time of migration. A more
ridiculous proclamation never could be imagined! At
the time it was promulgated it was almost certain death
to any native who would shew himself to an European,
and it was also death to any European that might fall
within the reach of the spear or waddy of the aborigines.
This proclamation, purported to be printed to warn tribes
of men who were ignorant of its meaning, and with
whom there was no intercourse whatever.   Black Tom,*
in a conversation that he had with the Governor, rela-

---

* An aborigine named Black Tom, who was brought up by Mrs.
E. Hodgson, went out with the first party who were sent in pursuit
of his countrymen, after the proclamation of Martial Law.
The Lieutenant Governor being desirous to make use of Tom, as
a negociator with the savages, questioned him very particularly; on
the cause of the hostility of the aborigines against the whites. The
following dialogue took place, as reported by a by-stander :—
Tom.—" A'nt your stock-keeper been a kill plenty black fellow ?"
Governor.—" But your countrymen kill people that never did
them any harm—they even kill women and children."
Tom.—" Well, a'nt dat all same's white un ? A'nt he kill plenty
black un, a woman, and little picaninny too ?"
Governor.—" But you know, Tom, I want to be friendly and
kind to them, yet they would spear me if they met me."
Tom (laughing).—" How he tell you make a friend along him ?
A'nt he all same a white'un ? 'Pose black un kill white fellow, a'nt
you send all your soddier, all your constable after him ? You say,
dat black a devil kill a nurra white man, go—catch it—kill it—a'nt
he then kill all black fellow he see, all picaninny too ? A'nt dat all
same black fellow—a'nt you been a take him own kangaroo ground ?
How den he like ?"
Tom laughed most immoderately on hearing the proclamation
read, particularly at the idea of the tribes applying for passports
to travel through the settled districts.
Tom says—" You been a make a proflamation, ha! ha! ha! I
never see dat foolish—(meaning I never saw anything so foolish.)
When he see dat ? He can't read, who tell him ?"
Governor.—" Can't you tell him, Tom ?"
Tom.—" No! me like see you tell him yourself, he very soon
spear me."
The party to which Tom was attached, having met the Governor
and his suite near the coast, on an excursion which His Excellency
was making to the eastward, both parties encamped for a night at
the same place. Tom was invited to the Governor's tent, when a
dialogue to the following effect took place :—

tive to this proclamation, fully shewed its absurdity; and
the reasoning of a savage demonstrated a shrewdness

Governor.—" Well, Tom, do you think you will be able to find
your countrymen, and persuade them to come in ?"

Tom.—" Can't tell Mata Guberna, I try. 'Pose I see track, den
I find him, and party catch it—den I bring him Hobart Town."

Governor.—" Very well Tom, you must do your best, and if you
bring them in, I will reward you handsomely—besides giving you
the whale boat which I promised you." (It may be worthy of remark that Tom never got his boat.)

" Tom.—Dat very good, Mata Guberna! Pose I catch dat black
un, what you do wid him ?"

Governor.—I will make friends with them, Tom, and tell them
that I have given all this part of the country (pointing out a line on
a map), to themselves, where no white man will go near them ; and
if they want to go to the east coast, the magistrates will give them
a pass, so that no white man will trouble them, and I will give them
food and blankets.

Tom. —" Aye, Dat very good, Mata Guberna, you take it all,
him kangaroo ground yourself, gived him nurra mob kangaroo ground.
Pose he walk dere, an't nurra mob make fight, you call it war,
and kill him right out. You give it him blanket, bread, tell him
walk about. Dat very good—by an by, pose he see you, den he
spear you. I tell a you dat black un nebber make a friend along a
you, he nebber take dat word from you (i.e. he will never take your
word for that). Dat way nebber do."

Governor.—" Well, Tom, I will send them to Maria Island."

Here Tom burst out into a loud laugh. " 'Riah Island ! ! I like
a hear you talk dat b——y foolish—ha ! ha ! ha ! A'nt he go dere
himself come back again, often he like. I tell you dat, him own
Wallaby ground—he make't catamaran, come back so soon as yourself. Dat way nebber do Mata Guberna."

Governor.—" Well, Tom, I will put them in prison, and keep them
there."

Tom here looked unutterable things. " Put him in a gaol, Mata
Guberna !! You take it him own country, take it him black woman,
kill 't right out, all him litta child—den you put him in your gaol.
Ah, Mata Guberna, dat a very good way. 'Pose you like dat way
—'pose all same dat black un ! I nebber like dat way. You better
kill it right out."

Governor.—" Well, Tom, I will send them to one of the islands
in Bass's Straits, and keep them there." Tom enquired the distance
from the main land, and whether there was game on the island, being
satisfied of this, he continued.—" You send him dat hyland, and
take't all him own country—what you give him for him own country ?"

Governor.—" I will give them food and blankets, and teach them
to work."

L

which could not have been expected from a man, whose species have always been represented as little better in intellectual knowledge than mere brutes. The proclamation had the effect of adding outrage to outrage; and a few months afterwards, when martial law* was proclaimed, the

---

Tom.—(Laughing.) "You make't black un work!! I nebber see dat, Mata Guberna." Here Tom pointed to a fly that was on the table. "You see dat man, Mata Guberna."

Governor.—Yes, Tom, I see a fly.

Tom.—"' Pose you tell dat man work—you tink he work for you ?"

Governor.—" No, Tom, I do not think he would."

Tom.—"Well, black un all same; he nebber see work, you nebber make dat black un work, he too d—m lazy."

Governor.—" Well, Tom, he can go and hunt, and come back when he likes, to get food and blankets, and I will send people to take care of the children, and teach them to work."

Tom.--" Aye, dat very good way, litta one work by and by. I like dat way. Now I like catch all dat black un."

Tom next day set out with the party, and in a few days came up with a tribe which had been committing several outrages, and had recently speared a man at Malony's Sugar Loaf. The party, consisting of six soldiers and two prisoners under the charge of Mr. Gilbert Robertson, Chief Constable of Richmond, captured Eumarrah, the chief of the Stoney Creek tribe, three men and one woman, destroyed a great number of dogs, about 100 spears, and twice as many waddies. The natives had 36 pairs of blankets, which they had stolen, with a variety of cutlery, and other plunder.

* (By His Excellency Colonel George Arthur, Lieutenant Governor of Van Diemen's Land and its Dependencies.)

A PROCLAMATION.

Whereas, the black or aboriginal natives of this Island have, for a considerable time past, carried on a series of indiscriminate attacks upon the persons and property of divers of His Majesty's subjects; and have, especially of late, perpetrated most cruel and sanguinary acts of violence and outrage; evincing an evident disposition systematically to kill and destroy the white inhabitants indiscriminately, whenever an opportunity of so doing is presented,—and whereas, notwithstanding the proclamation made and issued by me on the 15th day of April, last past,—and that every practicable measure has from time to time been resorted to, under that proclamation, and otherwise, for the purpose of removing the aborigines from the settled districts of the Colony, and for putting a stop to the repetition of such atrocities,—repeated inroads are daily made by the natives into the said settled districts, and acts of hostility and barbarity there committed by them, as well as at the more distant stock-runs, and in some in-

destruction of these creatures became, as it were authorised by the Chief Authority. Years have now elapsed since

stances upon unoffending and defenceless women and children.—
And whereas, also, it seems at present, impossible to conciliate the
several tribes of that people; and the ordinary civil powers of the
magistrates, and the means afforded by the common law, are found
by experience to be wholly insufficient for the general safety; and
it hath therefore become at length unavoidably necessary, for the
effectual suppression of similar enormities, to proclaim and keep in
force martial law in the manner hereinafter proclaimed and directed:—
    Now, therefore, by virtue of the power and authorities in me in
this behalf vested, I, the said Lieutenant Governor, do by these
presents declare and proclaim, that from and after the date of this,
my proclamation, and until the cessation of hostilities shall be by
me hereafter proclaimed and directed, martial law is, and shall continue to be in force against the several black or aboriginal natives,
within the several districts of this Island; excepting always the places
and portion of this Island, next mentioned, (that is to say)—
    1st.—All the country extending southward of Mount Wellington
to the ocean, including Bruné Island.
    2nd.—Tasman's Peninsula.
    3rd.—The whole of the north-eastern part of this Island which
is bounded on the north and east by the ocean, and on the south-
west by a line drawn from Piper's River to Saint Patrick's Head.
    4th.—And the whole of the western and south-western part of
this Island, which is bounded on the east by the river Huon, and
by a line drawn from that river over Teneriffe Peak to the extreme
Western Bluff; on the north by an east and west line from the said
extreme Western Bluff to the ocean, and on the west and south by
the ocean.
    And, for the purposes aforesaid, all soldiers are hereby required
and commanded to obey and assist their lawful superiors; and all
other, His Majesty's subjects, are required and commanded to obey
and assist the magistrates, in the execution of such measures as
shall by any one or more of such magistrates be directed to be taken
for those purposes, by such ways and means as shall by him or them
be considered expedient, so long as martial law shall continue to
exist. But, I do, nevertheless, hereby strictly order, enjoin, and
command, that the actual use of arms be in no case reorted to, if
the natives can by other means be induced or compelled to retire
into the places and portions of this Island hereinbefore excepted
from the operation of martial law; that bloodshed be checked, as
much as possible, that any tribes which may surrender themselves
up, shall be treated with every degree of humanity, and that defenceless women and children be invariably spared. And all officers,
civil and military, and other person whatsoever, are hereby required to take notice of this my proclamation and order, and to
render obedience and assistance herein accordingly.

the promulgation of these two extraordinary documents;
and every reader must agree, that two more absurd proclamations never were issued by any British Government. Under the apparent pretext of charitable feelings
towards these poor deluded, and perhaps, misguided
creatures, were the utmost cruelties permitted. At first
the tribes were robbed of their land and their food—
their females taken from them, and violated; when, in
return, they became desperate from treatment they could
no longer bear, when they resisted the violation of their
wives and daughters they were destroyed; and when
resenting these ortrages committed upon them, they
suffered death on the gallows! Nor did the shameful
conduct of the Colonists stop here; for a proclamation
divided their country, and prescribed imaginary bounds,
over which these ignorant creatures were not to step
without a passport from the Chief Authority, on pain of
forcible expulsion. In the proclamation of martial law,
the boundaries fixed were of a most extraordinary nature,
and embraced a vast portion of the Island, over which
the natives were prohibited from trespassing. When it
is recollected, that within ten or fifteen miles of Hobart
Town, the country is yet unexplored, the cruelty of this
sweeping proclamation, by which these poor creatures
were expelled from their own soil, may be more readily
imagined by the stranger. The customary plan adopted
towards them, after the passing of the martial law, was
that of attempting to capture the chiefs of the warrior
tribes. The Civil Authorities, aided by a few of the

Provided nevertheless, and it is hereby notified and proclaimed,
that nothing herein contained, shall, or doth extend to interrupt or
interfere with the ordinary exercise of the civil power, or the regular course of the common law, any further or otherwise, than as
such interruption shall, for the purpose of carrying on military operations against the natives, be rendered necessary.

Given under my hand and seal at arms, at the Government
House, Hobart Town, this first day of November, one thousand
eight hundred and twenty-eight.

"GEORGE ARTHUR." (L.S)

By His Excellency's command,

J. BURNETT.

military, occasionally guided by one of the sable natives,
scoured the bush, and when the mobs were fallen in
with, it depended on the leaders of the party in what
manner the natives were to be treated; occasionally
they were all shot, or had their brains knocked out by
the butt-end of the muskets—other more merciful leaders
captured them, and brought them to Hobart Town to
await the destination the Executive Council might think
proper to award them.* The effect of the proclamation

---

* After tracking a party of natives from near the Sand-pit River,
round by Prosser's Plains, and the Blue Hills, down past Mr. Hobbs's,
at M'Gill's Marsh, the party under Mr. Gilbert Robertson, on arriving at Mr. Hobbs's, were informed, that several robberies had
been committed by the natives within a few days, at Kitty's Corners,
and Malony's Sugar Loaf, and that a party of natives had been seen
down near the junction of the Little Swan Port, and Eastern Marshes
River; Mr. Hobbs's overseer accompanied the party for some miles,
in the direction that he had seen the natives go. Tom soon got upon
a track, which the party followed until about 3 o'clock in the afternoon
of the next day, when they heard a most unearthly shout, which Tom
instantly recognized as a native's cry, and suddenly starting, and
holding up both his hands, said, in a most energetic whisper—
"Stop!—lie down!—dat a black un, he been a huntin" (hunting.)
The party halted, and Mr. Robertson and Tom went a-head to re-
connoitre, when they discovered several natives round a small fire,
one of whom Tom recognized as a chief. Mr. Robertson then retired about a mile from the place where he had at first halted, and
placing a hill between him and the natives, remained there for the
night. It came on to rain about 9 o'clock, when the natives were
heard chopping the trees, to get bark for a hut. As soon as the sky
began to break, the party were in motion, but Tom, missing his
way in the dark, they had to march above a mile knee-deep in water.
When they got out of the water, and about 100 yards from the fire,
which was then visible, the party formed for the attack. Mr. Robertson, Tom, with Thomas Arthur, a prisoner, who had been
released from prison at Tom's request, and Robert Lee, another
convict, who had been picked up by Mr. Robertson on the coast,
opposite Maria Island. These four formed the centre, and there
were three soldiers of the 40th regiment on each flank, at a considerable distance, so as to surround the fire, which they did with
the greatest precision at the same moment, but not a native was to
be seen. On looking to the right, another fire was discovered, about
100 yards off, the party, who could not see to communicate by signs,
and who durst not speak, again dispersed in the same order, and
made for the last discovered fire. Mr. Robertson, having outrun
the others, got first to the *back* of the hut, which he had not pre-

of martial law was, to destroy, within twelve months
after its publication, more than two thirds of these wild

viously seen, when five furious dogs rushed out upon him, and almost at the same instant the natives came tumbling out at the back
of the hut where he stood. He then fired off his musket, for the
purpose of frightening them, and causing those that were inside to
run the other way, where the rest of the party were coming up ; before
the smoke of his fire had dispersed, another shot was fired from the
hut, and he saw one of the natives who had run past him, fall into
the scrub, Mr. R. instantly seized a lad who was scrambling through
the bark, and dragged him into the hut, where he found Thomas
Arthur, Robert Lee, and Tom, with a native man and woman,
secured. The boy whom he took, then directed his attention to a
sheet of bark, under which a stout man was found, lying flat on the
ground. By the time the captives were bound with strips torn from
the blankets, which were found in great abundance in the hut, the six
soldiers came up, they said they had lain down in the scrub, when they
heard the firing—they then ran in the direction the natives had run,
and one of them, named Clark, found the poor wounded man lying at
the back of a tree. The monster broke his musket over the skull of the
poor wretch, and cut him dreadfully on the top of his head. The
ball had struck the bone at the back of the ear, and passed upwards,
without entering the skull, or breaking any bone, leaving a very
deep flesh wound. The natives expected that they would be shot as
soon as they were tied, and Tom recommended this as the best
mode of disposing of them, describing them as a very " bad mob,"
who had killed many of his tribe. When they saw that they were
not to be killed, they begged for bread and sugar, and Tom was
then the most anxious to supply their wants ; they made a most
hearty meal, consuming all the provisions which the party had, and
an enormous quantity of kangaroo, of which they had a great store
about the hut—while they were eating, Tom, who acted as interpreter, informed Mr. Robertson of the name and rank of the captives. The wounded man was the chief, named " Eumarrah,"
which evidently is not a native name, and, as Tom explained was
borrowed by the chief from Mr. Hugh Murray, of the Macq·arie,
and pronounced as above. The others had all English names one
being called Jemmy, another Jack, and the woman Dolly. There
was another, who was lame, and had no English name. Tom being
asked what station this man occupied in the tribe, after declaring
him useless as a hunter or a warrior, on being farther pressed, he
said, " Oh! he very good a lawyer—he eat all a urra (other) fellow
catch ;" and this poor fellow, who was a very humourous tricky
chap, was ever after known as " The Lawyer." Tom had been a
long time in prison, and it was a common saving amongst the thieves
that, the lawyers who defended them on their trial, got all the profits of their plunder.

At sun rise the party were perfectly ignorant of the part of the

creatures, who by degrees dwindled away till their populous tribes were swept from the face of the earth.

The year 1829 may be considered as one of the most

---

country they were in—even Tom could not tell which was the nearest settlement. In this dilemma, they desired their captives to point out the direction of the hut which they last robbed, which they readily did, and following this direction, they arrived at Mr. Dudgeon's stock-hut, at Molony s Sugar Loaf, close to Pressnell's hut, which had been robbed the preceding day, and the overseer speared by " Eumarrah." The poor captives were conducted first to Richmond, and thence to Hobart Town. Mr. Robertson was called before the Executive Council, and thanked for his services. On his recommending to the Governor to shew some marks of respect to " Eumarrah," with a view to conciliate him, and make use of him in bringing in the other tribes, His Excellency replied, " I would not attempt to conciliate that man."

Mr. Robertson.—" What will you do with him ?"

Governor.—" If you can find evidence to prove all those outrages you speak of, I would have him tried, and executed, if he is found guilty."

Mr. Robertson.—" Consider, Sir, that this man was defending his country against cruel intruders, he is now a prisoner of war, and your Excellency, by executing him, would be guilty of a worse murder than ever he committed."

Here the Chief Justice looked up, and said sharply—" Mr. Robertson, do you consider that those men who were tried and executed here were murdered ?"

Mr. Robertson.—" I do, indeed, your Honor."

Here the Council looked at one another, and the Governor said— " Mr. Robertson, you may withdraw, but do not leave the house."

Mr. Robertson then retired, and " Eumarrah" was ushered into *the presence* with his companions in captivity. After some time Mr. Robertson was re-called, when he found " Eumarrah" and the others, excepting Tom, squatted on the floor. Tom was acting master of the ceremonies and interpreter. The Governor said, " The Council has resolved not to try your friend " Eumarrah," Mr. Robertson, and you can take him with you to Richmond, under your own immediate protection, with power to confine him in the gaol for safe keeping. The Captives were removed to Richmond, where they were kept in the prison, but brought out every day to Mr. Robertson's house, where they spent the most of their time with his children. Jack and " The Lawyer" became quite familiar, and were much attached to the family, and the children were equally fond of them. " Eumarrah" maintained a sort of reserve, becoming a dignified savage in adversity, but he afterwards went out with Mr. Robertson, as a guide, in company with Jack and Tom, and all proved alike faithful and useful, being convinced that it was

prosperous the Colonists have ever yet enjoyed : with the exception of the continued war with the blacks, there was nothing to disturb the tranquility of the Colony—nothing to excite the Colonists. It was during this year that Van Diemen's Land made one general rapid stride in improvements of all kinds. There had been large arrivals of prisoners and these were anxiously sought after by the settlers in the interior ; as also by the tradesmen in the townships. The export of provisions continued on a large scale, and yet so abundant was the

---

for the benefit of their countrymen to submit. He was a man whom nature had endowed with a superior mind. He twice made his escape, but voluntarily returned to join the whites, and was attached to the parties under Mr. G. A. Robinson, who succeeded Mr. Gilbert Robertson. "Eumarrah," with Dolly, Jack, and " The Lawyer," and Tom, and some others who were captured by Mr. Batman, and familiarized with European habits, by a residence of several months at Richmond, contributed greatly to the success of Mr. Robinson, in removing the natives, he being, by the labors of his predecessors, furnished with means which neither of the former possessed. " The Lawyer" was a most amusing fellow. Mr. Stephen, the present Attorney General, and Mr. Pitcairn, having gone on a visit to Richmond, were desirous to see the natives. They were brought from the gaol. When they came up, Mr. Stephen enquired which was " The Lawyer," and making him a very handsome bow, said, " Good morning, Mr. Lawyer." The person thus addressed, exactly mimicking the bow and motion with the arm, of the speaker, replied in the same tone, " Good a morning, Matta Lawyer." Mr. Stephen, turning round to Mr. Lascelles, said quickly, " How the devil does the fellow know that I am a lawyer ?" The other as quickly repeated, addressing Mr. Robertson, and pointing to Mr. Stephen, " How de debble dat fellow kuow I am a lawyer?" and seemed much amused at Mr. Stephen's astonishment. Mr. Pitcairn then pointing to " The Lawyer's" dress, said, " our learned brother looks very respectable." The other, pointing in a similar manner to Mr. Pitcairn, said " our learna broder look a murry 'spectable." All those poor fellows, including Tom, are dead, Dolly is still alive at Flinder's Island, Jack had become like one of Mr. Robertson's own family, and was taken away from him by the Government, in what he represents in a most unjustifiable manner; Jemmy, on being removed from Richmond to join Mr. Robertson's party in the interior, was most brutally treated by a constable named Prior, belonging to the Oatlands Police, and by him chained all night to an iron pot—he escaped in the morning, and has not been since heard of—he was an active good-natured fellow.—*M.S.S. Journal.*

supply, that the cost of the rations of each prisoner in Government employ was only about 4d. per diem. The expense of the assigned convicts to farmers was not nearly so much, on account of the food being raised on the several estates : and the cost of provisions of convict mechanics to master tradesmen, might be reckoned at about 6d. each man per diem. The price of labour still continued high, therefore the loan of assigned servants was a most valuable donation on the part of the Government. Many master tradesmen this year laid the foundation of handsome fortunes. Such was the demand for labour, that had ten times as many prisoners been sent out, every one of the number would have found masters eager to take them from the Government. The free mechanics, during this year and the following, would not accept work at less than 10s. per diem; and the commonest labourers obtained 5s. or 6s.; the great demand for labourers caused the number of Crown prisoners in Government employ to be merely such as were absolutely necessary for the carrying on of Colonial works, and to form the necessary appendages of the different departments. The Commissariat expenditure, or the sum required from the Mother Country for the maintenance of convicts in Government employ, was this year reduced : and the duties levied, and taxes imposed, on the Colonists, had the effect of transferring to the Colonial Treasury Chest, a considerable surplus fund, after paying the Colonial expenditure.

This year an Act of Parliament for the administration of the Colony succeeded one, the time for the enforcement of which had expired previously to the arrival of its successor. Happily for the Colonists there was no sittings of the Council during this year, and fortunate would it have been for Van Diemen's Land, had the Council terminated the "experimental"* legislation with the year 1828, when a sufficient sample of "experimental" legislation had been offered to the Colonists

---

* His Excellency, in 1835, when referring to the Acts previously passed the Council, makes use of this extraordinary term.

M

to prove beyond doubt that a Council so constituted was incapable of passing laws requisite for the Government of the Colony.

This year the newly established British settlement at Swan River held out considerable inducements to this and the Sister Colony, to open a new trade. It was considered that the young adjoining settlement would require much assistance from both, in the way of provisions and stock. It was with these expectations that several enterprising individuals engaged largely in the Swan River trade, and as high prices were quoted for every article in the new settlement, large profits were calculated upon as certain. The result of this commerce was most unfortunate. The prices at which food sold at the Swan were extraordinarily high; but there was no means by which remittances to foreigners might be obtained. As to money, that was soon all expended, and an exchange of nearly valueless British machinery was taken at a loss, for food and live stock, forwarded from this Colony. This trade scarcely lasted two years, and incurred ruin to some of those engaged therein. This year large exports were made of corn, sheep, potatoes, bacon, hay, hides, skins, and wools, and what with the exports to New South Wales and the Swan, commerce was remarkably thriving.

The Government brig *Cyprus* was captured in the month of August by the convicts, on their way to the penal settlement of Macquarie Harbour, * by which not

---

* PIRATICAL SEIZURE.—The *Cyprus* was on her passage to the penal settlement of Macquarie Harbour, conveying 31 prisoners under sentence of transportation to that place : and having on board a large supply of provisions for the settlement; when the prisoners mutinied and took possession of the vessel and carried her out to sea.

The *Cyprus* went into Research Bay, on Monday, the 9th of August, in consequence of the wind being then foul, which prevented her from proceeding on her voyage round the coast to Macquarie Harbour ; the evening being very calm, Lieutenant Carew, Mr. Burn, the mate, Mr. Williams, one soldier, and one prisoner, went into the small boat to fish in the Bay, leaving the Captain, the soldiers, and sentinels on board, together with the ship's's crew.

only was a very serious loss incurred by the Government, but the prisoners at the settlement almost left in a state

---

This was about six o'clock in the afternoon, some time before dark. At the moment the fishing boat was distanced from the vessel about two hundred and fifty yards, there were no persons on the ship's deck, except the two sentinels on duty, each having a musket with fixed bayonets, and a soldier without arms—the rest of the soldiers and the serjeant, (together with all muskets and ammunition), being between decks, taking supper; and the master of the vessel and Mrs. Carew in the cabin; at this moment there were five of the prisoners on deck likewise. They had been allowed to come up as an indulgence, as was granted to all the other prisoners in their turns, to take the benefit of the air. These prisoners consisted of Walker, Pennel, M'Kan, Jones, Fergusson, and a carpenter, (with the exception of the latter), who assisted the ship's carpenter at his work, all these men were double ironed! This man, together with Walker and Wood, who assisted the sailors to work, was therefore allowed to sleep with them, and of course to walk the decks, and were so doing at this period! Fergusson here availed himself of the opportunity which presented itself by calling on his fellow prisoners walking the deck, and saying that if they did not embrace that opportunity, he would discover their previous plots; for that they had six favourable opportunities already, and did not avail themselves of either. They instantly rushed upon the two sentinels and knocking them down, released the prisoners who jumped upon deck, and fastened down the hatchway on the soldiers, and knocked down Captain Harris, who had come up to see what was the matter. The soldiers instantly fired shots up through the hatchways, at the prisoners, and one of the balls passed through Walker's jacket. The pirates then poured down boiling water on the soldiers, and threatened to throw down a kettle of lighted pitch to smoke the ship, unless they immediately surrendered. The soldiers could not stand up in the little place they were in; and, being deprived of light or air, and threatened with being instantly smothered, had no other alternative than to surrender their arms; upon which they were let on deck one by one; when they were put into a boat, and guarded by another boat, containing armed prisoners, until they were put on shore, when they repeated the same means, until they put the forty-five persons on the land. The whole time, from the first attack, until they shouted " the ship's our own," did not occupy more than eight or ten minutes!!! One of the sentinels, named Scully, had his head cut in four several places.

When Lieutenant Carew came alongside, to go on board, they refused to admit him, and Pennell levelled his piece at him, but it missed fire several times, the soldiers having wet the powder in the muskets before giving up the arms. They then demanded Lieutenat Carew's commission, which, in order to satisfy them, he said was on board. Upon the whole of these unfortunate persons being landed,

of starvation from the loss of provisions taken away in the brig by the pirates.

His Excellency appointed a site for a market, in the open space at the end of Collins-street, a more desirable spot could not be fixed upon, as it was centrically situ-

the pirates sent on shore only 60lbs. of biscuit, 20lbs. of sugar, 4lbs. of tea, 20lbs. of flour, and 8 gallons of rum ; together with a lighted stick and a tinder box, one musket, and a few rounds of ammunition ; but, although many were the entreaties, they refused to give them their trunks, or clothes, or other necessaries ; even Mrs. Carew's or her children's things, who were left so destitute, that Mrs. Carew would not come on shore, on the return of the *Oppossum* in the harbour, until after dusk. These persons, forty-four in number, remained thirteen days on that desolate and forlorn part of the island, exposed to all the inclemency of the weather, both night and day, upon such a very scanty allowance, which did not, of course, last them many days. Thus seventeen prisoners voluntarily went off in the *Cyprus*, besides Brown, one of the sailors, whom they hand-cuffed, and forced to go with them ; all the rest of the prisoners they forced on shore, not knowing there was so large a quantity of provisions on board as actually was. Walker was appointed Captain, Fergusson, who dressed himself up in Lieutenant Carew's uniform, and put on his sword, was appointed Lieutenant, and Jones the Mate! They purposed making regulations when they got out to sea, and to make canvas clothing for the sailors, as they supposed there was a considerable quantity of canvas on board. Morgan and Knight, two more of the sailors, were also pressed, and ordered by Walker to remain on board until next morning. They, however, treated them very well, and endeavoured, by making them drunk, to prevail upon them to go with them ; but they sternly refused, and were therefore put on shore next morning. M'Kan, one of the ringleaders, first picked out ten men, as they were determined to take no more ; but the remaining seven prevailed upon them to take them, as if they were put on shore, they said they would all suffer, for having assisted in capturing the vessel ; upon which they were permitted to remain on board, though they apprehended they would come short of water. Walker, Fergusson, and Jones, promised to give Morgan and Knight, (the two sailors whom they pressed) the jolly boat, to go on shore in the morning ; but a James Cam refused, saying that they might be becalmed off the coast, and wisely added, that the jolly boat might enable the Lieutenant to send an express to Hobart Town, and cause them to be re-taken. Pennell, Jones, and Watts, became quite intoxicated the same night ; and, at half-past five on Saturday morning, they gave three cheers, and sailed with a fair wind, and were out of sight in two hours, blowing hard from the North-west, and it was supposed that they bent their course for Valparaiso.—*Colonial Times.*

ated, as regards the town, and excellently well adapted for the shipping. From the want of some enactment, doing away with the general system of hawking, the market did not answer the expectations of the towns-people, and to this day the large square remains a complete useless waste.

The aborigines this year adopted a new system of revenge, and it is generally believed they were taught by some of the runaway convicts, to destroy by fire the stacks and houses of the settlers—they also occasionally burnt standing ripe crops.

The year 1830 is one of the most important in the history of the Colony. It has been seen that hitherto Van Diemen's Land had advanced rapidly, but in a legitimate and healthy manner—commerce had not been forced, neither had any improper stimulus been given to the settlers in the interior. The merchants had imported the necessary articles of dress and luxuries for the use of the Colonists, and the farmers had grown corn, and fed sheep and cattle, wherewith to pay for goods requisite for their establishments; but during this year an unwholesome stimulus was given, by means of several " experimental" laws, and impolitic Government measures—the compiler of this work will take these *seriatim*, and point them out as they were adopted.

The Legislative Council—that body which had been happily so tranquil during the preceding year—now commenced active operations, and a whole series of laws were passed,* some of them uncalled for, others unnecessary, and several that have proved highly injurious to the settlement. It will be, however, the duty of the writer to confine himself to two of the most important, that of the Impounding, and the other the Usury Act. It might be asked by the Colonial reader, why no mention should be made of the ridiculous Slaughtering Act, which will not allow a farmer to sell his veal, his sucking pigs, or his rabbits in Hobart Town—it might be asked, why no mention is made of the harrassing and

* Sixteen in number.

oppressive Habouring Act—of the imbecile Dog Act—
of the semblance of a Jury Act—or of the arbitrary
House of Correction Act, &c., but the compiler's reply
is simply, that although such laws may have depressed
many—although they may have been considered oppressive, and some of the clauses tyrannical, still, as they were
confined to individual Colonists, and did not injure the
welfare of the Colony generally, they are of minor
import, and cannot obtain sufficient commentary in a
work of this limited description.

The Act of Council, usually denominated the " Uusury
Act," excluded from operation in this Colony, the laws
of England relative thereto. Previous to the framing of
this Act, the Bank interest, as at present, was only ten
per cent., and the interest allowed by the Supreme
Court, that of eight. This legal rate of interest, if it
may be so called, was fixed by proclamation during the
administration of a former Governor. Although, ten
per cent. was considered as the current interest, still it
often happened, that a higher rate was privately obtained.
The securities offered the Banking Establishments, were
only bills of three months date—the Directors, in consequence of some bye-laws, never discounting any paper
exceeding that term; consequently, money for longer
dated bills, or money raised by way of mortgage, was
obtained from private individuals, who frequently, though
not then legal, obtained a much higher interest. No sooner
however, had the new Colonial law passed, than persons
connected with the Derwent Banking Establishment,
and also private individuals, communicated with their
friends iu different parts of the world, explaining, that
a *higher legal rate of interest* could be obtained in Van
Diemen's Land than in any other British colony. Capital
soon poured in from all parts, the *bait* held out induced
the Indian Capitalists, and the Stock-jobbing Money-
lenders of England, to lay out, at usurious interest in
Van Diemen's Land, large sums of money. The great
increase of pecuniary wealth, induced many individuals
to speculate beyond reason ; others, without one farthing
capital, by means of the facility offered, started up in

extensive business—interest, or rather the rate of discount, to these latter, was of trifling consideration—
they had nothing to lose, but there was a chance of
gain! The farmers too, finding with what facility money
was to be had, abandoned their labours; and by obtaining
at first trifling sums, by means of mortgaging their estates, lived like wealthy and indolent men, little expecting the result. These farms, at first mortgaged for
trifles, in a few years passed from their former owners.
What with the ease with which money was obtained, and
the apathy which was most prevalent on the part of the
settlers—who, instead of bringing their families up to
such labour as ought to be expected from the settlers in
the interior of a young colony, purchased piano-fortes
for their daughters, and race-horses for their sons—
"the goose was killed for the sake of the golden egg." The
rapid strides which the settlers had made in former years,
by perseverance and industry, was now to be wasted by
the introduction of foreign capital. At first the interest
asked by the legalized usurers, was merely twelve or
thirteen per cent., then it increased to fifteen, and very
soon, twenty per cent. became common. Nor did this
iniquitous system stop here; for before long the half
ruined Colonist took his last parchment deed to the
usurer, to pawn—to raise funds to pay interest on former
loans; and when no other security was at command, the
land passed from himself and his children, and became
the property of the absentee. It will, perhaps, be said,
that the greater the introduction of capital, the lower
the interest of money *must* be, and that therefore this
borrowed capital must have kept down the rate of interest, and thus considerably assisted the Colonists in
their mercantile transactions—but this is not the case,
experience has proved the contrary. The wisdom of
past ages has, with regard to most countries, found it
necessary to fix a rate of interest of some kind. In some
countries this rate is fixed by law, in others by the price
at which Government securities may be purchased—in
all countries a variation to a trifling extent takes place
according to the demand or otherwise, for money. In a

young colony, however, where the " fly-wheel of prosperity" has raised labourers to be men of large landed
property, such temptation as usury, by which unsound
speculations might be entered into, ought not to be allowed.   In England experience has taught that money
could not, as a general rule, be lent out at above five per
cent. benefitting thereby both the lender and the borrower:
in Van Diemen's Land experience of former years has
taught us, that nearly double that interest could be obtained, advantageously to the employer of the capital, and
to the borrower. Colonial manufactures—fishers—and
agriculturists could perhaps lay out money advantageously, at eight or ten per cent., and benefit themselves considerably thereby : some speculations might
even succeed when money might be borrowed at double
that rate ; but take the Colony as a whole, and fix a
rate of interest at which the borrower might benefit
himself, and the capital be secured, and seven or eight
per cent. will be found the most advisable rate of interest. It is not so much the high rate that has cramped
the energies of the Colonists, it is the introduction of
the *foreign* capital, by which absentees have obtained
possession of the soil, and who consequently draw rents
therefrom, and expend such sums elsewhere.   If the
capital lent out at usury had been purely Colonial, the
Sheriff might have sold the farms, and the lender of the
money would have become the possessor, and yet no
loss sustained to the Colony, but to the individuals only
who were ruined thereby.

A more impolitic Act of Council than the one referred
to, could not have passed—the emigrant with capital,
instead of farming—instead of employing his money in
developing the resources of the Colony, lent all out on
usury, for he could not obtain nearly so much interest
by any other honest means.   The terms too, on which
these usurers have been grinding the Colonists, is a
matter of astonishment that such has been sanctioned
by those in authority.   The several Banks have been
made instrumental in furthering usury ; true, their dis-
counts have been still at ten per cent., but then the

twenty and thirty per cent. gentry have had their paper discounted in preference to the regular tradesman : the directors of the several Banks could not refuse to select the best security, and thus were they, for the interest of the shareholders, *obliged* to discount the usurer's bills at ten per cent., which bills probably ten minutes previously had been cashed by them, deducting some thirty or forty. Again, the manner in which the system of mortgaging has been carried on, is truly distressing.   In most parts of the world good security, such as land or houses, is sure to obtain a preference—here the system has been the reverse, the Banks have discounted without security at ten per cent., whilst the usurer invariably advances only *one half* the value on *undeniable* security.   The abominations of usury introduced the still greater abomination of law charges.   Some *gentlemen of the profession* are among the most notorious usurers, and these—not satisfied with lending money on an estate worth double or treble the sum wanted, at a rate of twenty or thirty per cent. interest—by means of legal plunder, such as warrants of attorney, mortgage deeds, transfers, and such like, not unfrequently have cleared fifty—nay, sixty per cent. for money they have thus lent. And this has been no secret work—the law allows such transactions.*

The other most impolitic Act passed during the year 1830, was the Impounding Law. It has hitherto been seen that vast quantities of corn have been annually exported to New South Wales, and other places, and that sheep and salt provisions, formed very considerable articles of commerce. The facility with which the settler obtained money, it has been already shewn, prevented his customary exertions and enterprise in procuring wheat ; and by the passing the Impounding Law, the ultimate destruction

---

* During the year this work was published, the lawyers' rate of interest had somewhat increased, rather than otherwise; for from a recent publication it appears a gentleman of the profession, who shall be here nameless, charged forty per cent. discount on a bill of £52, and *attendance* 6s. 8d.   This bill, in all probability, was discounted at a Bank ten minutes afterwards, at ten per cent.

of the export trade of meat followed. In the "good olden times of a year previously," every settler who possessed a few hundred acres of land, had a flock of sheep—nay, many such settlers often possessed herds of cattle, but no sooner was the Impounding Law passed, by which all cattle and sheep were to be impounded from off Crown land,* than such farmers were compelled to sell their flocks and herds, or let the poundkeeper sell them to his own friends and relations. The adoption of this law was of advantage to the large over-grown land owners. Those individuals who possessed twenty or thirty thousand acres of land naturally wished for the adoption of a law by which none, save themselves, could supply the Colonists with food—the race of small industrious farmers were to be destroyed by the grasping prosperity of some half score of individuals, whose rise in the Colony has been as sudden as it has been extraordinary.

The effect produced by the passing of these two laws, will be seen, when recording the events of the few subsequent years.

In addition to the impolitic Acts of Council, just referred to, other measures were adopted, unfavourable to the Colony. The large balance in the hand of the Colonial Treasurer, was pointed out to the Home Authorities, as a certain proof of the prosperity of the Colonists, and His Excellency the Lieutenant Governor was highly complimented by the Home Authorities, for his financial measures. In former years, there appeared no chance whatever of the Colony paying off the debt incurred by advances made through the Colonial Agent, but the dispatches of His Excellency now pointed out that the large annual surplus of income might hereafter be disposed of in such a manner. The flourishing accounts sent to the Secretary of State during this year, were ultimately attended with the most injurious consequences; for, owing to the prosperity of the Colony being

---

* About fourteen fifteenths of the land in the Colony is yet unlocated—it was on the unlocated land, that herds and flocks of former years were depastured.

so great, the Home Government thought it advisable to discontinue the stimulus formerly held out for emigration, and in the following January, an order was issued at the Colonial Office, stopping the *giving* away of any more land, and ordering for the future the *sale* of all Crown land, for which purchasers could be found.   It will be necessary, a few pages further on, to offer some general remarks on the land question, and therefore further reference, at present, is unnecessary.

In September, of 1830, the black line was projected, and proved a very innocent amusement for the various Government officers, as also for a very large portion of the settlers, and their convict servants. That something was necessary, either to intimidate the blacks, or to capture them, there cannot be a question; and although the " *line*" proved a failure, yet it was undertaken with the best intentions.   The great movement against the blacks had been made a subject of newspaper discussion for some time previously to its operation; the Government papers, of course, supported the proposed undertaking, and commented on the practicability, as also on the policy of such a measure—but there were journals that described the whole attempt as a master-piece of absurdity.   The whole Island appeared in commotion during the months of September, October, and November ; and the black war, and nothing but the black war, was the subject of general attention.   A fresh declaration of martial law was gazetted on the 15th of October, * and about the

---

* *By His Excellency Colonel George Arthur, Lieutenant Governor of the Island of Van Diemen's Land and its Dependencies.*

‌ PROCLAMATION.

Whereas, by my proclamation, bearing date the 1st day of November, 1828, reciting, (amongst other things), that the black or aboriginal natives of this Island, had for a considerable time carried on a series of indiscriminate attacks upon the persons and property of His Majesty's subjects, and that repeated inroads were daily made by such natives into the settled districts, and that acts of hostility and barbarity, were there committed by them, as well as at the more distant stock runs, and in some instances, upon unoffending and defenceless women and children, and that it had become unavoidably

same time, a general Government Order issued, stating that the Colonists were called upon *en masse*, to come forth, and captnre the hostile tribes, and by one determined effort put an end to the *Guerilla* war which had

---

necessary, for the suppression of similar enormities, to proclaim Martial Law, in the manner therein hereinafter directed. I, the said Lieutenant Governor, did declare and proclaim, that from the date of that my proclamation, and until the cessation of hostilities, Martial Law was, and should continue to be in force against the said black or aboriginal natives within the several districts of this Island, excepting always the places and portions of this Island in the said proclamation after mentioned ; and whereas, the said black or aboriginal natives, or certain of their tribes, have of late manifested, by continued repetitions of the most wanton and sanguinary acts of violence and outrage, an unequivocal determination indiscriminately to destroy the white inhabitants, whenever opportunities are presented to them for doing so ; and whereas, by reason of the aforesaid exceptions so contained in the said proclamation, no natives have been hitherto pursued or molested in any of the places or portions of the Island so excepted ; from whence they have accordingly of late been accustomed to make repeated incursions upon the settled districts with impunity, or having committed outrages in the settled districts, have escaped into those excepted places, where they remain in security ; and whereas, therefore, it hath now become necessary ; and because it is scarcely possible to distinguish the particular tribe or tribes by whom such outrages have been in any particular instance committed, to adopt immediately, for the purpose of effecting their capture, if possible, an active and extended system of military operations against all the natives generally throughout the Island, and every portion thereof, whether actually settled or not. Now, therefore, by virtue of the powers and authorities in me in this behalf vested, I, the said Lieutenant Governor, do by these presents declare and proclaim, that from and after the date of this my proclamation, and until the cessation of hostilities in this behalf shall be by me hereafter proclaimed and directed, Martial Law is and shall continue to be in force against all the black or aboriginal natives, within every part of this Island (whether exempted from the operation of the said proclamation or not), excepting always such tribe, or individuals of tribes, as there may be reason to suppose are pacifically inclined, and have not been implicated in any such outrages, and for the purposes aforesaid, all soldiers and others His Majesty's subjects, civil and military, are hereby required and commanded to obey and assist their lawful superiors in the execution of such measures as shall from time to time be in this behalf directed to be taken. But I do, nevertheless, hereby strictly order, enjoin and command, that the actual use of arms be in no case resorted to, by firing against any of the

been so harassing and murderous in its effect.* In the first week of October, upwards of 3,000 individuals were in the field, 550 persons, including about 50 of the

natives or otherwise, if they can by other means be captured, that bloodshed be invariably checked as much as possible, and that any tribes or individuals captured or voluntarily surrendering themselves up, be treated with the utmost care and humanity. And all officers, civil and military, and other persons whatsoever, are hereby required to take notice of this my proclamation, and to render obedience and assistance herein accordingly.

Given under my hand and seal at arms, at the Government House, Hobart Town, this first day of October, in the year of our Lord, one thousand eight hundred and thirty.

GEORGE ARTHUR.

By command of His Excellency,

J. BURNETT.

* *Colonial Secretary's Office, Sept.* 25, 1830.

The reader will be, perhaps, amused with the gazetted orders for the grand operation of the black war—to those connected with military tactics, it must be amusing, if not instructive. It should be borne in mind, that Van Diemen's Land is even more mountainous than the Highlands of Scotland, and nearly the whole face of the country is covered with a thick scrub or jungle, in some places so closely matted together, as scarcely to be penetrable for a bandicoote. Bearing in mind the nature of the country, the folly of the undertaking must be apparent.

1.—The community being called upon to act *en masse* on the 7th October next, for the purpose of capturing those hostile tribes of the natives which are daily committing renewed atrocities upon the settlers ; the following outline of the arrangements which the Lieutenant Governor has determined upon, is published, in order that every person may know the principle on which he is required to act, and the part which he is to take individually in this important transaction.

2.—Active operations will at first be chiefly directed against the tribes which occupy the country south of a line drawn from Waterloo Point east, to Lake Echo west, including the Hobart, Richmond, New Norfolk, Clyde, and Oatlands Police districts,—at least, within this county, the military will be mainly employed, the capture of the Oyster Bay and Big River tribes, as the most sanguinary, being of the greatest consequence.

3.—In furtherance of this measure, it is necessary that the natives should be driven from the extremities within the settled districts of the county of Buckingham, and that they should subsequently be prevented from escaping out of them ; and the following movements are, therefore directed, first, to surround the hostile navtive tribes ; secondly, to capture them in the county of Buckingham, pro-

troops, were drafted from Launceston, and about treble
that number were raised in Hobart Town. The inhabitants of both these townships undertook the duties of the
military, and both places appeared nearly deserted. Most

gressively driving them upon Tasman's Peninsula; and thirdly, to
prevent their escape into the remote unsettled districts to the west-
ward and eastward.

4.—Major Douglas will, on the 7th of October, cause the following chain of posts to be occupied, viz.—from the coast near St.
Patrick's Head, to the source of the St. Paul's River, and by that
river and the South Esk, to Epping Forest and Campbell Town.
This line being taken up, the parties composing it, will advance in
a southerly direction towards the Eastern Marshes, and will thoroughly examine the country between their first stations and the
head of the Macquarie, and on the afternoon of the 12th of October,
they will halt with their left at a mountain on the Oyster Bay Tier,
on which a large fire is to be kept burning, and their right extending
towards Malony's Sugar Loaf. To effect this movement, Major
Douglas will reinforce the post at Avoca, and this force, under the
orders of Captain Wellman, will be strengthened by such parties as
can be despatched by the Police Magistrate of Campbell Town, and
by the roving parties under Mr. Batman, and will receive the most
effectual co-operation from Major Gray, who will, no doubt, be
warmly seconded by Messrs. Legge, Talbot, Grant, Smith, Gray,
Hepburn, Kearney, Bates, and all other settlers in that neighbourhood.

5.—Major Douglas will also, on the 7th of October, form a
chain of posts from Campbell Town, along the south-west bank of
the Macquarie, to its junction with the Lake River. These parties
will then advance in a southerly direction, carefully examining the
Table Mountain, range on both its sides, and the banks of the Lake
River, and they will halt on the afternoon of the 12th, with their
left at Malony's Sugar Loaf, and their right at Lackey's Mill, which
position will already be occupied by troops from Oatlands.

In this movement Major Douglas will receive the co-operation of
the Police Magistrate of Campbell Town, who will bring forward
upon that portion of the line extending from the high road, near
Kimberly's, on the Salt-pan Plains, to Malony's Sugar Loaf, the
force contributed by Messrs. Willis, W. Harrison, Pearson, Jellicoe,
Davidson, M'Leod, Leake, Clarke, Murray, Horne, Scardon,
Kermode, Parramore, Horton, Scott, Dickenson, R. Davidson,
Cassidy, Eagle, Gardiner, Robertson, Hill, Forster, with any
other settlers from that part of his district, while that portion of the
line extending from Lackey's Mill to Kimberly's, will be strength-
ened by Messrs. G. C. Clarke, G. C. Simpson, Sutherland, Ruffey,
Gatenby, G. Simpson, C. Thompson, H. Murray, Buist, Oliver,
Malcolm, Taylor, Mackersey, Bayles, Stewart, Alston, Bibra,

of the young men in Government employ volunteered to
join the troops in the interior, and the parties forming
the " black line," composed as they were, of a curious

Corney, Fletcher, Young, O'Connor, Yorke, and any other settlers
resident in that part of the district, who will on their march have
examined the east side of the Table Mountain.

6.—In order to obviate confusion in the movements of this body,
the Police Magistrates will, without delay, ascertain the strength
which will be brought into the field, and having divided it into parties of ten, he will nominate a leader to each, and will attach to
them experienced guides for directing their marches, and he will
report these arrangements to Major Douglas, when completed.
The remainder of the forces under Major Douglas will, on the
afternoon of the 12th, take up their position on the same line, extending from the Oyster Bay range to the Clyde, South of Lake
Crescent, over Table Mountain. Its right under the command of
Captain Mahon, 63rd Regiment, resting on the Table Mountain,
passing to the rear of Michael Howe's Marsh. Its left under Captain
Wellman, 57th Regiment, at a mountain in the Oyster Bay Tier,
where a large fire will be seen Its right centre under Captain
Macpherson, 17th Regiment, extending from Malony's Sugar Loaf
to Captain Mahon's left, and its left centre under Captain Bailie,
63rd Regiment, extending from Malony's Sugar Loaf to Captain
Wellman's right.

7.—Major Douglas's extreme right will be supported by the roving parties, and by the Police of the Oatlands district, which,
together with the volunteer parties formed from the district of Oatlands, will be mustered by the Police Magistrate, in divisions of
ten men, and he will nominate a leader to each division, and will
attach experienced guides for conducting the march, and he will report
his arrangement, when completed, to Major Douglas, in order that
this force may be placed in the right of the line, to which position
it will file from Oatlands, by the pass over Table Mountain.

8.—Between the 7th and the 12th of October, Lieutenant Aubin
will thoroughly examine the tier extending from the head of the
Swan River, north, down to Spring Bay, the southern extremity of
his district, in which duty he will be aided in addition to the military
parties stationed at Spring Bay and Little Swan Port, by Captains
Maclaine and Leard, Messrs. Meredith, Hawkins, Gatehouse,
Buxton, Harte, Amos, Allen, King, Lyne, and all settlers in that
district, and by Captain Glover and Lieutenant Steel, with whatever force can be collected at the Carlton, and at Sorell by the
Police Magistrate of that district.

In occupying this position, the utmost care must be taken that no
portion of this or any other force shews itself above the tiers south of
Spring Bay, before the general line reaches that point, and the constables at East Bay Neck, and the settlers on the Peninsula, must with-

melange of masters and servants, took their respective
stations at the appointed time.   As the several parties
advanced, the individuals along the line came gradually

---

draw before the 7th of October, in order that nothing may tend to
deter the native tribes from passing the Isthmus. On the 12th, Lieutenant Aubin will occupy the passes in the tier which the natives
are known most to frequent, and will communicate with the extreme left of Major Douglas's line, taking up the best points of
observation, and causing at the same time a most minute recon-
noisance to be kept upon the Schoutens, in case the natives
should pass into that Peninsula, as they are in the habit of doing,
either for shell-fish or eggs, in which case he will promptly carry
into effect theinstructions with which he has already been furnished.

9.—Captain Wentworth will, on the 4th October, push a strong
detachment under the orders of Lieutenant Croly, from Bothwell,
towards the Great Lake, for the purpose of thoroughly examining
St. Patrick's Plains, and the banks of the Shannon, extending its
left on retiring to the Clyde, towards the Lagoon of Islands, and its
right towards Lake Echo.   This detachment will be assisted by the
roving parties under Sherwin and Doran, and by the settlers resideng
on the Shannon.

10.—Captain Wentworth will also detach the troops at Hamilton
township, under Captain Vicary, across the Clyde, to occupy the western bank of the Ouse.   For this service every possible assistance
will be afforded by the parties formed from the establishments of
Messrs. Triffith, Sharland, Marzetti, Yonug, Dixon, Austin,
Burn, Jamieson, Shone, Risely, and any other settlers in that district, together with any men of the Field Police who may be well
acquainted with that part of the country.

11.—A small party of troops, under the command of Lieutenant
Murray, will also be sent up the north bank of the Derwent, to scour
the country on the west bank of the Ouse.   This detachment will be
strengthened by any parties of the police or volunteers that can be
supplied by the police magistrate of New Norfolk, and from Hobart
Town.

12.—These three detachments, under the orders of Capt. Vicary,
Lieut. Croly, and Lieut. Murray, after thoroughly scouring the
country, especially the Blue Hill, and after endeavouring to drive
towards the Clyde whatever tribes of natives may be in those quarters, will severally take up their positions on the 12th of Oct., as
follows : viz. Lieut. Croly's force will rest its left on the Clyde,
where Major Douglas's extreme right will be posted, and its right
at Sherwin's.—Capt. Vicary's left will rest at Sherwin's, and his
right at Hamilton : Lieut. Murray's left at Hamilton, and his right
on the high road at Allanvale, and his whole line occupying that
road.

13.—The parties of volunteers and ticket-of-leave men from Ho-

closer and closer together—the plan was, to keep on advancing slowly towards a certain peninsula, and thus
frighten the aborigines before them, and hem them in,
so that their caption might be easily effected. It may be

bart Town and its neighbourhood, will march by New Norfolk, for
the purpose of assisting Capt. Wentworth's force, in occupying the
Clyde; and they will be rendering a great service by joining that
force in time to invest the Blue Hill, which will be about the 10th
of October.

14.—The police magistrate of New Norfolk will reserve from
amongst the volunteers and ticket-of-leave men, a sufficient force to
occupy the pass which runs from the high road, near Downie's by
Parson's Valley, to Mr. Murdoch's on the Jordan, and on the 9th
of October he will move these bodies by the Dromedary mountain
which he will cause to be carefully examined towards that pass,
which, on the afternoon of the 10th, he will occupy, taking care so
to post his parties, as to prevent the natives from passing the chain
on being pressed from the northward.

15.—Captain Donaldson will, with as little delay as possible,
make arrangements for advancing from Norfolk Plains towards the
country on the west bank of the Lake River, up to Regent's Plains
and Lake Arthur, driving in a southerly direction any of the tribes
in that quarter. He will also push some parties over the Tier to the
Great Lake, so as to make an appearance at the head of the Shannon
and of the Ouse; and on the 12th of October his position will extend from Sorell Lake, to Lake Echo, by St. Patrick's Plains. In
this important position he will remain, with the view of arresting the
flight of any tribes towards the west, which might possibly pass
through the first line. And as the success of the general operations
will so much depend upon the vigilant guard to be observed over
this tract of country, the Lieutenant Governor places the utmost
confidence in Captain Donaldson's exertions, in effectually debarring
the escape of the tribes in this direction; for which purpose he will
withdraw, if he thinks proper, the detachment at Westbury, and
will concentrate his forces on the position described. In this service Captain Donaldson will be supported by all the force that can
be brought forward by the Police Magistrates of Launceston and
Norfolk Plains, in addition to that which can be contributed by the
settlers in those districts.

16.—It may be presumed that, by the movements already described, the natives will have been enclosed within the settled districts of the county of Buckingham.

17.—On the morning of the 14th of October, Major Douglas
will advance the whole of the northern division, in a south-easterly
direction, extending from the Clyde to the Oyster Bay range: Captain Mahon being on his right, Captains Macpherson and Bailie in
his centre, and Captain Wellman on his left, while Lieutenant

O

observed that during this time, the inhabitants of Hobart
Town and Launceston formed themselves into regular
militia corps, some undertaking the duties of guarding
the Jail, others the Battery, whilst the great body

Aubin will occupy the crests of the tiers. The left wing of Major
Douglas's division will move along the tier nearly due south, to
Little Swan Port River, the left centre upon Mr. Hobbs's stock-
run, the right centre upon the Blue Hill Bluff, and the right wing
to the Great Jordan Lagoon. Having thoroughly examined all the
tiers and the ravines on its line of march, the divisions will reach
these stations on the 16th, and will halt on Sunday, the 17th of
October.

18.—A large fire will be kept burning on the Blue Hill Bluff,
from the morning of the 4th, until the morning of the 8th, as a point
of direction for the centre, by which the whole line will be regulated.

19.—On Monday, the 18th, Major Douglas's division will again
advance in a south-easterly direction, its left moving upon Prosser's
River, keeping close to the tier, its centre upon Prosser's Plains to
Olding's hut, its right upon Musquito Plain and the north side of
the Brown Mountain, which stations they will reach respectively on
the evening of the 20th, and where they will halt for further orders,
taking the utmost care to extend the line from Prosser's Bay, so as
to connect the Parties with the Brown Mountain, enclosing the
Brushy Plains, with the hills called the Three Thumbs, in so
cautious a manner, that the natives may not be able to pass them.

20.—From the morning of the 18th to the 22nd, a large fire will
be kept burning on the summit of the Brown Mountain, to serve as
a point of direction for Major Douglas's right and Captain Wentworth's left.

21.—On the morning of the 14th of October, the western division, under the orders of Captain Wentworth, formed on the banks
of the Clyde, will enter the Abyssinian Tier, and after thoroughly
examining every part of that range, will move due east to the banks
of the Jordan, with its left at Bisdee's, Broadribb's, and Jones's
farms. Its centre at the Green Ponds, and its right at Murdoch's
farm at the Broad Marsh, which stations they will severally gain
on Saturday evening, the 16th of October, and where they will
halt on Sunday, the 17th.

22.—Whenever Captain Wentworth's force moves from the Clyde
to the eastward, those settlers who do not join him will invest the
road of the Upper and Lower Clyde, and will keep guard on it
during the remainder of the operations, extending their left through
Miles's Opening, to Mr. Jones's farm.

23.—On Monday, the 18th, the western division will advance
its left, which will connect with the right of the northern division
by Spring Hill, the Lovely Banks, and the Hollow Tree Bottom.

were stationed at the Main Guard, from whence the various sentinels were posted for the Government House, and other public buildings. This grand military movement may be compared to a very large net being

---

to Mr. Rees's farm, on the west of the Brown Mountain, its centre over Constitution Hill, and the Bagdad Tier, and by the Coal River Sugar Loaf to Mr. Smith's farm, at the junction of the Kangaroo and Coal Rivers, its right over the Mongalore Tier, through Bagdad and the Tea Tree Brush, to Stynes' and Troy's farm, on the Coal River, which stations they will respectively reach on the afternoon of the 20th, and where they will halt till further orders.

24.—Whenever the right wing of Captain Wentworth's division shall have reached Mr. Murdoch's, on the Jordan, Mr. Dumaresq will abandon the pass at Parson's Valley, and will extend itself on Captain Wentworth's extreme right, advancing with that force, until it occupies the Coal River, from Captain Wentworth's right to the mouth of the river. A post of observation will be stationed on the mountain called "Gunner's Quoin," near the Tea Tree Brush.

25.—The Assistant Commissary General will provide rations at the undermentioned stations, viz. :—

Waterloo Point	Bisdee's farm
Malony's Sugar Loaf	Richmond
Lackey's Mill.	Mr. Rees's, Kangaroo River
Under the Bluff of Table Mountain	Olding's, Prosser's Plains
	Captain M'Laine's, Spring Bay
Bothwell	Lieutenant Hawkins's, Little
Hamilton	Swan Port
New Norfolk	Oatlands
Murdoch's (Jordan)	Tier, west of Waterloo Point
Brighton	Jones's hut, St. Patrick's Plains
Cross Marsh	Captain Wood's hut, Regent's
Hobbs's (Little Swan Port River)	Plains
Mr. Torlesse's	Mr. George Kemp's hut, Lake
Nicholas's, on the Ouse	Sorell
Green Ponds	Michael Howe's Marsh.

The arrangement at the different depots, for the conveyance of rations and stores to the parties employed, will be undertaken by Mr. Scott, Mr. Wedge, and Mr. Sharland ; and as the leader of each party will be a respectable individual, he will keep a ration book, in which he will insert his own name, and the names of all his party, which, on his presenting at any of the depots, stating the quantity required, the respective storekeepers will issue the same, taking care that no greater quantity than seven days' supply, consisting of the following articles per diem, viz., three ounces of sugar, half an ounce of tea, two pounds of flour, and one pound and a

drawn across the Derwent, and the net at last gathered
up in the small bay which forms the port of this town—
of course *all* the fish in the river would be secured in the
small bay—so thought the projectors of this scheme. The
blacks were to be frightened into the peninsula, and there
captured, without loss of blood, and then lodged in jail.*

half of meat, for each person, shall be issued at one time to any
party.

25.—The inhabitants of the country generally, are requested not
to make any movements against the natives within the circuit occupied by the troops, until the general line reaches them, and the residents of the Jordan and Bagdad line of road, will render the most
effectual assistance by joining Captain Wentworth's force while yet
on the Clyde.

26.—The assigned servants of settlers will be expected to muster,
provided each with a good pair of spare shoes, and a blanket, and
seven days' provisions, consisting of flour or biscuit, salt meat, tea,
and sugar; so, also, prisoners holding tickets-of-leave; but these
latter, where they cannot afford it, will be furnished with a supply
of provisions from the Government magazines.

27.—It will not be necessary that more than two men of every
five should carry fire-arms, as the remaining then can very advantageously assist their comrades in carrying provisions, &c., and the
Lieutenant Governor takes this opportunity of again enjoining the
whole community to bear in mind that the object in view is not to
injure or destroy the unhappy savages against whom these movements will be directed, but to capture and raise them in the scale of
civilization, by placing them under the immediate control of a com-
petent establishment, from whence they will not have it in their
power to escape, and molest the white inhabitants of the Colony,
and where they themselves will no longer be subject to the miseries
of perpetual warfare, or to the privations which the extension of the
settlements would progressively entail upon them were they to remain in their present unhappy state.

28.—The police magistrates, and the masters of assigned servants will be careful to entrust with arms only such prisoners as
they can place confidence in, and to ensure regularity, each prisoner employed will be furnished by the police magistrate with a
pass, describing the division to which he is attached, and the name
of its leader, and containing the personal description of the prisoner
himself.

By His Excellency's command,

J. BURNETT.

* The expertness and agility of these poor people, in their peculiar
way, is indeed astonishing. Peletegu, the chief lately apprehended
at the Shannon, who is now in the Hobart Town jail, displays the

During the advance of the lines, the despatches received
and sent, equalled in number those forwarded by the allied
armies during the last European war—in fact, every thing
was carried on, as if it were a great war in miniature : the
reports—the gazetted proclamations of the advance of
the lines—the stories told by the persons of their falling in
with the natives,* and so forth, kept the people alive,

most perfect good humour and cheerfulness ; and for a small reward
of sugar, or other desirable food, will sing and dance to entertain
the donor. He has a method of clapping the palms of his hands
and soles of his feet simultaneously on the ground, and immediately
making his frame bound in a perpendicular position four or five feet
in the air, and then dancing and singing round and round in a rota-
tory motion. He yesterday took up an old broom-stick, which lay
in the jail yard, and standing at a distance of about twelve yards,
threw it in the manner of casting a spear, right through a small hole
which had been accidentally made in the side of the sentry-box,
and this at the very first trial, although the orifice was scarcely half
an inch larger in diameter than the stick that passed through it.
At another time, taking up a small bit of lath, which some gentlemen trying to throw, could not cast with all their efforts, half the
distance, he struck it directly through and through the middle of a
hat set up about thirty yards off.—*Hobart Town Courier.*
		* GOVERNMENT NOTICE, NO. 203.
		Colonial Secretary's Office, Oct. 18, 1830.
The attention of the Colony, at present, being so much alive to
every circumstance connected with the aboriginal natives, the
Lieutenant Governor has directed the following narrative to be made
public, which His Excellency feels satisfied will be received with
much interest. By His Excellency's command,
					J. BURNETT.
	Mr. Bisdee's farm, White Hills, Oct. 16, 1830.
On the afternoon of Friday, the 15th inst. about half-past 4 o'clock,
as Thomas Savage, an overseer in the service of Mr. Bisdee, of the
White Hills, was at work splitting timber with another man, he
heard a noise which attracted his attention, and he proceeded in the
direction from whence it came, supposing the Lieutenant Governor,
whose arrival was expected, was approaching, and who, in fact, did
arrive just about that time—from that moment Savage's companion
saw no more of him. On Saturday morning, Savage had not returned. Mr. Edward Bisdee thought it probable that he had gone
to Mr. Jones's to enquire after a cow which had strayed away, and
therefore he was not particularly anxious; but as up to the middle of
the day, Savage was still missing, some search was made on foot,
and about 2 o'clock, a vague report was brought in that Savage had
been taken by the natives, who had let him go again. At this time

and caused a fund of amusement. One day the troops were told that large numbers of whites had joined the aborigines, that were flying before the lines ; at another

the Lieutenant Governor was on the point of mounting his horse to visit the several parties which were formed on the Jordan, and on his arrival at Jones's hut, he learned from a shepherd, that Savage had been there, and that he had been with the natives, and had proceeded with a small party up the tier leading to Miles's Lagoon. The Lieutenant Governor, accompanied by Mr. Frankland, Mr. Charles Arthur, and Mr. Edward Bisdee, instantly proceeded up the tier, which was rapidly ascended, and on their arrival at the Lagoon, named Miles's Lagoon, there they met Savage, half naked, who accounted for his absence nearly in the following words:—" I was working with my fellow servant, between 4 and 5 o'clock, yesterday afternoon, when I heard a very soft *coo-ee*, and thinking it was the Governor coming, I went to meet him, but very slowly, being bad with the rhuematism ; I walked a very little way, when —as it were instantaneously—I was surrounded by a mob of natives who raised their spears at me, and I should have been dead in a moment, had not a white man, who was standing by with a double-barrelled gun, called out, and they immediately desisted." The white man then spoke to me, and said, " don't be afraid, Savage, you was very kind to me in jail, about three years ago, and I won't suffer you to be hurt." The man I immediately recognized to be a convict named Brown, who was in prison about two or three years ago, and when I was in Mr. Bisdee's service, I used to be civil to him, and take him, now and then, something to eat. Brown is a fine stout man, well dressed, and shaved, rather light hair, rather pale complexion, he had on a good pair of shoes, cord trowsers, dark waistcoat striped up and down, short jacket, and was carrying a double-barrelled gun.

Presently, whilst he was talking to me, six more of the blacks came out of the bush, and joined us, and Brown then said, " I must go a little way along with them." I was so bad with rheumatism before, that I could not walk ; but the fright cured me, and I could walk as well as ever, and I began to consider how I could slip away— however, we walked along, talking. Brown told me, he had been with the natives about three years, and said, he was surprised at so many parties being out. I said, " I had remarked the same thing, and believed the Governor was determined to take all the bushrangers." I then said, " Brown, you know the Governor has promised to be kind to all these poor people, if they will be quiet—you had better bring them in." He said, " no, he had been twice deceived, and would not be deceived again ; but he might let the Governor know the blacks should commit no murders whilst he was with them," (remember, their spears were raised to kill poor savage, had they not been restrained in this particular instance, by the ever powerful

time there were reports of desperate struggles between the
blacks and some of the advancing parties, but the greater
part of these proved to be unfounded tales of terror. One

---

interposition of Providence !) and turning round, he appealed to
the mob.—" You never knew me kill, or commit a robbery," to
which they all replied, shaking their heads, "No! No! No!"
Savage had on a cap and a good pair of shoes, which Brown was
not restrained by gratitude from making him take off and give to one
of the men, whose face indeed was black, but his features were evidently those of a white man. He had on a shirt and trowsers, with
a single-barrelled gun in his hand—the name of Moore was on the
lock. This man never spoke during the whole time Savage was with
the mob. Brown had evidently the complete controul over the mob,
which did not exceed fifteen or twenty. One of the women was
Brown's *Gin*, and he seemed very fond of her. She was quite big
with child, and looked to be confined every hour. All the mob
were very fond of Brown, and did every thing he told them. Brown
said, " he was afraid to go to Launceston, he was so well known
there, but he had been frequently in Hobart Town, and there he
bought the clothes for the women," pointing to some petticoats which
the *Gins* had on. When the six men came out of the bush, one of
them was carrying the carcass of a sheep over his shoulders, and
half round his neck, just as they carry a kangaroo. The animal
had just been killed, and soon after Savage fell in with them, not
more than a mile from Mr. Bisdee's house, they stopped to make a
fire, and hearing the report of a gun, Brown said, " we must not
stay here, let us be off," and accordingly they crossed the Jordan,
and continued marching, until about 11 o'clock at night they reached
Miles's Lagoon, where Brown said, " Now, Savage, you may go,"
and we shook hands very comfortably all round. On being asked
whether he afterwards stopped to watch them, he said, " no, he was
half frightened to death, and was happy to get away." By the time
this information was given, it was nearly dark, but the Governor
descended the Tier with all despatch, and in the course of an hour
and a half four parties were sent off, with orders to proceed during
the night, ten miles beyond the Lagoon, as far as the Quoin, and
then to spread themselves out and scour the bush thoroughly ; and
supposing the natives to be tired with their long march the previous
night, and especially so the woman with child, it may be hoped
that they will be surrounded, or at least driven to the southward and
eastward, if that has not been already effected by the parties which
came over the Tier at day-light this morning. This singular occurrence has brought to light, that although the natives have been
guided by men worse than savages, they have had more than savage
instinct for their guide in the various murders and robberies which
they have committed. The tribe had no dogs with them.
    [It is scarcely necessary to remark, that the story of Savage was,

of the roving squadrons, under the command of a young
man of the name of Walpole,* captured two natives when
the troops were drawn up, waiting for the advance of Capt.

---

at the time, not believed, but by a few individuals; and from what
has since occurred, there can be no doubt but that the whole statement was trumped up to suit Savage's own interests.]—PUBLISHER.

    * Mr. Walpole had charge of a roving party, of ten men, and
had been sent inside of the line to scour the country, along the sea-
coast, to the southward of Prosser's Bay. On the evening of Monday, the 25th inst. he discovered the natives hunting, and watched
them making their fires and forming their encampment for the night,
in a deep scrubby ravine, to the south of the Sand Pit River, opposite the south end of Maria Island. The dogs of the savages made
a great noise, howling nearly the whole of the night, while Mr.
Walpole, and his party, were concealed at a short distance, not
wishing to attempt taking any of the tribe until morning. No noise
being heard near day-light, it was supposed the natives had taken
the alarm and gone in the night, and, in consequence, Mr. Walpole
advanced to the first hut, where he very unexpectedly saw five blacks,
all fast asleep, under some blankets, with their dogs. He seized
hold of one of the largest of the feet, which awakening the party,
they endeavoured to make their escape. The man, whose feet he
had hold of, made a violent effort to escape, and darted through the
back of the hut, carrying Mr. Walpole with him, into the gully or
creek behind—here he again tried to make his escape, by twisting
his legs and biting, and would have succeeded, had Mr. Walpole
not drawn a small dagger from his belt, and inflicted a slight wound
which so frightened him, that he was secured. The other taken,
was a boy of about fifteen years of age, and appears to be the son of
a chief, from the ornaments upon his body, cut with flints, or some
sharp instrument, into the skin. Two others were shot by the party
in making their escape into the scrub, on the edge of which their
huts were placed. This hut had been fixed as a vidette, or out-post
to a very numerous tribe encamped in the scrub, who took the alarm
on the firing, and made a precipitate retreat, leaving a great number
of spears and waddies behind, and baskets of their women. It is
supposed that the tribe amounted in all, to near 70 individuals.
The boy, when taken, wished them to let him go, as he said "there
are plenty more black fellows in the scrub," pointing to it. None of
them have yet succeeded in forcing their way across the line, although many attempts have now been made upon the cordon, in
various places, in all which they have been repulsed and driven
back. In one of these attempts, the sentry was speared in two
places, and they again tried to force their way. yesterday, at the
same spot, which is a favourite crossing place of the blacks over the
Prosser's River.—*Hobart Town Courier.*

Donaldson's division. During the time the line was stationary, which was for about fourteen days, the parties forming the line were close to each other, and their spirits were kept up by being convinced that hundreds and hundreds of the aborigines were before them, making towards the peninsula.

Many very curious anecdotes are related, as having occurred during the time the army was thus stationed :*

---

* Prosser's Plains, Oct. 26.

Yesterday morning, at 2 o'clock, the natives attempted to force their way through the line where Lieutenant Ovens's division was posted upon a rocky hill, on the south bank of Prosser's River, about five miles from the sea. The man on guard observed a black man in a stooping attitude, and a fire-stick in his hand, running past. It was raining very heavy at the time. He succeeded in getting before him, and again driving him to the southward of the line. Several other lights were observed at a short distance on the hill, so that it is probable a considerable body of the natives were endeavouring to force their way, the alarm was in a very short time passed along the line, and all were under arms, and on the alert during the remainder of the night, which was exceedingly tempestuous and rainy. This is the first time I have known the natives to move at night. No doubt they are aware of being enclosed, and have resorted to extraordinary merns of escape. The civil forces perform the duty most cheerfully, although the weather has been lately very much against operations in the field. The country through which we have penetrated is exceedingly difficult of access, and almost unknown, from the rocky nature of the ground, and scrub with which it is covered. Most of the pasties came into their places in the line in the most regular and perfect manner, which reflects credit upon the leaders, having no roads by which they could direct their march. Five roving parties, each consisting of ten men, have been sent into the country where the blacks are now enclosed, to discover their fires, and secure them if possible, they have now been gone four days, something is expected from them, as they were all picked men, under leaders who knew the country well.

Prosser's Plains, Wednesday, 27th October.

Since last writing you, the natives have made a second attack upon the line under the command of Major Douglas, and been again repulsed and driven back to the south, inside of the cordon. At 11 o'clock this forenoon, a party of six men made their appearance on a rocky hill, occupied by part of the Richmond force, and where No. 5 party were stationed, under the charge of Mr. Wise. The

P

frequent alarms were given, and detachments sent out to scour certain portions of the enclosed country, where native fires were said to have been seen; but most of these turned out to be idle rumours. Several times at night the whole body of troops would be firing their muskets, expecting a rush from the natives before them : and one dark night some young men, when hunting opossums, the report of their fowling-pieces, was considered by some of the troops as an alarm—a rush to the supposed danger took place, when the utmost confusion prevailed. At another time several rounds of musketry were fired from the troops, when ultimately it turned out that the cause of the alarm had been a black stump of a tree, at a little distance which had been taken by one of the military for a native trying to pass the line. At length the anxiously expected hour for advancing arrived. "The whole chain of posts moved forward simultaneously towards the new position, on the 18th November, and it was calculated that the extreme of the left wing would arrive at the mouth of the Sand-pit River, opposite Maria Island, on the evening of the 20th. The whole line then, reaching in a westerly direction over the tier of hills, towards the Iron Creek and Pittwater, was shortened to less than half the extent which it

---

sentry had just set his musket down, and was putting some wood on the fire, when a spear was thrown at him, which passed quite through his leg—having a billet of wood in his hand, he immediately threw it at the savage, and was turning round to get hold of his musket, when he received another spear, in an oblique direction, through the breast and shoulder, and instantly fell, giving the alarm to the next party, distant only about eighty or a hundred yards. These men came up, but the blacks succeeded in making their retreat good, from the first man, when running, and in the act of cocking his firelock, falling over a dead tree, and from the country in that place being so rocky and heavily timbered. One satisfaction is, to know that they are still within the lines.

There were only six blacks seen, all men. One carried a bundle of spears, and two others had a blanket each round their shoulders. Several small parties were immediately formed, and sent in pursuit, and traced them in the direction of the Brushy Plains, in the neighbourhood of which place, the grand mob is supposed to be.—*Courier.*

formerly occupied, between Sorell and Prosser's Bay."
Ten days after, an order was issued, that the long wished
for division of Captain Donaldson, would appear on the
morrow; and fresh instructions were published.* It

---

* *Camp, Sorell Rivulet, October* 31, 1830.
TO THE COMMANDERS OF CORPS.

The Colonel commanding requests, that the commanders of corps
will inform every leader under their orders, that the advance of
Captain Donaldson's division will, it is hoped, enable the final and
decisive movement to commence to-morrow. That His Excellency,
fully aware of the great privations and inconvenience which the
leaders, as well as those serving with them, have been suffering, by
so protracted a separation from their families and homes, has observed with real satisfaction the cheerful and praiseworthy alacrity
which has animated them in strfving to accomplish the present important undertaking.

The delay consequent on waiting for reinforcements, has been un-
avoidable, for, to have advanced the whole force from its present
position, would have assuredly risked the loss of the great advantage
which the labours of the community have obtained, in so successfully enclosing the two most dangerous tribes. A few days must
now terminate the great work in the most satisfactory manner, and
His Excellency earnestly hopes that the leaders will for the remaining short period continue to shew the excellent spirit which has all
along been so conspicuous in their parties, for they will perceive
that the advance of the scouring parties will render redoubled vigi-
tance necessary on the part of those who guard the line, as the na-
lives, when disturbed in the interior, will undoubtedly increase
their efforts to break through the position.

GEORGE ARTHUR.

Camp, Sorell Rivulet, October 31, 1830.

The expected arrival of Captain Donaldson's force this day, now
enabling the Colonel commanding to make the final movement for
the capture of the tribes within the lines, the following arrangements will take place :—

Major Douglas will form twenty-two parties of seven men each,
including leaders, and early on Monday morning they will take post
fifty paces in front of the line, according to the following order, from
the left, viz., and in front of Lieutenant Aubin's corps, will be
placed at equal distances four parties, viz., Messrs. Walpole, Pearce,
Thomas Massey, and H. Batman.

In front of Lieutenant Ovens, two parties, viz., Mr. Byers, with
half of Mr. H. Batman's party, and Mr. M. Fortoza.

In front of Lieutenant Groves, three parties, viz., Messrs. G.
Robertson, E. Blinkworth, and J. Moriarty.

is needless to go into further particulars, the line occupied this second station for many days, whilst about
fifty scouring parties, composed of ten men each, were
ordered to take the field before the line, and thus drive

In front of Captain Baylee, three parties, viz., Messrs. G. Scott,
Layman, and Jemott.

In front of Captain M'Pherson, four parties, viz., Messrs. Allison,
Cox, Helmslie, and Russel.

In front of Captain Mahon, two parties, viz., Mr. Doran, (Peter
Scott will be attached either to this party, or to Mr. Evans's), and
Mr. Thomas's.

In front of Lieutenant Pedder, four parties, viz., Messrs. Evans,
Harrison, Flexmore, and Jack Jones, all four under the joint direction of Mr. Franks.

Captain Wentworth will also immediately form fifteen parties of
seven men each, including leaders, and on Monday morning they
will likewise take post fifty paces in front of the line, in the following
order :—

In front of Lieutenant Croly, four parties, viz., Messrs. Paterson,
Brodribb, Emmett, and Sherwin.

In front of Captain Clark, (Richmond force), Messrs. Kimberley,
Espie, and Lackey.

In front of Lieutenant Champ, two parties, viz., Messrs. Stan-
field, junior, and Cassidy.

In front of Lieutenant Murray, three parties, viz., Mr. Proctor,
(if he shall not have returned Stacy), Mr. Steel, and Mr. Synnott.

In front of Lieutenant Barrow, three parties, viz., Messrs. Caw-
thorn, Mills, and Shone, unattached. Messrs. Lloyd and Kirby,
as soon as the advanced parties shall have been posted in marching
order, and with five days' rations, the vacancies in the line which
their advance will have caused, will be filled up by the whole remaining force closing to the left, and Captain Donaldson's force
will take up the ground which has been heretofore occupied by
Lieutenant Barrow, Lieutenant Murray, and by a portion of Lieutenant Champ's corps. This movement, regulated by the right,
must be made with the utmost possible care, under the superintend-
ance of Major Douglas, Captain Wentworth and Lieutenant Aubin,
so as to prevent the possibility of any gaps in the line.

By this movement, which should, if possible, be effected by
12 o'clock on Monday, the line will remain of its original strength,
and the scouring parties will be in readiness to advance, which they
will do as soon as the vacancies have been closed. These parties
will then advance towards the south-east, driving the natives in that
direction, or capturing them, and on the fourth day will reach East
Bay Neck, where they will receive further orders.

The investing line which remains in position, must, during these

the whole body of natives before them on the peninsula. The last position occupied about twenty miles, extending over some of the roughest ground in the Colony. The scouring parties, after examining the enclosed country, advanced to the neck of the peninsula, where being provided with one week's rations, they were ready to proceed on the peninsula, when intelligence was brought that the line had suddenly been abandoned, and the troops all marched on to Pittwater. The extraordinary manner in which the warlike movements ended, surprised many ; and it is said by some, that large numbers of the aborigines were on the peninsula, which had not been scoured. It is certainly beyond dispute, that there might have been hundreds before the line, and had the military movements terminated as proposed, it is possible the result might have been very different. The whole scheme proved a most complete failure, as any reasonable man might have anticipated. The loss on the part of the troops amounted to some four or five killed by accident, whilst but one prisoner of war was brought as a trophy into town, and even this one afterwards escaped into the bush. His Excellency, however, to finish the *farce* in all due form, issued a Government Order, thanking the Colonists for their exertions.* This expedition, it is believed, (for no offi-

---

four decisive days, put forth every effort to prevent the possibility of the natives passing through them, as the tribes will naturally redouble their attempts to pass when they are disturbed in the interior.

GEORGE ARTHUR.

* GOVERNMENT ORDER, NO. 13.

Colonial Secretary's Office, November 26, 1830.

1.—The first series of operations for the capture of the native tribes, having been now brought to a close, by the military and civil parties to East Bay Neck, and as the length of time during which those composing the volunteer force have absented themselves from their homes, renders the Government unwilling to wish them to extend their period of service at this conjuncture, when to remain any longer in the field would prove so detrimental to their private interests, they will now disperse, and the assigned servants of settlers who have not been able to be present themselves, will be marched back to their respective districts, under the charge of constables ap-

cial notification has ever been made in the Colony) cost upwards of £35,000. It may be as well to offer one or two remarks concerning this black expedition. In the first place, some of the forests and underwood, which

pointed for that purpose, with the exception of a small body, whom the Lieutenant Governor has judged it expedient to detain, for the protection of the settlements, and the further pursuit of the natives.

2.—The Lieutenant Governor cannot allow the forces to separate without observing, that although the expedition has not been attended with the full success which was anticipated, but which could not be commanded, yet many benefits have resulted from it, amongst which may be enumerated, the cordial and unanimous feeling which has distinguished every class of the community, in striving for the general good.

The knowledge which has been acquired of the habits of the natives, and which will so much tend to insure success in future operations; the opening of communications throughout the country, which was before their secure retreat, but which can no longer afford them the same security or confidence, and above all, the proof which has been given of the great personal sacrifice which the whole population were not only willing, but most anxious to make, for the purpose of capturing the savages, in order, by their being placed in some situation where they could no longer inflict or receive injury, that the race might be preserved from utter extermination; an event fearfully to be apprehended, so long as they continue to commit such wanton outrages upon the white inhabitants, and which every man of humanity and proper feeling would endeavour to avert.

3.—In touching upon the merits of the individuals composing the force, the Lieutenant Governor feels it difficult to attach to them the meed of praise which they have deserved, and when all have shewn so much alacrity, zeal, patience, and determination to overcome every difficulty, it were invidious to extol any in particular, although it is quite impossible to avoid noticing the extrordinary exertions which have been so cheerfully afforded by the Surveyor General, and every officer of his department. The conduct collectively of the whole community on this occasion, will be a lasting source of pleasure in the mind of the Lieutenant Governor, but His Excellency will not fail to bear in remembrance the separate merits of each in the proportion which his exertions have proved him to possess. In making this allusion to the conduct of the civil forces, he has the satisfaction at the same time to observe, that the orderly and soldier-like behaviour of the military, and the zeal and ability which their officers have displayed, in organizing and commanding the civil levies, merit the highest encomiums. The difficulties which the forces have had to surmount in such an impervious country, as that which has lately been the scene of their efforts, can only be

frequently impeded the march of the line, were almost impenetrable to the aborigines, who are accustomed to scramble through the scrubs on their hands and knees, like wild animals : but as to those in pursuit scouring the

---

understood by those who have seen it, and nothing but the excellent spirit of the parties, could have enabled them to overcome so many obstacles.

4.—The project of surrounding and driving the two worst tribes to a particular quarter, had succeeded to the furthest extent; and but for their untimely dispersion by a party who too hastily attacked them before a sufficient force could arrive to capture them, the whole measure would probably have been crowned with success.

5.—The Lieutenant Governor has, however, the satisfaction of announcing on this occasion, that a body of natives have been captured without blood-shed, on the northern coast, where there exists every prospect of the remainder of that tribe being secured. [A]

The recent treacherous conduct of a party of natives who had been received and treated with every species of kindness, but who endeavoured to repay their benefactors by murder and rapine, sufficiently demonstrates, that it would be in vain to expect any reformation in these savages, while allowed to continue in their native habits. It will, therefore, become an immediate subject of anxious consideration with the Government, whether it is not proper to place those who are now secured, and who amount to about thirty, together with any others who may be captured, upon an island from whence they cannot escape, but where they will be gradually induced to adopt the habits and feelings of civilized life.

6.—The circumstance of the late military movements not having been attended with the expected success, will not, it is hoped, cast any despondency upon the public mind, for the activity and cordiality which have been recently shewn by the community, afford sufficient earnest that the evil which has afflicted the Colony, must in the course of the summer be removed. The most active measures will be continued, for vigorously pursuing the object in view ; but as the Lieutenant Governor feels a strong persuasion that there are white men amongst the natives, His Excellency does not consider it prudent to detail any future operations in public notices.

By His Excellency's command,

J. BURNETT.

[A] The capture alluded to, had nothing whatever to do with the military movements.   Mr. Batman hearing the natives had attacked his farm, distant some hundred miles in the rear of the line, immediately returned, and fell in with a mob of natives, some of whom had escaped from him before ; he re-took them, along with several others, without bloodshed.—COMPILER.

country properly, the thing was impossible.* Had there
been 50,000 natives encircled in the space the line gradually enclosed, every one might have escaped, and
would have escaped to a certainty; and as a simile has
been given, by comparing the proceedings to a net, it
may be added, the meshes of the net were so large, that
whole shoals of fish could swim through, without any
obstruction.   The enthusiasm which the sound of arms
had kindled was not to be allowed to pass without advantage being taken; and if the Lieutenant Governor
did not perform the part of an able general, he shewed
the tact of an experienced soldier, in obtaining from all
parts of the Colony congratulatory addresses.   The Colonists, in the ebullition of their feeling, thanked His
Excellency for his personal exertions, and for expending
the public money which had been hoarded up uselessly
in the Treasury; indeed, as the expedition ended so un-
favorably, there was nothing else for which the Colonists
could thank their leader.   His Excellency's friends were
most assiduous in their exertions, and on reading over
the various addresses presented, it would really appear
that the whole body of Colonists had turned crazy in
consequence of the complete failure of this grand undertaking.

It may now be as well to trace the ultimate end of
the war between the aborigines and the Colonists.   For
some little time after the grand movement, scarcely a
native was seen or heard.   The great military operations
had, no doubt, the effect of frightening them: they
could not understand the meaning of such warlike movements on the part of men they had been accustomed to
make war against when acting only in small numbers.
This peace did not last long, and the following winter

---

* In order to shew in what manner some of the lenders of parties
scoured the woods, it may be as well to observe, that Captain E.
Dumaresq, instead of closing on the proposed line, advanced his
two hundred men on the main road from Brighton to Pittwater.
Other detachments frequently advanced in single files, leaving the
impenetrable wood for miles and miles unexamined.

depredations were as commonly heard of, as before the black war. The martial law, however, had reduced the number of the natives so very considerably, that it became evident, that most of the acts of aggression were committed by the same tribes. It was almost immediately after the black war, that Messrs. G. A. Robinson, Bateman, and Cotterell, commenced their praiseworthy and christian-like endeavours to bring in the whole of the aborigines; these persons were employed by the Government, with trifling salaries, and assistance given them, in rations, for their men and themselves. Their exertions have been crowned with success; and so that the evil has been removed, it may appear of little consequence in what way it may have been effected. It is but justice to these individuals, that a few words should' be offered, respecting the manner in which they effected their grand object. They proceeded, not with the sword, but with the olive branch. Their small companies, composed of four or five Europeans, with eight or ten of the aborigines, proceeded into the interior, and when the traces of the natives were fallen in with, they were followed, and when overtaken, the domesticated aborigines of the party explained to their wild brethren, that their embassy was for peace. The aborigines would then advance towards the party of Europeans, when persuasion on the part of the several leaders, aided by the gift of some trifling baubles, invariably induced them to join them, and proceed to Hobart Town, from whence they were drafted to Flinders Island. It may appear extraordinary that so few natives were captured, the whole number only amounting to about three hundred and ten men, women, and children; but no doubt the treatment these creatures had received, and the certainty of almost immediate death before their eyes, had rendered the remnants of the tribes most desperate. At the present writing, the aborigines are never heard of—indeed, Mr. Robinson has asserted, that there are less than a score now at large in the Colony. Perhaps this may be incorrect, as the intelligence

Q

which he received must be from the aborigines he
had captured, who, being probably at war with the
others, may have been ignorant of the number of
their enemies.   At Flinders Island there are now about
eightv aborigines.   These wild creatures live a life of
indolence, occasionally hunting the kangaroo, or passing
their time in their aboriginal custom.   It is generally
believed, that this race of human beings will soon become
extinct altogether, as the deaths are common, and the
increase nothing equal in proportion.   Little is known
as to the manner in which they are governed, and the
Colonists are not at all informed of the proceedings of
the Government towards them.   The labors of Messrs.
Robinson and Cotterell have been rewarded by various
donations on the part of the Government, by subscrip-
tions on the part of some of the districts, and by very
flattering addresses of nearly the whole body of Colonists   Their exertions. however, have made all lament,
that kindness and good treatment were not sooner made
the means of ridding the Colony of the sable owners
of the soil, and that the European musket and the
bayonet were the instruments that caused retaliation.
The whole affair is now ended, and thousands of lives
have been lost by hostile measures.   It is, nevertheless
very easy now to point out what plans *ought* to have been
adopted ; but it should be recollected, that when martial
law was proclaimed, the Colonists were suffering from
the " *Guerilla*" war ; and although the aborigines may in
most skirmishes have been worsted, still their depredations
were harrassing to the settlers, who considered themselves masters, of the Colony, and protected themselves
accordingly.   Nothing can be offered in extenuation of
the conduct of the first Colonists towards these bewildered creatures, and the historian must ever lament,
that he has to record outrages so inhuman and so unjust
on the part of a British community.

The year closed with public meetings all over the
Colony, the most remarkable of which was, the grand
one held at the Court House of Hobart Town, the pur-

port of which was, like all the others, to thank His Excellency the Lieutenant Governor for his personal and unwearied exertions during the war. On this occasion nearly all the influential Government Officers were present, and these, with some few leading townspeople, over whom they had influence, (after some trifling opposition) agreed to an address, the presenting of which the Colonists have repented ever since. One country gentleman* on this occasion, boldly opposed the voting of the address, he said that the whole proceedings of the line had been absurd, and that all had ended as any child might have anticipated—in a total failure. He ridiculed the idea of thanking Colonel Arthur for his personal exertions, he said there was such a thing as being "*actively mischievous,*" and that a " man might go to the top of Mount Wellington, with a harpoon in his hand to kill a whale, and his exertions in so attempting such an absurdity might be tremendous." Another country gentleman† moved, that the address should be named " the Address of the Traders and Professional Gentlemen of Hobart Town,"—but all opposition to the " cut and dried" resolutions and address was unavailable, and every thing was carried by a large majority, as the movers anticipated.

The commencement of the year 1831 resembled a calm after a storm—every thing was quiet and monotonously dull, the country settlers had retired to their farms, and the townspeople to their business—and within a few months the black war was only recollected as a subject for ridicule; the effect neither being felt by the Colonists, nor causing any diminution of the outrages on the part of the aborigines.‡

---

* T. G. Gregson, Esq.   † W. Kermode, Esq.

‡ The following particulars of a coroner's inquest, may give the reader an insight into the nature of the war botween the settlers and the aborigines—Captain Thomas was brother to Colonel Thomas, Member of Parliament for Kinsale, and came out to this Colony as agent for the Van Diemen's Land establishment. " The bodies of Captain Thomas and Mr. Parker were brought up to Laun-

The spirit of improvement was most conspicuous—roads were made in the interior, and the buildings in the townships were erected in great numbers, and in a style far superior to those of former years.   The grand

---

ceston from George Town on Wednesday last, having been found by means of a partly civilized aboriginal woman, who persuaded a woman of the tribe, who was taken prisoner by Captain Thomas's servants, to conduct them to the spot where they had killed them, two days previously.   The next morning, the bodies were removed from the boat to the Commercial Tavern, and a Coroner's, Inquest was instantly convened by Mr. Lyttleton, at the Police Office.   The Jury, having been sworn, proceeded to view the bodies, and upon their return took the following evidence :—

George Warren, sworn.—Started from George Town on Sunday last, by order of Mr. Clark, in search of Captain Thomas and Mr. Parker ; got to Port Sorell on Monday morning, the 12th instant, when I saw Dr. Smith and Ensign Dunbar ; two women offered to take us (that is, Alexander M'Kay and me) to the bodies they took us into the bush about two miles, when they stopped and cried, and would not go any farther, but pointed to the place where the bodies were to be found ; we went, and found the body of Mr. Parker on his back, the head towards the root of a tree ; he had on no hat, neckerchief, coat, or waistcoat ; saw blood under the head ; saw ten spear wounds in his body ; I found a spear at about ten yards distant from the body ; we then asked the women to shew us where the other body was ; on my way, I found the tail of a coat ; found Captain Thomas's body about one hundred yards off, among some long grass ; saw some wounds about the body, and a black stake under the head ; there were twelve wounds by spears, three in the right thigh, two or three in the right side, one in the back, &c. ; the head was not bruised so much as Mr. Parker's, but a quantity of blood was under him ; from the appearance of the bodies, thought they had been dead a fortnight ; part of the neck of Captain Thomas was destroyed by vermin ; some notes were lying about him ; (one produced ;) we left the bodies, and returned with the women to Dr. Smith, at Port Sorell ; on the way, the women appeared sulky : Dr. Smith then accompanied us to the bodies, together with several others ; this time, the women thought the soldiers had come to kill them ; one of the women said, (through the other who interpreted,) that Captain Thomas and Mr. Parker came to one of their tribes—that one of the black men took a gin, which the stout man, meaning Mr. Parker, had under his arm, and ran away with it—that one of her tribe speared Mr. Parker in the back—that Captain Thomas then ran away, but was overtaken and knocked down ; the bobies were removed to George Town ; the women told us ' Tum assisted in spearing them ; Tum is now in jail at George Town.

undertakings of Bridgewater and the New Wharf, occupied considerable attention on the part of the Government and the Colonists, and their completion was anticipated by all parties to be of vast importance. The

This woman exactly described the position the bodies lay in before reaching the place. (Here the skirt of a coat was produced, and certified as being part of that worn by Captain Thomas.)

Thomas Carter, sworn.—Assigned servant to Captain Thomas; I was at Port Sorell on the 31st ult.; I was at Port Sorell with Captain Thomas and Mr. Parker; I was in charge of the boat with three others of the crew; before Captain Thomas came down, two natives came into our tent: we were eating some damper; they called out for ' breadly ;' we told them to come in; they did come in; we gave them some damper and some cheese; at this period, or within a quarter of an hour, Captain Thomas and Mr. Parker arrived on horseback, and then Captain Thomas said, " have you seen the natives ?" I replied, " I have two in the tent ;" he then got off his horse; he asked the blacks if there were any more: when they held up all their fingers, and said, " good many more ?" Captain Thomas asked them to take him to them; which they readily agreed to do; Mr. Parker, however, fearful of trusting Captain Thomas amongst the natives by himself, walked behind at some little distance, with a double-barrelled gun under his arm; this is all I saw of Captain Thomas or Mr. Parker; about two hours after, the two native men who went with the Captain, returned with three others, besides two women and a man; M'Kay shook hands with them; in a few minutes we saw another woman, who we enticed to us, and gave her some bread; before we left (which was about two hours) we cooed, but were not answered; after having started, taking with us the horses belonging to Captain Thomas and Mr. Parker, about three hundred yards homewards, another native came up, whom we enticed, but he ran away before we reached Northtown Beach, where Captain Thomas resided; we then asked what had become of the white men ? they said " they had ' tabbity,' " meaning run away; we did not ask them before we started; the next morning Mrs. Parker sent out four men in search of Captain Thomas and Mr. Parker; after being absent two days and one night, they returned, but without success.

Dr. Smith sworn.—On the return to George Town of Chief Constable Freestone and Mr. Haims, (who had been in search of the bodies of Captain Thomas and Mr. Parker), on Thursday last, I was requested to see Mrs. Parker, who was very ill; I left George Town on Friday last, with Ensign Dunbar, and arrived at Port Sorell about 2 o'clock, where we found Mr. J. Thomas, Junr., and Captain Moriarty, on the beach, who had not found the bodies, but were waiting for a man (M'Kay) and a partly civilized native

foundation stone of the Orphan School at New Town
was laid during this year, and at the period of the compilation of these pages, this building is one of the most
magnificent of the kind to be found in any Colony in

woman; next morning they arrived, when we proceeded to Port
Sorell in search of the bodies, but did not succeed in finding them;
we then returned to Northtown Beach, with the exception of M'Kay
and the native woman, who were sent on to George Town, for one
of the native women, who had been taken there. He returned
with the two women, and upon his firing a gun, we sent a boat
over for them; M'Kay said one of the women had told them where
the bodies were to be found; and then went with Warren and the
two native women by my order; they returned in about an hour,
and said they had seen the bodies; I then proceeded with them and
a man of the name of Jones, to look at the bodies, about a mile up
from the Creek, in the direction of the Northtown Beach, but to
the left of the road; this was about four miles from Northtown
Beach; the women conducted me straight to a body, which I recognized to be that of Mr. Parker; I called one of the constables to
remove the dress, so as to enable me to examine the body; I found
on the breast five or six spear wounds, on the left side, near the
heart; every wound would have caused death; I found six wounds
on the back, and an extensive contusion on the side of the head;
we then proceeded with the women eastward about about fifty or
sixty yards, and found another body lying dead, which I recognized
to be that of Captain Thomas; upon removing his dress, I found
one wound very near the heart, and three others on the right side,
one of which had bled profusely; one wound by the clavicle; I
then had the body turned, and found five spear wounds on the back;
the upper part of the throat was eaten by crows or native cats; on
the following morning the bodies were conveyed by my orders to
George Town.

Thomas Carter, sworn.—Should know the two natives again that
took Captain Thomas and Mr. Parker away: two of these (pointing
to two of the three in custody) are them.

Thomas M'Kay, sworn.—I am attached to Mr. Robinson's party;
I left Port Sorell on Saturday week, by order of Captain Moriarty
and Mr. J. Thomas, jun.; on the following day I went to the jail
at George Town, where I saw the natives who were in custody; I
was informed by the women that the white men were killed; they
told me they were lying near the water; one of the bodies was lying
under a tree, the other in an open place; this was told me by 'Black Sal;'
I left George Town on Sunday, the 11th instant. accompanied by
Constable Warren, ' Black Sal,' and one of the native women from
the jail, and got to Port Sorell next morning; we then went into
the bush and found the bodies about two miles off, when we got

the world.   Several churches were also commenced in
the interior, and various other tokens of rapid improvement were evident.   The first stage coach that ever ran
on Van Diemen's Land roads, was established between

---

within about one hundred yards from the bodies, the woman (whose
name I 'do not know) stopped and pointed to where they were ; I
found the body of one man partly on his back, with his arm stretched
out; I went about one hundred yards further, and saw part of a
coat; a little farther, pointed out by a native woman, I found
another body on its back ; I did not examine it, but found a spear
not far distant from it ; I afterwards found another spear and a waddy
near the body, which I was told was that of Captain Thomas ; I
then returned to Port Sorell, told Dr. Smith, and returned with
him and others to examine the bodies.   On the road in search of the
bodies, the native woman before-mentioned described the situation
in which the bodies lay ; she told me that two of the natives came
down to the boat ; that the two men that were killed went into the
bush with the two natives ; that when they got into the bush, that
one man had a gun that would shoot twice (meaning a double-barrelled gun), that one of the native women (Wowee) seized the gun
by the lock, and twisted him round at the same time, and another
man hit him with a waddie on the head, and he fell down, that the
other, the smallest white man, ran away, when some of the natives
pursued and speared him, while others killed the one who was
knocked down, that the woman attempted to stop them from killing
him, but could not, and in consequence three women left the tribe,
and went to the cart with four of the men, natives, who had assisted
in the murder by throwing spears, &c., and that the man who first
struck the white man had run away, making an appointment with
the other natives, where to meet, should they have the opportunity
of escaping, but they were secured and sent to George Town in a
boat.   The names of the men who accompanied Captain Thomas
and Mr. Parker from the boat, were Wowee and Mackamee; he
(M'Kay) had seen them this morning.   The same woman also informed me that the gun had since been thrown into the water.
     Thomas M'Kay was then sworn for interpretation of the native
woman named " Mongareepitta," from whom he had obtained the
information contained in his evidence, and who discovered to him
the situation of the bodies ; but she had passed the preceding night
in company wtth the three men who were brought up from George
Town, and it appeared evident that a plan was laid to get them off
by contradicting her former evidence ; upon a repetition of the questions, she either confirmed her first statement to M'Kay, or gave a
third, but more frequently the former.   She was present (she said)
when the white men were killed—one of the white men had a gun
under his arm THere she identified the two men who accompanied

Hobart Town and New Norfolk, and another journal, "The Independent," made its appearance at Launceston.

the two white men into the bush.] Her tribe consisted of seven men and six women : Wowee and Mackamee were present when the first white man was killed, and the other ran away ; the waddies and spears were produced; but she would not allow that any of the men present had anything to do with the murder, but that they were sitting down.

This concluded the evidence, and after a short consultation, the Jury returned the following verdict—"'We find that Bartholomew Boyle Thomas, and James Parker, have been treacherously murdered by the three native men, now in custody, called ' Wowee,' ' Mackamee,' and ' Calamaroweyne,' aided and assisted by the re sidue of the tribe of Aborigines to which they belong, known by the name of the ' Big River Tribe.'—*Independent, Sept.*

It would appear that these aborigines were of the " Big River Tribe," of which there were six chiefs sent to Flinder's Island, two of the number are since dead. It may not be irrelevant to occupy a few lines in recording the names of some of the chief leaders, sent by the Government to the settlement at the Island, for, as in all probability, the race will become extinct in a few years, not only will these original possessors of the soil be no more, but their very names will be forgotten. The following is a list of the male aborigines at Flinder's Island :—Worethetitatilargener, Moulteerlargener, and Marenerlargener, the two former were chiefs of the Ben Lomond tribe. Teelapanner, Walenteerlooner, Panacooner, Wowee, Mackamee, and Calamaroweyne, (the last three were the murderers of Captain Thomas and Mr. Parker), belong to the Eastern tribe. Paroper, Nicermenic, Tymethic, Prerope, Pyntharyne, Peey, Toinchouc, Boobyluthic, Toindeburic, and Rowlapanner, are of the Western tribe, Toby Langta, Lamaima, Conapanny, and Packabanny, belong to the Oyster Bay tribe. Wymeric, a chief, and the only native of Cape Grim. The following have died since their transportation to the settlement :—Nickerumbaragener, Walmteerlooner, Prerope, (burnt), Cowndetabone, Timeateen, her husband and brother, Wymeric (burnt) and seven more of the Western tribe were burnt shortly afterwards; they were at the settlement but a short time. Three of Wild Mary's husbands, Kammy, who was formerly at Mr. Robinson's, at Hobart Town, the husband of the same woman, three orphan children, Wottycowyder's infant, Tobylangto's infant, three of Lamothic's brothers, Kitawa's mother, her brother, his wife and child, died in the space of twelve or fourteen days. The entire number of the aborigines removed to Flinder's Island, is 310—250 of which number were captured by Mr. Robinson. Some people say, the number on Flinder's Island now exceeds 100 ; their removal to King's Island is talked of, as they are much dissatisfied with Flinder's.—*Correspondent.*

A new charter for the administration of justice arrived, superceding the one of 1824; it contained a provision for the appointment of a puisne judge, naming also the individual. This gentleman was Mr. Baxter, the Attorney General of New South Wales. This nomination not being agreeable to the chief authorities, an act of the legislature * made short work of the affair, and altered the entire meaning and intention of the new charter, doing away altogether with the appointment from home, of the second judge, and continuing the administration of the Supreme Court, in the same manner as before, solely in the hands of the Chief Justice. This violation of the charter, excited a degree of surprise among the Colonists, who plainly saw that if such a charter could be so altered—its intention so defeated, and its purport rendered nugatory—that the charter itself was useless; and that the superior power—the Legislative Council of Van Diemen's Land had better frame a new charter, according to the *expediency* of the times. Subsequent events have shewn that the power vested in the legislature *is* supreme—that it is under no control whatever. Acts of Parliament have been unheeded —and a body of men chosen from among the friends and relatives of the Chief Authority, have passed enactments repugnant to British law—to colonial interests, and altogether rendering the Colony anything but British. The reader will be reminded of the extraordinary power' usurped by the Council in a few subsequent pages.

On the 23rd of May this year, a very large public meeting was held in Hobart Town, for the purpose of preparing an address to the Throne and both Houses of Parliament, praying for a change of measures. It is but justice however, here to remark, that the grievances complained of on this occasion, did not arise altogether from the administration of the Government by the local authorities, nearly the whole of the grievances originating in the orders received from the Secretary of State

---

* The only Act of Council passed in 1831.

R

for the Colonies. This meeting has been characterised as the " Glorious twenty-third of May," and the manner in which it was attended, and the talent displayed by the whole of the numerous speakers, could not be imagined by any individual, unless present on the occasion. The grievances complained of were several.* One of the most staunch of the leaders on this occasion, was an old " *Colonist*" connected with the Press. He stood forward nobly and boldly, but his abandoning the cause, nay, his turning into ridicule the whole proceedings of the meeting, is to be regretted, inasmuch as it un-

---

* 1.—Unnecessary and vexatious delays in issuing grants of land by the Crown.

2.—Complaints of the heavy quit-rent that is imposed by the Crown upon all granted lands.

3.—Severe strictures upon the general mode of conducting business in the Survey Department.

4.—A condemnation of a local Act of Council, by which the usury laws of England are excluded from operation here.

5.—An expression of the hardships the Colonists endure, in having no control whatever over the expenditure of the money that is raised from them by taxation.

6.—A sweeping censure upon the present Legislative Council, arising chiefly from the form in which that body is nominated.

7.—A complaint of the manner in which the Magistracy of the Colony is selected.

8.—The resolution upon this subject shall speak for itself. " That the free population of this Island consists of upwards of 13,000 persons, and increases annually at a rapid ratio. That this Colony and New South Wales form a striking contrast with every other Colony in His Majesty's dominions; being purely British and governed by British laws, but without a representation of the people. That from the extreme distance from the Mother Country, the interest and prosperity of the Colony require a British Constitution—a Legislation of its own, composed of Representatives, to be elected by the Colonists themselves."

9.—Was upon a subject, by no means peculiar to this Colony ; although perhaps the grievance has been carried at times, farther here, than elsewhere. It related to delays that had occasionally taken place in the administration of the law.

10.—Drew comparisons between the rate of duties on imported articles here and at New South Wales, shewing the great difference there exists against this Colony.

11.—Was a reference to the aboriginal question.

doubtedly assisted in keeping the Colonists from the enjoyment of those liberties which they had a right to expect —the extraordinary conduct of this individual, is indeed a matter of regret. The result of this meeting was somewhat singular—after unwearied exertions on the part of many, the address was most numerously signed and forwarded by an agent to His Majesty. On board the very vessel this agent took his passage, were several friends of His Excellency the Lieutenant Governor. Whether the address was ever presented—whether it was not thrown overboard during the passage, is a matter of doubt; but most certainly the prayer of the Colonists (even did the address ultimately reach the throne) has never been attended to; and to this day no notice whatever has been taken of the prayer of the whole body of Colonists.

The population of the Colony was fast increasing— at this period there were about 27,000 souls on the island, including prisoners. The commercial affairs were yet prosperous. True, the exportation of sheep and meat, ceased towards the end of the year, but yet there were large shipments made of wheat to New South Wales. The exports during 1831, approached closely in value to £200,000, and the Colonial Treasurer had a considerable balance in hand, (£20,000) from the year 1830, over and above the current expense of the Colonial establishments.

In a great measure owing to the accounts forwarded to the Home Government of the prosperity of the Colony, coupled with the very large surplus of idle money lying in the Colonial Treasury, the Home Government was induced to change the system of emigration; and here it will be necessary to request the attention of the reader to a subject of the most vital importance to the Colony —*the land question !*

In former years, when the island of Van Diemen's Land was scarcely known to those of the Mother Country, save as being a place to which convicts were transported, this penal settlement was but a " jail on a

large scale." Time, however, and the perseverance of
the prisoners, soon convinced the Home Government
that the Colony *might* be rendered an advantageous appendage to the British nation. Some few years after,
the great war of Europe was over, and the attention of
the Home Rulers could be more particularly drawn to
the capabilities of this distant settlement, it was considered advisable that the Colony should be thrown open
to free emigrants. The distance of the Colony, and the
name of Botany Bay, were for a time sufficient to deter
or frighten most individuals who were then migrating
to distant shores. It therefore became absolutely necessary that some considerable stimulus should be held
out, by which the desired end might be attained. No
doubt it was with these intentions, grants of land, differing in extent according to the rank of life of the emigrant,
were *given* on arrival. The rank in life was intended to
be calculated according to the capital such emigrant might
carry with him to the new settlement. In addition to
the *giving* away of land to such emigrant, a further
bonus was held out—he was promised *white slaves* to
improve and cultivate such land—these slaves were of
course the convicts. For several years, yet further
stimulus to emigration was offered; the settler was told
that, in addition to land given to him for nothing—in
addition to slaves to work that land, he should be supplied with food for himself and his family, and for his
prisoner servants also, till such time as the land might
enable him to be independent of other aid. Nor was
this all, the emigrant was still further told, that but a
trifling quit-rent should be imposed—a mere nominal
sum should be claimed by the Crown as rent, and further, that every settler who relieved the Government by
the employment and maintenance of convicts, should
have his quit-rent redeemed by such means. Under
these circumstances, many, many were induced to leave
their mother land, to migrate to these distant shores.
Even so late as the year 1826, the official documents
obtainable at the Colonial Secretary's office, in Downing-

street, held out prospects almost as favourable to the
emigrant*—what a change has taken place in ten years?
—but to proceed. By degrees, the regulations under
which the original settlers migrated to the Colony, were

---

* For the information of persons proceeding to New South Wales
and Van Diemen's Land, as Settlers, it has been deemed expedient
to prepare the following summary of the rules which His Majesty's
Government have thought fit to lay down, for regulating the grants
of land in those Colonies :—

1.—The division of the whole territory into counties, hundreds,
and parishes is in progress—when that division shall be completed,
each parish will comprise an area of about 25 miles. A valuation
will be made of the lands throughout the Colony, and an average
price will be struck for each parish.

2.—All lands in the Colony not hitherto granted, and not appropriated for public purposes, will be put up to sale at the average
price thus fixed.

3.—All persons proposing to purchase lands, must transmit a
written application to the Governor, in a certain prescribed form,
which will be delivered at the Surveyor General's Office, to all
parties applying, on payment of a fee of two shillings and sixpence.

4.—All correspondence with the Local Government, respecting
grants of land, must take place through the same office.

5—The purchase money is to be paid by four quarterly instal-
ments. A discount of 10 per cent. will be allowed for ready money
payments.

6.—On payment of the money, a grant will be made in fee simple
to the purchaser, at the nominal quit-rent of a peppercorn.

7.—The largest quantity of land which will be sold to any individual, is 9,600 acres. The lands will generally be put up to sale
in lots of 3 miles square, or 1920 acres. Persons wishing to make
more extensive purchases, must apply to the Secretary of State in
writing, with full explanations of their object and means.

8.—Any purchaser who, within ten years after his purchase,
shall, by the employment and maintenance of convicts, have relieved the public from a charge equal to ten times the amount of
the purchase money, will have the purchase money returned, but
without interst. It will be computed that for each convict employed, and wholly maintained by the purchaser for twelve months,
£16 have been saved to the public.

9.—Lands may also be obtained without immediate purchase, but
upon different conditions.

10.—Person desirous to become grantees without immediate purchase, will make their application to the Governor in writing, in a
prescribed form, copies of which are to be obtained at the Surveyor
General's Office, on payment of two shillings and sixpence.

privately altered. At first, the difficulty of obtaining
servants in proportion to the number of acres *given* to
the emigrant, was impossible; either the calculation
had been made without reference to the number of convicts in the Colony, or else too large a proportion of
land was offered to the free settler—but this is of trifling consideration. When, however, the tide of emigration, if it may be so called, was flowing on these
shores, the Home Government by degrees withdrew the
stimulus—at first, the rations for families on their first
landing, were reduced from six, to two months, and then
again, totally withdrawn. Regulations after regulations were published—the encouragement was no longer
offered, and, as if to destroy emigration altogether, the
Home Government, in 1830, positively ordered that no
more land should be given to the emigrant, but that
every acre should be sold. His Excellency the Lieutenant Governor naturally remonstrated against such a
decisive measure; which, on the one hand, had the effect
of almost destroying the possibility of future emigration;
whilst, at the same time, it was a death-blow to the

11.—The largest grant that will be made to any fresh settler
without purchase, is 2,560 acres, the smallest 320 acres.

12.—No grant is to be made to any person without immediate
purchase, unless the Governor is satisfied that the granted has the
power of expending in the cultivation of the lands, a capital equal
to half their estimated value.

13.—A quit-rent of 5 per cent. per annum, upon the value of
each grant of land, as estimated in the survey, will be levied on all
such grants; but such quit-rent will not commence to be levied,
until the expiration of the first seven years next succeeding the issue
of such grant; at the expiration of the above-mentioned seven years,
the grantee will become possessed in fee-simple of the grant, subject
to the payment of the quit-rent; or he will be entitled to redeem
such quit-rent, if he prefer that alternative.

14.—In the redemption of his quit-rent, the guarantee will have
credit for one fifth part of the sums which he may have saved to His
Majesty's Government, by the employment and maintenance of
convicts, and for the purpose of making this allowance, it will be
calculated that the Government has saved £16 for each convict employed by the grantee, and wholly maintained at his expense on his
land, for one whole year.

patronage, which would rendered the Chief authority more
despotic, (if he so willed it), than any turbaned sultan
in the universe.

It is now the intention of the author to discuss the
land question generally—to show how land has been
located and resumed, and to throw a light upon some
portion of the jobbing carried on, and then to offer a
few necessary remarks as to the propriety of making the
quit-rents the means of raising the Colonial revenue.

There can be no doubt but that the plan, according
to which land has hitherto been located, has been exceedingly unfair and injurious, and under such a system,
it cannot be wondered that the most extraordinary instances have occurred of oppression and injustice. When
land was first *given* to the free emigrant, it has already
been observed, very considerable stimulus was held out,
rations and workmen being allowed to the new settler,
in proportion to the number of his family, and the quantity of acres given to him. But even in these times,
when land was not of much value, the grossest jobbing
prevailed—and so has it continued ever since, only
varying according to new promulgated regulations. In
former times, the free settler, on landing, called upon
the Surveyor General, and a map was immediately laid
before him—but that was all!—for as to any further information being afforded, *that* depended upon other circumstances. If the new comer had no friend to show
him how to proceed, he would immediately go in search
of land in the interior—he would then return to the
Survey-office, with the knowledge of perhaps a dozen
spots suitable to his fancy; the first he would be told
had already been taken—the second was a township reserve—the third a private reserve, and so on; in fact,
the whole number of selected places, he would find either
reserved or located, although no mark whatever, to that
effect, might appear on the charts. After much waste of
time, and very considerable expense and inconvenience, the
new settler would by chance fix upon some distant spot,
which being so remote, was totally valueless in the esti-

mation of the Surveyor General, and this land the settler was ultimately allowed to possess. If, however, a settler arrived who had a friend to counsel him the business was soon settled, and a hogshead of wine, a piano-forte, or a harp, or such like present, would point out on the chart in the Survey-office, the most desirable land in the Colony. In former times, the free emigrants brought with them orders to locate land, but in later years this was not necessary, for a Land Board was appointed to fix the rate of quit-rents, and to examine the amount of capital the fresh settlers might bring with them ; and the Local Government had the authority to *give* away the land in proportion to the capital introduced. Here also fraud was most common ; the capitalist entitled to a large grant, would often find an almost beggar that came out with him in the same ship, receive a like quantity adjoining him. It was a common practice for individuals to borrow sums of money, and to shew the bank receipts to the commissioners—and when the location order was issued, the money, of course, was returned to the lender. The favouritism too, practised, will scarcely be believed by any individuals not fully aware of the true circumstances of the Colony—some friends of those in power would have large grants given them, besides suburban, and township allotments in numbers, in every township in the Colony, if they so pleased to have them ! Government officers, without bringing with them one farthing of capital, have had the most extensive *gifts* of land ; whilst the industrious capitalist, the real settler, has had his time and money frittered away with the difficulties and negligence he has had to combat with at the Survey-office. The land patronage, too, has been so disgracefully made use of, that Government officers and friends of those in authority or favor, have had large additional grants for " *improvements made*," when the applicants for such additions have not even seen the land first given to them, nor cultivated an inch thereof, or expended thereon one farthing. Whilst land of the finest description and the most valuable, has been squan-

dered on men holding Government situations, who were
necessarily prevented from residing thereon, or improving the same, every obstacle has been thrown in
the way of the capitalist, who unfortunately has had no
friend at the Colonial Court. Bandied about from one
office to another, if a fortunate settler obtained the
number of acres his property entitled him to, he would at
length proceed in search of land, and after the shuffling
of the Survey Department, and much labour and expense,
would have the spot marked out on the chart as his
own. But when this was done, the reader will imagine
his troubles were ended, and that he might consider the
soil he selected, as his own property ; but this was not
the case ;—the settler would occupy the land—would
cultivate it, and expend every halfpenny he was worth
thereupon, trusting his children would reap the benefit
thereof ; year after year would pass by ; no entreaty of
his could obtain the measurement of the land by the
Government surveyors ;* the settler continued to cultivate, and when one of the department did condescend to
come and point out his boundaries—the settler would
then find himself a ruined man—he would then find he
had for years, unknowingly, been cultivating land, the
property of another man ; this, reader, is not a solitary
case, but numerous such, unfortunately, could be adduced.

The manner, too, in which the authorities have occasionally *resumed* land, is much to be regretted ; but in
history, the truth ought to be told, and if men have
acted wrong, it is, nevertheless, the historians duty to
record the fact, and not to slur over unpleasant truths,
because men who have so acted, yet hold the highest
official situations. With regard to the resumptions of

---

* One particular instance occurs to the writer. A farmer arrived
with his wife and family, in 1822, he had 500 acres of land located
to him, somewhere near Richmond. His endeavours to persuade
the Government surveyors to measure it, were futile—last year, 1834,
he sold the land to one of the district surveyors, and within one
month of the time, the purchaser measured his own land.

S

land, they are numerous, but not one single instance can be named, where a Government officer ever had an inch of land taken from him, although it is notorious that any Government officer, of any standing, has had one or more grants *given* him, and which (with but very few exceptions) have been sold, contrary to the Colonial regulations, as also contrary to the orders of the Home Government. If, however, no land has been resumed belonging to Government officers, there are unfortunately many instances where the resumption of the land of settlers, has been attended with the most melancholy consequences. The writer will draw the attention of the reader to *one* case only; as it is the one more generally known than any other in the Colony! and this must suffice, as the confined nature of the work will not allow further examples to be given.*   A merchant of the name

---

* The resumption of the land belonging to Captains Wight and Kerr are rather extraordinary instances :—

CAPTAIN BORTHWICK WIGHT, about the year 1828, applied for a grant of land, when His Excellency Colonel Arthur permitted him to locate 2560 acres, after having proved that he brought sufficient capital into the Colony to claim a grant to that extent. The grant was measured to him a year or so afterwards. He placed upon it a regular farming establishment under the charge of a free overseer, and employed a gentleman, whose estate adjoined his own, as agent, to see that every thing was properly attended to. Captain Wight went to very considerable expense in fencing—he had part of the land in cultivation, and purchased, among other stock, 2,000 sheep, for which he gave 20s. each. During one of Capt. Wight's trips to England, the Government resumed the land, and granted it to Mr. Henry Nicholls, who shortly afterwards sold it. The land was resumed, because the owner *did not reside in the Colony, according to the stipulated regulations !* It is a well known fact, that Captain Wight has brought more capital into this Colony than have all the Darlings and the Dumaresqs, with all their cousins put together ; indeed, at the present writing, his property in purchased land and houses is very considerable ; but he has no influence save with the merchants, to whom he has been known as a regular visitor for the last fifteen years ! So much for the want of influence !—*Colonial Times.*

CAPTAIN KERR.—This gentleman arrived in the Colony about the year 1827—he was entitled to a grant of 2,000 acres of land, which he located on the Big River. The land was measured to

of Hammond arrived in the Colony, in the year 1823, when he obtained a grant of land of 2,000 acres, and forthwith proceeded to stock and improve the same : he held the land three years, when his business required his visiting England. After making the necessary preparations for his departure, empowering an agent to manage his affairs and his estate, he left the Colony with the intention of almost immediately returning. His business required more time than he anticipated, and he did not return to the Colony till 1828, when, to his astonishment, he found his land had been resumed by the Government, and given by Colonel Arthur to a *then* friend of his, holding the situation of Colonial Secretary. It was in vain Mr. Hammond claimed his land—in vain did he for a time keep forcible possession—it was useless for him to " kick against the pricks ;" unfortunately, he had chosen an enviable spot for his grant,* and it was required for one more influential—a favourite. Redress was denied him ; almost a ruined man he died of a broken heart, leaving a wife and young family scantily provided for. The resumption of this land destroyed the family—not only did the father die of a broken heart, but the mother, after sinking by slow degrees into a life of vice and misery, followed her husband to the grave,

---

him. Captain Kerr died some years since, leaving his property to his son. It was necessary that Mrs. Kerr should visit England, for the purpose of arranging some family affairs. She intended to return, as soon as circumstances would permit. Messrs. Hopkins and Thompson were appointed trustees for the child, whose father had not been dead many months, before the land was resumed by the Government, and the brother of the surveyor of the district is now the possessor of a portion of it ! Reader, ask us not why the land was resumed—ask us not how it was again located ?—for these are questions which can be best answered by the district surveyor and the Government ! So much for Captain Kerr's child's *want* of influence !-—*Ibid.*

* The land selected by Mr. Hammond, was on the South Esk river, adjoining the properties of Captains Montagu and Foster, both nephews by marriage, of Colonel Arthur. The land given to the latter gentlemen was never cultivated or improved by them, but sold almost immediately obtained.

attended with the most heart-rending circumstances;
one child died before her, and fortunate would it have
been for the other (a female) had she also been in the
grave.   It would appear as if those possessing this land
were doomed to be unfortunate.   The individual to whom
Colonel Arthur gave these 2,000 acres, was the Colonial
Secretary, J. Burnett, Esq., and it was in consequence
of his having sold the land to another Government officer, possessing about some 30,000 acres, that in a few
subsequent years he was obliged to seek leave of absence, and Colonel Arthur placed in his room his near
relation, Captain Montagu, whom, the reader will recollect, was the first individual the present Governor appointed to office on his arrival.*   It has been observed,
that civil officers holding Government situations, have had
large tracts of country *given* them, and that they evaded
the orders from home, by selling such land almost immediately it was located to them—Mr. Burnett did no
more than the Surveyor General, or the Crown lawyers
themselves, or Colonel Arthur's relations ; but Mr. Burnett had become obnoxious to the Chief authority, and
his removal was considered expedient.

It is to be regretted that so much power—so much
patronage had ever been allowed to remain in the possession of any one individual, for it enabled him to rule
with a rod of iron ; and coupled with the great additional
patronage vested in the Governor, of assigning convicts only to such persons as he might approve of, gave,
as has already been observed, more power in his hands
than that vested in any turbaned sovereign of the universe.   The reader has yet only been shewn the manner
in which land has been located generally, and one instance given of resumption ; but it is necessary now
to draw the attention to an extraordinary case, just the
reverse to that cited, in which influence has been opposed to all rules and regulations—to justice and com-

---

* Captain Montagu has been designated the " official warming
pan," having been appointed to so many situations before he was
confirmed to any one by the Home Government.

mon sense.   One of the distant relations of the late
Governor of New South Wales, a Captain E. Dumaresq,
was Surveyor General prior to the appointment of G.
Frankland, Esq.   It is commonly rumoured, that for
certain services rendered by General Darling, to the
Lieutenant Governor of this Colony, that this said gentleman should receive " the equivalent"—whether this
be true, or not, the writer will not presume to say, but
suffice that Mr. Dumaresq has been most fortunate ; he
has had a large location of land made to him—an additional location for improvements—(which improvements
were in every sense of the word, *imaginary*) large numbers
of township allotments, and suburban allotments in all the
townships he has thought proper to name—besides the
lucrative and gentlemanly berth of Police Magistrate of
the richest district in the Colony.   Without any conspicuous talent, or any other good reason why such
patronage should be bestowed upon him, this gentleman
for many years was allowed to enjoy every species of the
good things in the gift of the Lieutenant Governor : nor
was this all, his desire to further the interests of his
family, induced him to apply to the Government for a
grant of land and township allotments for a cousin of
his, whom he said lived in India—this gentleman, be he
whom he may, has never visited these shores.   The
Lieutenant Governor was pleased to sanction such gifts,
and this gentleman, *said to be* a Mr. William Anley, of
Calcutta, had given him two thousand five hundred
and sixty acres, adjoining the fast-improving township
of New Norfolk, besides several valuable allotments in
Hobart Town and other places.   Mr. Dumaresq, of
course, acted as agent to this cousin, and selected as a
tenant, a man of the name of Handly,* who was formerly in his employ, and for whom he had obtained his
indulgence.   At the present writing, not one inch of
this land is in cultivation—not a building is erected
thereon; and although this *foreigner* has never visited the

* Many people considered this Handly, was the Mr. Anley, the
owner of the soil.

Colony—although Mr. Anley, or his agent, had the land given him in 1830, and although a regular demand has been made to have the land resumed, or put up for sale, according to the instructions of the Secretary of State, such demand has been treated with contempt by the Government. It would appear that such is the claim of this Mr. Dumaresq on the Governor, or Government, that a cousin of his, whom no one of this Colony ever saw, can maintain possession of a large grant and allotments, whilst numerous settlers have been refused one inch of land, and others have had their land resumed, because they have not resided thereon, although they have lived in the Colony ; or, because they have quitted the Colony, even with the intention of returning to settle therein.

The land jobbing system, which has been carried on with impunity, would astonish, were it possible to be made public ; men who ten years since were almost pennyless, have by some unaccountable means become landholders of 10 to 30,000 acres ; surveyors, whose salaries were nominally but trifling, have been most fortunate in the jobbing, and have amassed wealth with a rapidity truly astonishing. What is the most extraordinary portion of the system which has been allowed, is, that the Government Surveyors have been permitted to measure their own land, either granted or purchased—and in a very large grant a few hundred acres more or less, is of trifling import ; it would be invidious to point out any one individual as having so done, when the system to this day is general. The land jobbing has been carried on from the very highest to the very lowest of Government Officers, even His Excellency, the Lieutenant Governor, besides possessing large funded property, is a very extensive landowner* ; and with such

---

* The landed property known to belong to Colonel Arthur in the Jerusalem district alone, amounts to about 12,804 acres, viz.—
Carrington, on the charts Davey 3,000
Hill's ....Ditto....Nightingale 500
Two grants ....Ditto....Underwood 1,600

an example before them, some of his leading friends have outstripped him in the number of acres, if not in the value of the property.

The Colonists look to the land granted as glebes with much suspicion. Every township has more or less land set aside for the clergyman—generally speaking, the quantity is about 400 acres. About twelve months since it was currently reported, that orders from the Secretary of State had been received, commanding that the ministers should receive compensation for such glebes, and that these almost waste lands should be sold : compensation of some kind *has been* given, but the Church still possess the interest in the glebe lands, not one of which has been offered for sale. These lands for the most part are the very best that can be selected, and generally in

One grant, on the charts, Clitheroe's		350
Ditto ....Ditto.... Blinkworth		220
Ditto ....Ditto.... Phillips		100
Ditto ....Ditto.... Maddox		500
Ditto ....Ditto.... M'Donald		100
Ditto ....Ditto.... Walkinshaw..............		1,200
A veteran's grant Ditto.... Eves....................		100
One grant .... Ditto.... Hunt's		1,000
Tolmay purchase Ditto.... Tolmay		640
Lot 82, purchased from the Crown, Pitcairn..........		818
Lot 87........ Ditto............ Ditto............		756
Lot 88........ Ditto............ Ditto............		640
Lot 89........ Ditto............ Ditto............		640
Lot 90........ Ditto............ Ditto............		640

12,804

There are, besides these, several other grants of land. said to belong to His Excellency in the distrtct of Jerusalem, but the writer is not certain that public report is correct.

The extent of the landed property of His Excellency the Lieutenant Governor, must not be judged from the above-named grants, because these point out his property in one district only ; whereas, other of his extensive landed estates are to be found in most parts of the island—one property alone, that of Cottage Green, situated at the New Wharf, in the vicinity of which place some hundred thousand pounds of public money has been expended, is extremely valuable ; the area is about thirteen acres, and if it were put up for sale, would realize about twenty thousand pounds.—*Correspondent.*

the immediate vicinity of the townships.   The Colonial
Chaplains, having but an uncertain interest—an interest
so long as they may remain in the district—it follows, as
a matter of course, that no tenants will rent these glebes,
except for trifling sums; no man in his senses will
plough and grow the corn for another one to reap—
therefore, in most cases, these glebes produce a mere
nothing, and if sold would realize a very considerable
amount.

Before offering any remarks on the system of selling
land, as now adopted, or of the advantages a land revenue would be in preference to any taxation, it will be
as well to offer a few remarks on the *grants* of lands.
It is very generally supposed that there is at present no
valid title whatever to land in the Colony, and that a bill
must be passed through the Houses of Parliament, empowering the Local Government to issue grants of any
validity.   Every Government of this Colony has found
fault with the illegality of the documents issued by its
predecessor, by which the possessors of land have held the
same ; and in all probability the administration which will
succeed the present, will in a like manner object to those
now being issued.   The difficulty lies in the alienation of
Crown land without Parliamentary sanction ; and if the
Colonial lawyers are correct, it would appear that the
same difficulty occurs in a Colony for His Majesty to
give or grant away land belonging to the Crown, as it
would be were the land situated in the British dominions.
It need scarcely be added, that as land becomes more
valuable, the disputes among the Colonists about boundaries, &c., which could now be settled by valid grants,
will be more numerous, and their consequences highly
injurious.   If, however, the Colonists generally complain loudly of the precarious nature of their titles, there
is yet one branch of the community who benefit considerably thereby, viz. the lawyers ; and it would appear
also, that these members of society were considered as
most deserving of support and patronage.

The sale of land has been attended with the most un-

happy results.   The jobbing of former years was pernicious, but the order to sell land is likely to prove still
more so.   Under the old system a few favorites were
most fortunate, but then the Colony benefitted by emigrants arriving with capital ; now emigration may be
fairly considered as at an end—there is now no inducement whatever for any capitalist to leave his native
land and become a settler in a desert.   It will be necessary to explain more fully why it is that capitalists are
not likely to arrive in the Colony under the present system.   A man possessing thousands can live comfortably
in Europe ; he can enjoy the comforts and the luxuries of
civilized life—such a man is not likely to leave all that
he has cherished for years, to migrate to a distant Colony
like this, when the very name of Botany Bay is enough
to frighten most people.   The emigration of large capitalists to these shores is therefore out of the question—
not so the possessor of a few hundreds.   The latter,
finding no prospects in the Mother Country by which his
trifling capital may support himself and his offspring, is
recommended to turn his attention to distant colonies.
Suppose the man about to emigrate possesses some £500,
he has read of the wealth produced by industry and capital in the Colonies—perhaps Van Diemen's Land is
pointed out to him ; he is told five shillings an acre will
purchase land.   Five shillings an acre ! he exclaims
with astonishment, and he thinks then of the value of
space in London, where it is worth thousands.   With
false delusion, with flattering hope, he pictures to himself what a *gift* land *must be* at such a price.   He has
been accustomed to envy the possessor of the fields of
Hackney or Clapham, and five shillings an acre rings in
his ears, and he at once imagines his fortune made.
With most flattering prospects does he pay one or two
hundred pounds for the passage of himself and family ; and
after incurring the risk of life and property by a dangerous
voyage, he arrives in the Colony with perhaps £350 in
gold. He lands at the wharf—which way is he to turn ?
Perhaps he may be a stranger to every human being in

T

the Colony! After sauntering about the town he finds
himself at an inn, where he settles and remains inactive for
a week or two, not knowing which way to proceed to obtain the fields and the pleasure grounds at five shillings
per acre! Roused from his lethargy by the rapid diminution of his funds, he proceeds into the interior to examine the *dorado* of his imagination: he visits the
farms of the old settlers, and they appear to him most
desirable—he then inquires of them where there is land
unlocated on which he may fix? The settlers tell him
there is none in the neighbourhood, that he must proceed twenty or thirty miles further into the wild bush,
before any good land may be had. Perhaps, however,
the new emigrant has learnt that portions of land in a
settled district are not all taken, whereon he proceeds to
search for such. Find it wherever he will, and his *dorado*
dreams are at an end—the land will be either so heavily
timbered, or rocky, that it will almost overcome the
stoutest heart. But let us suppose him to overcome all
difficulties, and that he be fortunate in selecting land
not reserved for any Government or private purposes.
He returns to town, communicates with the Surveyor
General, and demands that so much land shall be put
up for sale; if he has chosen the land adjoining the property of a settler, he has to contend with a competitor;
but if he has proceeded far in the wilderness, he will
have none to oppose him. The due forms having been
attended to—which forms require some considerable
delay—the land is ordered to be measured by the surveyor of the district, and then the land is gazetted as for
sale. According to the Government Order, no land is
to be sold without advertising the same for three months;
so that what with the delay before seeking for the land
—before the district surveyor may please to measure the
same, and before the expired time for 'publishing the
sale—the very least time all these take is twelve months
—and on what has the new comer and his family been
subsisting?—on the capital. On landing, it is presumed
he had £350 in gold, and being a prudent man, he

thought it advisable to apply to purchase the smallest
lot the Government will sell, viz., 640 acres—he calculated, that at *five* shillings an acre, this would cost him
£160, and that he would have nearly £200 to stock, and
expend in cultivation; but as time advanced, his capital
decreased, and before the sale takes place, he will be
fortunate if the £160 remain.   Supposing, however, he
attends the auction, if he has selected land adjoining a
settler, the latter will be there also, and run up the price
against him, so that the nominal value of his own estate
may be encreased.   The amount of the purchase money
therefore, soon exceeds the money of the new emigrant,
and he returns to his inn with the worst of prospects.
If, however, he has selected land distant from any settler,
he will be allowed to purchase the same at the minimum
price, without opposition ; but can he cultivate or stock
the purchased land?   No! the whole of his capital is
sunk, and uselessly so ; and the man becomes a beggar
in a strange country.   One would imagine that the
Home Government considered that land was of itself of
intrinsic value ; but this is not the case—it is the population and the improvements which make it valuable.
An estate within two miles of Hobart Town is now
offered for sale, consisting of 2,560 acres, and but
the sum of £800 is alone demanded; whilst on the
very spot on which this work is published, a. piece of
ground of some thirty foot frontage, and some
sixty feet in depth, is worth a couple of thousands.
The Home Government, when the order for selling land
was issued, must have imagined that the land itself
was of a value, and the Home Authorities must have
been misled, as many settlers have been, by considering
that this country resembled the environs of a crowded
capital.   The Home Rulers little imagined that the
average cost of clearing land amounted to upwards of
£6 the acre.   True, in some spots the plough may turn
up the soil without one farthing having been expended
thereon, whilst other lands have cost from £10 to £20
per acre, in the grubbing up and the burning off the

thickets, with which the greater part of the best soils are covered.

The selling of land in this Colony very much resembles the killing the goose for the golden egg. Hitherto, valuable patches have alone been put up for sale, such have realized high prices : the settler who may have had an unlocated spot adjoining his grant, has sometimes wished to purchase the same, and he has requested to have it sold ; at other times the surveyors have pitched upon unlocated patches in centrical situations, and these have been recommended for sale, to raise funds. Lands so situated, have realized large amounts, but when all such have been sold, what can be done with the barren —the waste—and the wilderness ? Having alluded to the manner in which a modern emigrant is situated on his arrival, under the present system of land selling, it is scarcely necessary to observe, that such men are induced to emigrate under false pretences—they have been led to believe, either that land was to be *given* for nothing, or else that it might be bought like merchandize without delay ; and were it possible to enumerate the numerous individuals who have been ruined by visiting these shores, since the new system has prevailed, it would astonish the reader. The selling the land is not only injurious to the new emigrant, but also to the old colonists. The latter have taken root in the settlement, under the belief that encouragement would still be given to emigration—the improvements have been carried on by them, under the belief that such improvements would be valuable, by the introduction of capital and population ; and consequently the suspension of the stimulus to emigrate, will reduce the value of property, because landed property can only increase or decrease, according to the density of the population, and the wealth of the community. One of the Hobart Town Journals, in a rather playful mood, once recommended a plan of paying off the national debt of Great Britain. The Journalist stated that she-oak timber was worth twenty shillings a ton in Hobart Town—that there were so many tons of

wood on each acre, and that there were so many millions of acres in the Island; therefore, valuing the whole
number of tons at the market price, not only would it
give an amount equal to the national debt, but a sum
over and above, sufficient to support all the European
Governments for the next thousand years.   The same
calculation might be made with reference to land.   A
frontage in Hobart Town or Launceston, is worth from
£10 to £20 per foot—so is she-oak worth 20s. per ton
on the Old Wharf; but what is the value of the she-oak,
now growing behind Mount Wellington, where there are
no inhabitants?—and what is the value of land at the
same place?   The same answers must be given to both
questions—the wood and the soil are valueless without
population!

The conduct evinced by the Government towards the
pensioners, is also deserving of remark in these pages.
Men who have grown old and decriped in serving
their King and their Country—men who have been
disabled by wounds honorably obtained in battle, have
been most unhappily deluded to visit these shores
under expectations the most deceptive and distressing.
The pensioners were told that if they would abandon
their pensions and settle in Van Diemen's Land as
Colonists, they should have grants of land given to
them, and also a free passage.   Many such pensioners, deceived by the *bait*, have left a home in England
to come and perish in poverty and misery in Van Diemen's Land.   Arrived here, their *dorado* dreams have
been followed by the awakening truth, that a landed estate in this Colony, and a landed estate in the Mother
Country, are far from resembling each other.   The
broken down pensioner, on his arriving, in nine cases
out of ten, gave up all hopes, and in despair, his little
grant to which he was entitled, was soon sold, and
the proceeds spent in the liquor shops—and he became
a beggar of the worst description.   The Government
finding that the pensioners invariably *sold* their 100
acre grants, and thoughtlessly squandered away the pro-

ceeds, issued an order that no such sale should be binding, and that no pensioner should dispose of his grant, unless after having resided thereon a certain number of years. The effect of this order was still more distressing—how was it possible for an old veteran to live on his grant—in the wilderness ?—the man was without food or a dwelling, or means to build the one or obtain the other. To place him in such a situation was to order him to be starved. The result of this order was that the sales did take place in spite of the threatened invalidity ; but of course the veterans suffered, for their locations were sold but for a mere song. Representations however were made, that the order respecting the residence of the veterans on their grants, was impolitic, and the proclamation itself was countermanded—but not before many of the Authorities reaped an advantage ; these latter, knowing that the former order was to be cancelled, purchased all the veteran's grants that were saleable, and the price paid was a mere nothing; when a week or two after, these poor deluded men found out, when too late, how they had been deceived.

In a new Colony like this, it is the duty of the Authorities to watch over the interests of future generations, and to plan and adopt such measures as are likely to be beneficial to mankind. The granting away land indiscriminately, without reserving any for public services would be unwise in the extreme—but then the public reserves hitherto made, have not been of that description likely to be of a permanent advantage—for instance, an order one year, issued that glebes should be given to the Clergy, and a succeeding administration in the Mother Country, commanded that such glebes should not be attached to the Church, but that the clergy shall be dependent on the revenue, and not be allowed to meddle in secular affairs. The Colony is yet to be moulded ; and with care and attention, the best of results may ensue. The number of acres now located is about two million, and perhaps nine millions yet can be given, that can be rendered serviceable. Of the mil-

lions of acres already granted, about eighty thousand are
in cultivation—the reader will therefore perceive, that
it is not yet too late to make regulations which may encourage emigration ; neither is it too late to place the
Colony in a prosperous position, for future posterity. It
has occurred to the writer, that the whole of the Colonial revenue ought to be chargeable upon the land. by
this means the ports of the Colony would be free in every
sense of the word. By the adoption of a land tax or
quit-rent, the necessary revenue would fall upon the
property—in fact, the revenue ought to be raised by a
property tax ; and in the establishment of a new Colony,
such a property tax may be well enforced without any
difficulty. Opposed to this measure, there will be found
numbers, but of whom will these consist ? Of course of
the large and influential land proprietors—the ten and
twenty thousand acre gentlemen will cry out most lus-
tily against such a tax on their large incomes—but it is
worthy of consideration, whether or no these Antipodean Princes are of more consequence than the remaining portion of the Colonists ? The quit-rent question
has often been discussed at public meetings and otherwise : it has been considered as objectionable in the extreme, and the compiler of this work is of the same
opinion—because the quit-rent *now* presumed to be *raised*,
is for purposes injurious to the Colonists. The money
levied by the sale of lands, and by the enforcement of
the quit-rent, is now most injudiciously appropriated to
the introduction of pauper emigrants, the very worst
class of people that can be introduced into any Colony.
If, however, the quit-rent was to be enforced for the
maintenance of the necessary forms of Government, none,
save the large landed proprietors, would object. The
middling class of society, (of which class there will soon
be none, if the present system prevails) will not feel the
enforcement of a trifling rent to the Government—
indeed, the duty on the articles now consumed by them,
will not be chargeable on those articles, whilst a similar
sum only will be collected from them as quit-rent. The

poor man will be encouraged by the adoption of such a measure ; whilst the large overgrown landowner will be, as he ought to be, compelled to pay largely towards the revenue; and, as said before, it remains to be decided whether the Colonists generally, or the Antipodean Princes, are of most consideration in the eyes of our Home Rulers. It is the extensive landowners that are now considerably blighting the energies of the Colonists—these men will tell you, that but for them there would be neither wool, nor meat, wherewith to feed the population ; but the small quantity of wool shipped in proportion to the number of acres located, and the high price of meat, are quite sufficient facts to explode such reasoning. The truth is, that these landowners are yearly extending their properties, and to such a degree, that before long the whole located parts of the Colony will be in the possession of a few individuals : men who, ten years since, had but a few acres, have by means of selling the wool and the carcase of sheep, been able to purchase adjoining grants belonging to smaller settlers, for mere trifles ; and as each year succeeded, so have their estates encreased by thousands of acres. These twenty thousand acre gentry have scarcely any portion of their land cultivated, and the very largest sheep establishment requires but few servants to attend to the flocks. Were these estates divided, and cultivated, it need scarcely be observed, that double the quantity of wool, and double the quantity of meat, might be brought to market—without referring to the numbers that might have been employed in the cultivation of the land and the rearing of the stock. The English reader will perhaps imagine the fine sheep walks which he hears of in Van Diemen's Land, are level plains, open to the sun, and of a grassy green, like those to be seen in England ; but it will be necessary to observe, that more than three-fourths of this Island is covered with timber, either fallen or standing—and as to the native grass, it can be scarcely termed herbage at all. In England, a hundred acres of ordinary land will keep three hundred sheep, while in Van Diemen's Land, a similar quantity will not keep fifty from starving. Should the Home Government order the Colonial revenue to be levied by a property tax of the description alluded to, a few other considerations are deserving of attention. The land uncultivated, and as nature left it, ought to be more severely taxed than the soil on which labor and capital have been expended—the former has been almost useless to society : whilst the latter has assisted in the maintenance of the inhabitants. Besides, every turf turned up is a service rendered the Colony, if it only be considered in respect to the clearing of the country, and the beneficial change of pasture which will result from the turning the soil. Much as the proposition will be opposed by the overgrown landed proprietors, the compiler of this work feels satisfied, that in a few subsequent years the best results must follow the enforcement of a fair and equitable quit-rent, by which the whole Colonial expenditure might be levied. Should the Home Government abolish the present system of *selling* land— which experience will soon point out as absolutely necessary to save the Colony—emigrants would flock to Van Diemen's Land as they did five years since; and supposing that the *giving* away of land can be managed without introducing the corruption and the jobbing hitherto so prevalent, the greater part of the Island would soon be studded with villages and farms, containing an industrious, a healthy, and a loyal British people. No doubt that five or ten years of encouragement would find half the Island located, and the greater portion to individuals possessing less than one thousand acres. Till such time as five millions of acres are located, the revenue might be raised as at present, viz., by the duty on spirits and tobacco ; but when that quantity of land should be given, then the revenue should be drawn from the real property by means of a quit-rent. If three pence per acre were fixed upon land under cultivation, and sixpence an acre upon all such as remained in a natural state, a sufficient sum would thus be raised for the sup-

U

port of a Government suitable to the number of its acres, and its inhabitants. There would be then a stimulus to cultivate the soil, and instead of one hundred sheep requiring two hundred acres of land, as at present, the artificial food, or rather the advantage gained by regularly cleared grazing grounds, would be great, and each hundred acres then would maintain, as in England, three hundred.

Before abandoning the land question, one or two points may be slightly adverted to. The vast encreasing landed properties now possessed by several individuals, are likely in future years to endanger the welfare of the Colony, by rendering their proprietors the only possessors of property ; and it is worthy of consideration, whether it would not be advisable to pass some enactment, by which only a certain number of acres could be held by one man. Without diving further into the subject, it may be remarked, that there are abundant precedents for such limitation of landed possessions, in the establishment of ancient flourishing colonies. It is also deserving of consideration, that now is the time to set aside grants of land for schools and charities, and other national establishments; but the placing aside a certain number of acres for such like institutions is not all that is necessary—such grants should be let for a term of years on improving leases, so that when the Colony would be ripe for the formation of such institutions, the property set aside might become valuable, and return ample funds, in the shape of rents, for the purposes required. The glebe lands having been (as it is understood) ordered for sale by the Home Government, it is worthy of consideration, whether such glebes had not better be let on improving leases for a term of years, till every acre of each could be brought into cultivation, and then they would be desirable farms to rent. The whole of the above suggestions are offered with the best intention, namely, for the improvement of this, our adopted Colony ; but whatever change does take place in the land system—and a change there *must take place*—the grand objects to be aimed at should be, the prevention of jobbing, and the doing away with the system of allowing the patronage to any individual in the Colony of giving or granting land, except according to a fixed rule, which would allow of no infringement.*

---

* In a work, entitled, *Illustrations of the present state and future progress of the Colony of New South Wales*, published at Sydney, the following trite observations are made, relative to the land question :—

If there is any regulation that more immediately affects any recently arrived emigrants, as well as the adult children of inhabitants of small fortune, and the freed man, it is certainly that regulating the disposal of crown or waste land. It is impossible for a sober-minded man to conceive how any person can make it the only study of his life, to get more land than he and his immediate successors can possibly want ; and what makes this far more astonishing is, that this has been done in a country and in times, when the future fate, and the direction which that country may take, were quite uncertain, as those of the Colony are, even to the present moment. Let us suppose, that the British Government at any future period shall direct its favourite attention to any other part of our continent ; let us also suppose, that the British Government (as has already been spoken of) should withhold from us the transmission of its prisoners, what would be the fate, or what then would be the result of these exorbitant and inappropriate grants of land ?—Nothing less than that such persons, who now possess from 20,000 to 50,000 acres, would have a thorough conviction, that they were the sole cause of the Colony not having prospered while circumstances were propitious. Such land jobbing, briberies and corruptions, are the reasons, why the Home Government has been *induced* to adopt a regulation for the disposal of land, which is quite unparalleled in the annals of history. *The King of Great Britain selling land in a country belonging to the Papuas ! !* † Neither the annals of Cortes nor Pizarro, the (belligerent) occupants of South America, exhibit such an anomaly ! At the present time, after 300 years of colonization—after the formation of towns containing nearly 200,000 of inhabitants, the Brazilian Government sells no land, but grants it gratuitously. But in this country, where the greatest part around the metropolis is still

---

† " Let the Government revert to the grantings of land on a fair and equitable quit-rent. But how much beneath the dignity of an imperial Government like that of Britain, to descend to the driving of land bargains, with the yet tender and infant colonies, it has otherwise the generosity to plant."—*Hobart Town Almanack for* 1835, *p.* 206.

During the year 1832 the industry and enterprise of
the Colonists were most conspicuous. The settlers continued to improve their farms, and Hobart Town had
buildings erected therein of a description far superior to

an impenetrable brush, when a proportionally insignificant population of 80,000 people is scattered over an area of so many thousand
square miles,* the abuses—the crying abuses of the Local Government, and the advantages taken by the governed, have caused the
Home Government to sell land in Australia! And thus it is a fact
which characterises the spirit of the present age, that not even the
solitudes and wildernesses of the whole fifth part of the Globe, were
found sufficient to satiate and fill up our rapacity and avidity. These
regulations, when first promulgated, became the object of general
disapprobation, with the exception of those only, whose interests
were promoted by them. A public meeting was held at Parramatta,
(December, 1832) for the sake of protesting against them, however,
the spirit of apathy and sloth, occasioned this meeting to fail of its
desired success.

The greater proportion of emigrants are necessarily poor, and dis-
contented with their circumstances in the home country. Who but
these would emigrate from all the social comforts of European life,
to these wild and far distant shores? And then again, to find a few
wealthy emigrants for whom the laws are made, contrary to the interest of the far greater number, who are not wealthy! If such persons arrive in this Colony for the purpose of establishing an agricultural concern, they must:—

First.—Go an immense distance from Sydney to choose their
land, because, as it has been already said, all other land has either
been granted or jobbed away. Thus then, the primitive produce of
a distant farm scarcely remunerates the grower. Settlers, for instance, in Argyle, Port Macquarie, &c., find it not worth their
trouble to bring wheat or maize to the market, &c.

Second.—After a troublesome inspection and selection, the new
comer must apply for the land, and wait three months, (or one
month, if he applies within six months after his arrival, according to
a recent regulation) exposed to heavy expences, and subjected,
perhaps, with a wife and family, to the seductive and contamina-
ting influence of such a constituted Colony.

Third.—But even after his having happily passed over this time
of idleness and temptation, he may have the mortification to find at
the sale, that some wealthy or land jobbing man of that neighbourhood offers a price, which he cannot afford. Besides this ;

Fourth.—The terms of payment are most harrassing; ten per

* The amount of land disposed of by the Government amounts
already to 3½ millions of acres.

any yet attempted. Produce of most kind was obtainable at a cheap rate, but at such a price as remunerated such settlers as were fortunate enough to have good roads to their farms.

Several important public measures occupied the consideration of the Colonists ; among the most important, was the subject of the quit-rents. Meetings in all the settled parts of the Island were convened, for the purpose of petitioning the Lieutenant Governor to use all endeavours with the Home Government, either to abolish

---

cent. deposit, and the residue in one month after, although it is notorious, that

1.—Farms are to be bought occasionally from private persons, at the minimum rate of five shillings per acre, and still less.

2.—Farms of 2,000 acres, upon which £200 have been spent in improvements, have been sold by the Sheriff for £90. Further, it is well known, that

Fifth.—The greater part of the latter purchases are transacted here with a credit, which is extended in some cases so far as three years, and often a considerable part of the purchase money can remain upon mortgage.

I therefore assert most confidently, that these regulations have not been made at all with a view of benefitting, neither do they benefit the community at large. And to demonstrate this assertion, I would remark, that at the time when every body who could, was gorged with an exorbitant portion of land, agricultural, grazing, and other produce, became uncommonly cheap, as some of them still remain. At the same time, the outcry against such continued land jobbings, and corrupt granting of land, arrived at its highest pitch. Now the persons who were then in power, and who themselves, their families, and their hangers-on, were intimately concerned in so unexpected a depression of prices, availed themselves very cleverly of this circumstance, to find out some means of making their grants more beneficial to themselves. And I am deeply, sincerely, and apodictically convinced, that no better or more efficacious means for their personal and mercantile scope could have been devised, than the regulations which were adopted with respect to the sale of Crown lands. These regulations enable such individuals to say to the man of small capital : " If you will have land, waiting for it three months, with the risk of not getting it at all, land far distant from every town and place of sale, if you will have land which you must pay for in a month,—Go and buy it from the Crown."—" But if you will have land immediately, near towns, and with a liberal credit, on mortgage—buy it from *us.*"

altogether the system as it existed, or else to have the tax modified. The landowners complained that the early Colonists possessed the land with scarcely any quit-rent payable thereon; whilst, at the same time, the best soil had been selected by them—that the emigrants of later years had arrived when the best parts of the Colony had been located, and that for inferior ground they were called upon to pay a large annual tax. There can be no doubt but that the quit-rents would in some cases be extremely harrassing; but those complaining the loudest were the large landed proprietors; and as the rich ought to contribute the most towards defraying the expense of every state, so far the enforcement of the tax would operate well. It has already been observed, that the greatest objections to the selling of land, and the calling in the rents, are, the manner in which the funds so levied are employed, in bringing out a useless class of pauper emigrants; and it is decidedly the opinion of the writer, as also of most unbiassed persons, that a more proper plan of raising the revenue could not be adopted, than by the deriving a small annual tax from each landowner. To read the sad complaints of the speakers at the various meetings during this year, it would appear, that land was not worth the quit-rent, and it would also seem as if some of the speakers would give up their large estates, if the land tax was not resumed. The Home Government has thought proper not to attend to the prayers of the landowners; and yet not a single individual ever talks of abandoning his estate—indeed, were the large landowners more severely taxed, it would be advantageous to the Colony, it would reduce principalities, whereon but a few individuals are maintained, and change those barren and waste principalities to prosperous farms and happy villages. It is beyond dispute, that had the land about Perth and Norfolk Plains been granted in small lots of five hundred acres to various industrious individuals, instead of seventy thousand acres to one family,* and thirty to another, there

---

* The family of the Archers is said to possess upwards of 70,000 acres between three brothers.

would have now been no scarcity of bread; for that part of the country alone could grow more wheat than would serve this Colony, as well as the whole of the Sister Settlement.

In August another public meeting was held in Hobart Town, and was numerously attended, when an Address to His Majesty was framed, praying for a Legislation by Representation.* This Address has shared the same fate as the memorable one of the 23rd of May. Among the public mearuaes of this year, a Life Assurance Com-

---

* *To the King's Most Excellent Majesty.*

MOST GRACIOUS SOVEREIGN : —We the Landholders, Merchants, and Free Inhabitants of the Colony of Van Diemen's Land, in Public Meeting convened and assembled, by the Sheriff of Van Diemen's Land, beg leave to approach your Majesty, by means of this Address, with the renewed assurances of our loyalty and devotion to your Royal Person, and to your illustrious House.

The Colonists assembled in Public Meeting, on the 23rd May, 1831, for the purpose, amongst other things, of praying your Majesty to grant full and ample enjoyment of their birth-right, by extending to this Colony Legislation by Representation, and although your Majesty's answer to that petition has not yet been made known, and the most sanguine hopes are entertained that your Majesty will grant the enjoyment of that right, we nevertheless are bound by the present situation of the Colony, and the prospect of pecuniary embarrassment, which is impending over us, to reiterate our prayers at the foot of the Throne, together with some of the grounds upon which we look with confidence to the complete enjoyment of those privileges, which as Britons, we have a right to possess.

From the most authentic accounts which we have been enabled to obtain, it appears that although the Colony has only been established 30 years, yet that the free population amounts to 14,000, and that the revenue by direct and indirect taxation, exceeds the annual sum of £90,000, while the Colonists possess no voice or control, as to the raising or expenditure of this sum of money, but the same is wholly exercised by the Executive Government.

We abstain from enumerating many grievances under which the various classes of the Colony have been, and still are suffering, because we feel assured that they will be removed so soon as we are put into possession of this one important enjoyment.

We have recently witnessed with alarm, the abstraction of a considerable portion of our Colonial Funds, by means of Bills drawn by the Colonial Agent in London, upon the Colonial Treasurer of the Colony, although the law expressly declares that the Revenue shall be applied to local purposes only ; and we humbly represent

pany was started, and this institution would no doubt,
have been fairly established, to the benefit of the community, had not one or two individuals objected to the
principles upon which it was to be grounded, and by
means of starting an opposition Company, destroyed both.

The Infant School was this year founded by voluntary
contributions; and, considering the destitute state of
many children, (by reason of the nature of the society)
the School has been of the greatest service to the rising
generation.   At this period the establishment of a College was also proposed, and several public meetings held,
in order to form plans by which an institution so desirable might be formed.   It is to be lamented that nothing has yet been done towards the establishment of the
College!   It is at the present time most advisable, as
already stated, that certain portions of land should be
set aside for the purpose of defraying the annual expense of a College; for the gift of ten or twenty thousand
acres at the present time would cost only the trouble of
obtaining the signature of the Secretary of State for the
Colonies.   The land so given ought to be held in trust
by the Colonial Government, and the whole of it let on
improving leases far a term of years.   A College at the

to your Majesty, that the continuance of such a system will speedily
bring this infant Colony to ruin.

We glory in the institutions of our Mother Country—we feel
that pride, which swells the heart of every Briton—we know that
these feelings are not inherent, but are the effect of education, and
the enjoyment of those rights which belong to a British Constitution.
We desire to bring our children up with the same feelings, and to
transmit to them and their posterity the same rights which we have
enjoyed.   But, Sire, we feel by experience, that unless we are permitted to enjoy the blessings of a British Constitution, our efforts
will be in vain, and our posterity will only be Britons in name, and
that which is most justly your Majesty's glory and our boast, will be
lost to our posterity for ever.

We therefore most earnestly pray and beseech, that Your Majesty will be most graciously pleased to extend to this British
Colony, the full and complete enjoyment of our rights, as
British subjects, in granting to us a Legislation, by means of
a full and fair Representation, in such way and manner as
to Your Majesty may seem meet.

present time may, perhaps, be unnecessary; but in a
few years the rising generation will be ready for such an
institution, and by that time the land would return funds
by way of rentals towards defraying the whole expense
of the establishment. Some persons have suggested that
this National Institution should approach rather to a
School than to a College; but there can be no reason
why more than one such Public School should not be established. The founding such a College would at the
present time cost nothing, but the *giving* away of waste
land, and the Colonists can see no reason why a tenant
should not pay rent for the maintenance of a Public
School equally the same as he would do for the sole advantage and benefit of a private landowner.

Numbers of emigrants of all kinds arrived this year,
the greater part of them have been a burden to the Colony. The flattering accounts sent to the British Government of the prosperity of this settlement, led the
Home Authorities to believe that population was alone
wanted to establish a Colony of importance. An Emigration Committee, as it was termed, was appointed by
the Lieutenant Governor to draw up a report on this important question—a report was accordingly drawn up,
but it has never been made public in Van Diemen's Land.
During the whole proceedings of this Emigration Committee, or, as the members termed themselves, the Im-
migration Committee, the Colonists were loudly exclaim-
ing against the introduction of emigrants without capital; the Colonists vainly pointed out that paupers at
Home would be paupers here, and that without any assistance from the Mother Country, they were soon likely
to have more poor of their own to maintain than the
Colony could support. The Committee went blundering
on, determined to work on theory rather than adopt the
more reasonable plans suggested by practice. Encyclo-
pœdias were culled over, and all works on Political Economy were rummaged up, on which to frame the celebrated report. The result of the proceedings of this
Committee have been most injurious, most distressing!

Numbers of pensioners—men unable to work—have been deluded here by the favorable prospects held out by these blundering Political Economists. Numbers of families also, have left comfortable homes in the Mother Country, to come out here to live in this settlement, divested of the privileges so genial to British feeling, and abandoned by all ties of kindred and association. The veterans have assuredly been the greatest sufferers. Most of these men have arrived in this Colony with the expectation that Van Diemen's Land was a land of promise—these men have come on these shores almost pennyless and unfriended ; the little money they had scraped together was expended in a few days, and within a week after their arrival, some have been seen soliciting charity in the streets. These men must have envied the more fortunate British convict. The veteran was, soon after landing, destitute of food and clothing, and knew not where to find shelter ; whilst the British convict was furnished with plenty of wholesome food, with warm cloathing, and comfortable dwelling.

At this period arrived the first vessel chartered with free women. The manner in which they were selected and treated on landing,* is a disgrace to those whose

---

* On Saturday, the free females were landed from the *Strathfield-say*. Of all the disgusting, abominable sights we ever witnessed, nothing ever equalled the scene which took place on that occasion. It is well known, that the females of the *Strathfieldsay*, are of a far superior order to those hitherto sent us by the Home Government—poverty being the greatest crime of the greatest part of them. It is true that a small portion of the number are not of that description, which ought to have been allowed to have associated with the innocent ; but that indiscriminate mixture of virtue and vice, is not, at present the subject before us. Early on Saturday morning, it was known all over the Town, that the free women were to be landed at mid day. The *Strathfieldsay* was bedecked with all the colours on board, and great was the preparation. About eleven o'clock, some of the women were stowed in one of the ship's boats, and then another boat went alongside, and was filled—and others followed in succession. Those who had first left the vessel, had to remain on the water upwards of an hour, before all the boats were stowed, when they were all towed together towards the New Jetty. At this time the mob waiting to witness the landing of the women, could

duty it was to make the necessary arrangements. About one hundred respectable females were by flattering prospects induced to leave their friends and relations, to better themselves in an almost unknown land—poverty, no doubt, was the chief inducement for such abandonment of all that was dear and cherished—such young

not be less in number than a couple of thousand. As soon as the first boat reached the shore, there was a regular rush towards the spot, and the half dozen constables present, could scarcely open a passage, sufficient to allow the females to pass from the boats; and now the most unheard of, disgusting scenes ensued--the avenue opened through the crowd was of considerable length, and as each female passed on, she was jeered by the blackguards who stationed themselves, as it were, purposely to insult. The most vile and brutal language was addressed to every woman as she passed along—some brutes, more brutal than others, even took still further insulting liberties, and stopped the women by force, and addressed them, pointedly, in the most obscene manner. Any woman, with one spark of the feeling of modesty, must have felt this degradation of the most terrible kind, and the consequence was, that by far the greater portion could bear the insults no longer—scarcely a female was there, but who wept, and that most bitterly; but this, again, was made the subject of mirth, by the brutes that were present. One of the poor creatures was so overcome, that she absolutely fainted—but there was no hand to assist—no one present who appeared to have any power in preventing these disgraceful scenes. After the females had passed through the long passage, the ordeal was not over; for men singled out the girls they fancied, and went in pursuit of them, annoying them, till they arrived at the door of the house, wherein these friendless beings expected to find security. The greater portion of the most insulting of the men, were those, apparently prisoners; indeed, it appeared as if the whole town had been picked, to select the lowest ruffians, expressly for the purpose of insulting these helpless females. It is true, there were one or two young men present, who ought to have known how to behave themselves—one in particular—a clerk belonging to a Government department, who will do well to take advice in time—otherwise, it will be to his cost. On arriving at *Bellevue*, the house *said to be prepared* for their reception, the rabble still loitered about, as if still further to insult. There had been plenty of time to prepare every thing for the reception of the women; and yet, we understand, the poor creatures had not any dinner till half-past six in the evening—and as to their bedding, we are credibly informed, that at five o'clock, a few dozen blankets were provided, and as many bed ticks,. in which the girls were set to put straw, so that they might have something better than the bare boards to lie down upon. During

females must have had extraordinary courage to have bidden adieu to their native country, when all before them was an ocean of uncertainty. When the purveyors of this cargo found a difficulty in persuading a sufficient

the whole of the night, the neighbourhood was in complete confusion—the most disorderly scenes were witnessed—men were seen pestering the purlieus of the place. Nor did the Sabbath allow a peaceable moment—on the contrary, during the whole of Sunday, a mob, somewhat similar to that seen the day before at the New Jetty, surrounded the house—scarcely could a girl stir herself, but the most obscene language was addressed to her. Those who strolled about the Town, shared no better fate, for at every step, and at every turning, knots of blackguards were assembled, whose only pleasure seemed to be, in trying to be more disgusting in their conversation than their companions. Sunday evening and Sunday night, were spent in a similar manner to the previous, with additional increase of noise and disorder—nor was it till Monday, that a female could leave her temporary lodging, without having the most disgusting language applied to her by some of the bystanders, who considered it all very fine sport. Never was there a worse managed affair, nor, in any civilised society, such outrages on common decency. Where were the scrupulous, conscientious, pslam singers, could none of these stand forth, and protect innocent females from insult, contamination, and ruin? Talk of squeamish-minded men, not receiving money for the support of a public institution, because it was raised by innocent theatrical representations—are there such conscientious men in Van Diemen's Land, and, will it be believed, none of them were present to protect—to save virtuous females from insult, infamy and destruction? Shame on all those concerned—we know not who they are, nor does it matter. Mrs. Arthur and one or two more ladies, assisted all in their power, but so soon as the ladies left, so soon did the scenes of infamy re-commence. Why was not a different time chosen for their disembarkation, and different arrangements made? Contrast the landing of these free females, with the landing of three hundred and twenty convicts the same morning. At seven the prisoners were landed—they were in an orderly manner marched up to the prisoners' barracks. They were immediately supplied with rations—their clothing was good. His Excellency arrived and addressed them at considerable length. Sleeping berths were provided—they received no insult. We cannot conclude these remarks, without repeating, that the whole affair was improperly managed, and no one can say, what misery and distress may ensue in consequence. We do sincerely hope, that should another such increase be made to our population, that some degree of caution will be manifested, and that scenes like those, partly only described, may never again disgrace the Colony.—*Colonial Times, August* 19, 1834.

number of respectable females to undertake the voyage,
the work-houses and the London streets were scoured,
in order to make up the number, and enable these traders in human flesh to obtain the money proferred by the
Government on the despatch of the vessel. Thus the
first cargo was a mixture of all classes—there were to be
found the offspring of the once wealthy, and the most
destitute prostitute of the London streets—these were
mingled together, and before the voyage was completed,
before some little distinction could be made, many a fair
creature had fallen into a gulph of vice and infamy.*

The Colony is yet greatly deficient in females, there
being, according to the last census taken, very nearly
three males to every female : consequently, any measure
by which the deficiency may be made up, must be beneficial to the *morality* as well as to the interests of the
community. The great aim, however, should be, to class
each sort of females separately.† The Colonists have
found the introduction of female prisoners highly advan-

---

* How many parents and relatives may now say in Great Britain,
" Well, our daughter has left us, and we shall, perhaps, see her
no more, but she has bettered her lot, and whereas with all her labor here she could not even make a supportable existence, she is now
in a young and thriving country ; there her exertions and her qualities will be best valued—perhaps, in this very moment, more tender
ties have united her for ever—" Halt, careful good parents, you
mistake greatly ! Don't you see this pale barefooted girl, which ar-
rayed in all the tawdriness of ill-gotten trumpery, is walking beyond
this unnclean and dark street—this is the person you spake of. This
is the fate of many, far too many of these poor unfortunate creatures. To speak candidly, the conveying of ship-loads of young
females to a distance of 16,000 miles, under the command of, and
surrounded by a crew of (to say the least) rough sailors, the innocent, tender, and childish girl to be mingled up in the same berth
with the consummate wretches of London—these are things we
would call at least unnatural ; neither does whole antiquity (with all
her Paphos and Lesbos) exhibit any spectacle of this kind. The
plan for conveying ship-loads of single women round the globe, is,
therefore, unnatural in its very outset, and by very careful arrangements only, both at home and in this Colony, can this be so far
corrected, as to lose, at least, some of its dstresssing origin.—*Dr.
Llotsky's Pamphlet on Female Emigration.*

† It is obvious, and has been proved in many instances, that fe-

tageous, and it is worthy of consideration, whether every class of females might not also be beneficial ; but let the author recommend, that should another cargo be sent out, that virtue and infamy should not be huddled together, but that the greatest distinction should be made.*

The Colonists this year began to feel the effects which were certain to follow the introduction of usury among a small community. In an address voted to the King, for a Legislative Council, during this year, the Colonists stated that a Representation of the people, alone could relieve them from the impending distress—indeed, certain ruin was most apparent.

The exports amounted to about £200,000, the Current Expenditure to £100,000, and the importations exceeded £400,000. The doing away with the *giving* of land, as already shewn, stopped the emigration of capitalists,

---

males tired by the long confinement and annoyance of the passage, have accepted situations which were not congenial, and many have been misled by this hurry into houses of notorious bad character. The poor stranger, secluded within the walls of the Lumber-yard or the Bazaar, has nobody whom she can ask, respecting the master, into the house of whom she is about to enter; and, on the other hand, the upright mistress has nobody to ask respecting the behaviour of the female during the passage, than (abominable to say) a rough master of a ship, or the (as it has often proved very questionable) male superintendent. These certainly are not the fit persons with whom sensible and decent females of any rank in society, would wish to confer. If the matron and monitress would remain with the females, a mutual understanding between the mistresses, Committee of Ladies, and the Emigrants would become more easy and natural. Besides, the different works, which have been carried on during the passage, should not be interrupted in the temporary abodes of the Emigrants, by which means the industrious girl would become conspicuous, and the work she is able to perform, would be before the eyes of the public. As the simple making of a fine shirt, is paid with four shillings in this Colony, the expenses for maintaining these females would not be so heavy, and the industrious girl being occupied in this way, would not be so anxious to enter without previous consideration, the first best place offered to her.—*Dr. Llotsky's Pamphlet on Female Emigration.*

* As soon as the females had embarked on board the *Sarah*, the superintendent appointed the married women to fill the various offices

whilst the exertions of the Emigration Committee threatened an increase of population, and further demand for imported goods. The difference between the imports and the exports was for a time made up by money lent on usury borrowed from the foreigner.* The flattering account of the Colony had reached the money jobber in London; he and the Indian nabob were both told that twenty per cent., nay more was to be obtained on the very best security. The Colonists also began to feel the injurious effects of the impounding law; instead of exporting provisions to New South Wales, on the contrary the Sister Settlement now partially supplied Van Diemen's Land with food of all kinds—wheat alone excepted, a small quantity of which was taken in exchange for the salt provisions. Large importations of Sydney horses were also made this year, and the speculators at first derived considerable benefits. The number imported soon brought down the value of the animals; and those concerned, after a short time, gave up the trade altogether.

The deficiency in the Colonial Treasury was discovered in the month of October, the extent of which deficiency the Colonists were never informed, but it is generally believed that a commission has been appointed to investi-

usually held by the sailors—for instance, the rations were given out by them—they also officiated as matrons. The whole of the females and children had their sleeping-berths altogether distinct, and apart from the men : but what is more novel—the husbands were the guardians and protectors of their wives and children, and at the same time, of the single women ; for this purpose, the men kept regular watch during the whole voyage, so that there were always three husbands on deck guarding the women, and to each hatchway was stationed one of the married men.— *Colonial Times, Feb.* 25, 1835.

* Owing to the high rate of Colonial interest, persons at home have recently found it advantageous to send out their money to be lent on mortgage of land or other property. No security can indeed be better than which an improving colony like this affords, where every year adds to the value of the territory. The consequence is that considerable sums are now periodically sent out to be invested in this way, and during the last year it is estimated that upwards of £50,000 have been lent out to settlers in the Colony.—*Hobart Town Almanack,* 1834.

gate the particulars.* The *Colonist* newspaper was started this year, supported by a party of gentlemen opposed to the Government of Colonel Arthur. Subsequent pages will shew how obnoxious this journal was to those in authority.

The conduct manifested by the authorities towards Mr. Gordon, the senior magistrate, of the Colony, excited surprise among the thinking part of the community; certain ambiguous reports, relative to the financial department of the Police Office, at Richmond, were buzzed about, and ultimately found their way to the chief authority, and without calling upon Mr. Gordon for any explanation of his conduct, a council suggested his removal from the office of Police Magistrate. The charges made against Mr. Gordon were, that he had not paid the Field Police the salaries due, and that he had not accounted for certain police fees and fines. In consequence of this charge he was compelled to resign, to avoid the disgrace of being suspended from office.† On investigation, it however turned out that Mr. Gordon had advanced money on account of the public service, and that the Government had no claim whatever upon him for fees or fines.‡ The individual employed in investigating the affairs of the Richmond Police District, was a young man of the name of " Mason," (an adventurer) possessed of no known property, and scarcely heard of until his name

* This year, 1835.

† See Mr. Gordon's Pamphlet.

‡ It appears that warrants to the amount of £600, being the salaries due to the Richmond Police for six months, were stopped by the Governor, in consequence of the alleged irregularity in the accounts, which irregularity was afterwards shewn to have arisen from the acts of the Muster Master and Chief Police Magistrate. The withholding this money gave rise to the complaints for non payment of the salaries due to the persons employed in the Richmond Police, which being brought under the consideration of the Executive Council, in the absence, and without the knowledge of Mr. Gordon, that tribunal recommended that he should be suspended, and the Governor, by letter, called upon to resign, without giving him any opportunity of explaining or qualifying his conduct, which the sequel shewed he was perfectly able to have done.—*Correspondent.*

was inserted in the commission of the peace, and his appointment gazetted, as Muster Master and Assistant Police Magistrate.* This inexperienced youth was ordered to investigate the accounts of the Richmond district, and thus report (if not decide) upon the charges preferred against the oldest magistrate of the Colony, who had held that situation with honor to himself, upwards of eighteen years. It may be necessary to observe that about this time, it was generally understood that orders from home had been received, to abolish the situation of Private Secretary to His Excellency, and that the individual then holding that office was a Mr. Parramore, a gentleman, in whose name it is believed, large properties belonging to His Excellency, appear on the charts at the Survey Office. Mr. Parramore was generally understood to be Colonel Arthur's land agent, and the Carrington Estate, and other large properties, known to belong to the Lieutenant Governor, are in the immediate vicinity of Richmond. Scarcely had Mr. Gordon been compelled to resign, than Mr. Parramore was appointed his successor, and remained in that situation until the arrival of Mr. Morgan, whom the Secretary of State for the Colonies, appointed to that situation, when Mr. Parramore became virtually what he was always considered to be, the general land agent of the Governor. It would appear that the Police Magistracy of Richmond was a situation much valued by the chief authority, for since the arrival of Mr. Morgan, many endeavours have been made to render that gentleman's office any thing but " a bed of roses," and at the completion of these pages, Mr. Morgan enjoys the advantages derived from the Police Magistracy strictly, because he has allowed no means for his enemies to make a case against him.

The year 1833 was not conspicuous for any marked political feature. The effects of the impolitic introduction of usury began to be more and more felt: and usury and the law charges allowed by the Supreme Court, were the two principal subjects which engrossed the

---

* See Mr. Gordon's Pamphlet.

public mind.   Fresh capital still flowed into the Colony.
from all quarters, but not in proportion to the demand.
It now became apparent the monster usury was destroying itself, and that no profits in any business,
were equal to what could be made according to law, by
the employment of money.   All kinds of manufactures
dwindled on, during this and the following year, till finally
the different manufacturers either became bankrupt, or
found that they could not compete with the high rate of
interest, and the cheap price of labour in other countries.
The merchants and traders presented a petition to the
Lieutenant Governor,* pointing out to him the ill

---

* That your Memorialists viewed, with feelings of alarm and regret, the introduction into the Council, during the last Sessions, of
an Act, declaratory that the Usury Laws did not, and should not,
extend to this Colony, being firmly persuaded that it was necessary that a wholesome restraint should be imposed upon the system
of Money Lending, and the rates of Interest exacted.

Your Memorialists beg to represent, that interest has been exacted upon the loans of money from fifteen to thirty-five per cent.
per annum ; and that the continuation of the system has brought
many persons to ruin—encouraged speculation to a ruinous extent,
and materially lessened credit.

Your Memorialists wish further to state, that capital cannot, in
the legitimate course of trade and commerce, be employed, so as to
return an interest beyond fifteen per cent. ; and that, in the case of
money loans at fifteen per cent., it amounts almost to an impossibility that the borrower can return the principal and interest ; and
with this acknowledged fact, your Memorialists view, with increased
alarm, the employment by absentee capitalists of large sums of
money in this Island, varying from fifteen to twenty-five per cent.,
upon which the interest annually is remitted from hence to England
and India—and ultimately the principal will also be withdrawn
from the Island, by which, not only individuals, but the credit of
the Colony must eventually, at no distant period, be greatly injured.

Your Memorialists wish to urge, that the reasons which exist in
the Mother Country, where there is a superabundance of capital,
for the repeal of the usury laws, do not apply here ; and that the
facilities of evading the laws in England are equally inapplicable in
this Colony.

That in England, Ireland, the East and West Indies, and in the
States of America, fixed rates of interest, according to the circumstances of each state, are established by law ; and although the
introduction of foreign capital may be desirable, when it can fruc-
ify to advantage to the Colony, yet your Memorialists are of opi-

effects which had arisen, owing to the abrogation of the English usury laws, and prayed His Excellency would introduce into Council a bill to define some specific rate of interest. This petition, although most numerously signed, was unattended to by His Excellency, and the evil was openly permitted to work the most baneful effects that could be produced, on an industrious community.

The Members of the Legislative Council were assembled during this year, when several Acts of Council were passed. It will be remembered, that in 1831, a new charter for the administration of justice arrived in the Colony, containing in it a provision, by which Mr. Baxter was appointed Puisne Judge. This latter gentleman, for reasons not necessary to mention, was re-shipped to England, and the charter requiring two judges, in the enforcement of the laws, the charter itself may be said to have remained in abeyance till Mr. Montagu, the then Attorney General, was appointed from home, to succeed Mr. Baxter in the situation of the Puisne Judgeship. One celebrated Act of Council, the Police Act, was this year passed by the Council : and their Honors, the Chief Justice and Puisne Judge, entered a manly protest against one of its clauses, which they were of opinion, was repugnant to the law of England, in so far as it rendered liable to apprehension, and detention, any mariner, however peaceable and orderly, who might be found in a public house, or in the streets, after the hour of nine, and before sunrise, if not provided with a pass from his master, or other person in charge of the ship. This protest—this shew of apparent

---

nion, that a fixed rate of interest of ten per cent. per annum is a sufficient remuneration for the use of money, quite as much as the settler and merchant can afford to pay ; and any exaction beyond that rate tends materially to check the rising prosperity of the Colony, and compels the borrower either to live upon his capital, or to resort to artificial means to sustain his credit.

Your Memorialists, therefore, strongly urge the necessity of introducing into the Council, and passing into law, an Act to regulate and define the rate of interest.--*Colonial Times, Oct.* 1, 1833.

respect for British law and British feeling—was appreciated by the Colonists as it deserved ; and happy would
it have been, had these gentlemen protested against
laws which were the following year passed, and which
were contrary to British law, in every sense of the word.
The protest of the Judges, as to the objectionable clause
in the Police Act, was met by the Chief Police Magistrate,
who, in an official correspondence to the Lieutenant
Governor observed, " that if free sailors be allowed to
perambulate the town, at all hours, without passes, there
would be nothing to prevent convicts, habited as mari-
ners, (who might be out after hours, for unlawful purposes) stating themselves to be sailors, and thus defy
the police." According to this shewing, convicts had
only to disguise themselves as gentlemen, and they
would preclude all chance of capture ; for surely no man
habited as a magistrate, would be touched by a convict
constable*. The good sense manifested in the protest
of the Judges, was not attended to, and the absurd and
childish reasoning of the Police Magistrate was deemed
sufficient to order the enforcement of a clause, which is
a disgrace to a free British settlement.

Mr. W. Gellibrand was reinstated in the Magistracy, and replaced in exactly the same station he
before held. The reader will perhaps not have borne
in mind that in the year 1827, " His Excellency had
been pleased" to dispense with this gentleman's services,
as a magistrate. At this period, however, the offer was
again made to him, and he accepted it *conditionally* that
he should be placed in the commission as he before
stood, having but few seniors to him in the Commission
of the Peace. The mere fact that this gentleman was so
replaced, shews that His Excellency conceived his former conduct to him demanded some kind of reparation,
and it is highly to His Excellency's honor, that he could
bring his mind to reinstate in office a man he considered
he had injured.

*Nine tenths of the constabulary are British convicts, enjoying
no indulgence whatever.

A monthly Magazine appeared this year, published in Hobart Town.   It was a very creditable production, but it did not receive the anticipated support, and after wavering for eighteen months, the proprietor ultimately abandoned the publication.   Few local occurrences of any import or interest occurred, with the exception of the destruction by fire, of the ship *Thomas* in the port of Hobart Town.*

---

* On Saturday morning last a number of the inhabitants of Hobart Town witnessed one of the most splendid and most awful sights imaginable—the burning of a ship (the *Thomas*) on the water. The general impression is, "that this awful visitation was not the result of accident." That there was, from the first commencement, the most extraordinary apathy manifested, every one can testify ; and in lieu of any attempt at either saving cargo or ship, each one looked on, admiring the awful sight, without in any way seeking to arrest the raging element, or to preserve the property from being sacrificed. The vessel, which was lying in the stream, was first discovered to be on fire about three o'clock in the morning, when Captain Hanley was awoke by the cry of fire. He immediately huddled his clothes together, and went on deck, where he dressed himself as rapidly as the occasion would permit. Soon the intelligence spread—the passengers and crew, consisting of the captain, the first mate, and two seamen, the remainder being ashore, were on deck, and the boat hauled alongside. The flames, at this time, were confined to the after part of the ship. Captain Turcan, of the *Mary*, and the mate of the *Stakesby*, with their boats' crews, were soon alongside, and after some little confusion, the whole of the passengers were taken away from the burning ship, and lodged on board a vessel in the harbour. About half-past four the fire reached the powder magazine, when an explosion of four barrels of powder took place. The poop was blown up, and the vessel shook from stem to stern in a terrible degree, rtunately, no lives were lost. The captain was standing, at the time, near the poop, and several persons were on deck. Soon after the ex-explosion had taken place, the fire took to the mizen-mast, which soon went by the board. The vessel now appeared to be deserted ; and only two boats were seen near her, till some time after six o'clock. About half-past five, the lower part of the main-mast being burnt through, fell overboard—the spangled fringe of the burning rigging looking most splendid—the early part of the morning was extremely dark, and the grandeur of the blazing elements appeared most splendid. At about seven, more boats left the shore for the vessel. Captain Moriarty despatched a government boat to the Lumber-yard : where, after some little delay, men were procured to cut the cables of the vessel. This was done, and a little after eight o'clock, she was towed burning to Sandy Bay Point, at which place she grounded in four or

Two new journals made their appearance in Hobart Town in February, viz., the *Hobart Town Chronicle*, and the *Australasiatic Review*—the former dwindled into insignificance, and expired in a very short time; and the latter property in the course of a few months was united to the *Tasmanian*, which journal was from thence published under the name of the *Tasmanian and Australasiatic Review*.

The succeeding year 1834, was ushered in with any thing but favourable prospects; the ill effects of over-trading, occasioned partially by the introduction of usury, became daily more manifest, and threatened con-sequences ruinous to the community. The Colony, how-ever possessed resources which were not apparent, and these coupled with the still further introduction of capi-tal, to be advanced at a high rate of interest to the Colo-nists, carried the mercantile and trading community well through this year: and although many men considered " *a crisis*" (as it was termed) was at hand, the introduc-tion of such capital delayed its occurrence for a time.

It was at the commencement of this year, that Mr. Bryan's case caused considerable sensation. The particulars are simply these. Mr. William Bryan, an Irish gentleman, well connected, and possessing consi-derable property, arrived in the Colony, in the year 1824. He became a settler on the other side of the island, and was appointed to the magistracy in 1828.

---

five foot water, where she continued burning till three or four o'clock on Sunday morning. It is said by some, that Captain Hanley is not insured, and others contradict this statement. Should the former be correct, we lament that such a serious loss should fall on any one man only. We trust, however, it will turn out that the captain has been more cautious, and that the vessel is, at least, partially in-sured. The cargo she had on board, was chiefly rum—of which she had about one hundred puncheons—and a small portion of her original cargo for Sydney—all of which, with a trifling exception, were destroyed. A few deals, which were stowed low down in the hold, were saved, when she was scuttled, after having grounded off the point. A few casks of salt too, and two or three puncheons of rum have been picked up, and it is hoped that others may yet be found on the coast.—*Colonial Times, Sept.* 24, 1833.

In the month of November, 1833, a secret examination took place in the Police Office, Launceston, when something transpired, which induced the Police Magistrate, (a personal enemy of Mr. Bryan) to forward to the local Government, representations supposed to be prejudicial to Mr. Bryan's character, who was at the time in Hobart Town. The latter, feeling indignant at the conduct of the Magistrate towards him, tendered his own resignation as a Magistrate.*

---

* GOVERNMENT NOTICE.
Colonial Secretary's Office, Nov. 28, 1833

William Bryan, Esq., having on the 7th November instant, tendered his resignation as a Justice of the Peace of this Territory, under circumstances which, in the opinion of the Executive Council, render the acceptance of the same impossible ; His Excellency, with the advice of the Legislative Council, has directed Mr. Bryan's name to be erased from the Commission of the Peace.

By command of His Excellency the Lieutenant Governor.

J. BURNETT.

Colonial Secretary's Office, Nov. 29, 1833.

SIR,—I am commanded by the Lieutenant Governor to inform you, that in consideration of the circumstances, under which you tendered the resignation of your Commission as a Justice of the Peace of the Territory, upon the 7th instant, as well as from facts elicited by the several depositions in the case of Samuel Arnold, taken in the Police Office, at Launceston—your most improper conduct to the Police Magistrate there—and your advertisement in the public papers, His Excellency, with the advice of the Executive Council, is under the painful necessity of refusing your resignation, and of directing your name to be erased from the Commission of the Peace.

I am, therefore, to intimate to you, that His Excellency has no further occasion for your services as a Magistrate.

I am also to add, that it has appeared indispensable to the Government, that the convicts assigned to your service should be forthwith withdrawn.—I have the honor to be, Sir, your very obedient servant,

J. BURNETT.

To W. Bryan, Esq.

Derwent Hotel, November 30, 1833.

SIR,—I have to acknowledge the receipt of a letter from the Colonial Secretary, addressed to me, " by command of your Excellency," intimating your refusal to accept my resignation as a

At this period the Council was formed, virtually of the Lieutenant Governor, the Chief Justice, and the Colonial Secretary. After no doubt, mature consideration on the part of the Government, it was thought advisable that the

---

Justice of the Peace of the Territory, and alleging for such refusal— First. " the circumstances under which I tendered my resignation." Second, " facts elicited by the several depositions in the case of Samuel Arnold." Third, " my most improper conduct to the Police Magistrate. And Fourth, " my advertisement in the pub.ic papers."

These are the alleged grounds for *refusal*, and form a pretext for offering me a wanton and gratuitous insult ; and I am accordingly informed, that " your Excellency, with the advice of the Executive Council, is under the *painful necessity* of directing my name to be erased from the Commission of the Peace." With regard to the first observation, contained in the Colonial Secretary's letter, I have merely to remark, that I acted from a sense of what was due to my character, as a gentleman and a man of honor, and I still feel, notwithstanding your Excellency's displeasure, that, if I had pursued any other course, I should have forfeited the esteem of every honorable mind. As I am in utter ignorance as to the nature of the second allegation, it is out of my power to offer any observation thereupon ; and I can only regret, that your Excellency should have deemed it expedient to withhold from me all information, and the opportunity—which concealment precludes of offering explanation.

The *secret* examination of a *convict*, under a charge of felony, by a *personal and a malignant enemy* (who may perhaps have the means of procuring *free pardons*, as in the case of the late Mr. Humphrey) cannot fail to excite alarm ! And I have a well-grounded reason to apprehend, that the " facts" elicited in Arnold's case, may have been the effect of intimidation, or the hope of reward. Under these circumstances, I can only *challenge investigation*, and express my utter abhorrence of the *system* of *Secret Inquiries* and *Free Pardons*, to procure evidence from prisoners, as subversive of all security, and affecting the peace and welfare of society.

You are pleased to assert, " that my conduct to the Police Magistrate at Launceston was most improper." This charge is without the slightest foundation in fact, I am bound to believe your Excellency has been led into some error.

The advertisement in the public papers contains, in my opinion, a very sufficient reason for its publication.

I am induced to hope, from the decision of the *Sydney Judges*, that the law will protect me from your Excellency's power, in the design you have formed, of wresting from me my convict assigned servants. To hold out such a threat upon an *exparte statement*, and without affording me even the means of refuting the allegation, leaves me no hope of redress but from the law.

most marked displeasure of the Government should be shewn towards Mr. Bryan, and forthwith an order was issued to remove the whole of that gentleman's assigned servants—this order was immediately carried into effect! Such a sudden blow as this, few men in the Colony could sustain without ruin! At the time this order was issued Mr. Bryan was gathering in his harvest, which, for want of hands, was in the sequel entirely destroyed; his shepherds too were taken from him, and his sheep, in consequence, were scattered over the whole adjacent country, and lost in hundreds. This was a blow of the Executive Council, no doubt considered by the members, as necessary to mark their displeasure at the conduct of Mr. Bryan! The Executive Government however, acted upon *ex parte* statements—Mr. Bryan not being called upon to defend himself from the charges made against him by secret enemies. About the same time, the trial of a man named Arnold, an assigned servant to Mr. Bryan, took place at Launceston, when the man was charged with the crime of cattle stealing, and found guilty. On the Court breaking up, the Launceston Police Magistrate expressed himself in very uncalled for terms, respecting his fellow Magistrate, Mr. Bryan, then absent in Hobart Town. Mr. Lyttleton said something to this effect, that " it was not the man Arnold, but his mas-

---

The Government and General Order, which you have caused to be published, with a view to cast a reproach upon my character, adds one more to the many arbitrary acts, of which the Colonists have so much reason to complain.

I cannot, however, allow myself to suppose, that your object was to defeat my actions against " the Police Magistrate of Launceston," for defamation in one case, and in another for conspiracy; although the " *Order*" is calculated to have such a tendency, emanating as it does from your Excellency and Mr. Chief Justice Pedder; before whom my actions will, in all probability, be judicially investigated, and who will then have to sit as Judge between the parties, having previously decided upon the question by *exparte* matter, and to a certain extent become a party to the very acts from which I am seeking redress.—I have the honor to be, Sir, your most obedient servant,

WILLIAM BRYAN.

To His Excellency Lieutenant Governor Arthur, &c.

ter, who ought to have appeared that day in the Court House." This expression was immediately conveyed to Mr. Bryan, who lost not a moment in returning to Launceston, and demanding an explanation. For this purpose, he requested a friend of his, Mr. Lewis, to wait upon the Police Magistrate, to request an explanation, or as Mr. Lyttleton himself afterwards swore, in the Supreme Court, that Mr. Lewis waited upon him to "appoint a time and place to meet Mr. Bryan, to give the satisfaction due from one gentleman to another." For this offence, the friend of Mr. Bryan, was prosecuted, and by a military jury found guilty of endeavouring to incite the Police Magistrate to commit a breach of the peace; and the extraordinary sentence of eighteen months imprisonment, and a fine of one hundred and fifty pounds was passed upon him, by His Honor, the puisne Judge, Montagu. It is scarcely necessary to advert to the extraordinary proceeding of the Court during this trial; Mr. Lewis considered that he had been prevented from making his defence,* in a manner suitable to the exigency

---

* Mr. Lewis was then called upon for his defence, and commenced as follows:—

May it please your Honor. Gentlemen of the Jury, I am placed before you this day under very peculiar circumstances, with all the tact and talent of the Attorney General to oppose me. I stand here alone, to oppose the well known " crushing" qualifications of that gentleman—qualifications, of which he has frequently boasted, even before he was invested with the terrific powers of Grand Jury and Attorney General. The Counsel for the prosecution, gentlemen, has told you that I scandalously endeavoured to excite Mr. Lyttleton to commit a breach of the peace. " We judge of others by ourselves," is an axiom of Adam Smith. When the Attorney General mentioned my attempt, as he calls it, to procure a breach of the peace, he forgot that it was but the other day he sent a message similar to the one which I am charged with conveying, to Mr. Roderic O'Connor.

His Honor here stopped Mr. Lewis, and said, that for the speech he had just delivered he should fine him ten pounds.

Mr. Lewis.—I can make no defence at all, your Honor, if I am not allowed to enter into particulars.

His Honor.—I perceive, Mr. Lewis, that you are reading from a document, and therefore the offence of using indecent and very improper language, which you have just committed, is evidently pre-

of his case. At the period at which this trial took place, Mr. Bryan had appealed to the laws of his country, for redress. Shut out from obtaining justice from the Executive Government, he appealed to the Supreme Court. He brought civil actions against the Launceston Police Magistrate, and also against the nominal agents, who had deprived him of his assigned servants. The British Parliament had, long previous to this period, (if the English papers can be believed) considered that Trial by Jury existed in Van Diemen's Land, the same as in England, but such *was* and *is not* the case. The Counsel for Mr. Bryan moved the Court for Trial by civil Jury, in every issue between the Government and his client; but their honors the Judges both decided that Mr. Bryan should not have such Juries. It must be borne in mind, the awkward situation in which His Honor, the Chief Justice was placed on this occasion. As member of the Executive Council, he had already decided against Mr. Bryan, and had approved of the Government punishing that gentleman, by depriving him of his assigned servants —as Judge therefore, did he sit upon the bench, to decide a question, upon which he had already come to a decision. The very man to whom Mr. Bryan appealed, for the impartial administration of justice, that very Ex-

meditated. If it were an extemporaneous address, I should feel disposed to make much greater allowances than I can do consistently with my duty in the present case, clearly appearing, as it does, to have been premeditated. If you will take my advice, Mr. Lewis, you will consult with your friends, and time shall be allowed you for the purpose, as to the propriety of a revision of the paper from which you appear to be reading.

Mr. Lewis having accepted His Honor's advice, he was [directed to retire into the Counsel's room, where he was followed by his friends, and shortly afterwards by Mr. Gellibrand.

Mr. Lewis remained out of Court a considerable time, during which time the Court waited for him most patiently, and upon his return, he addressed His Honor to the effect, that after consulting with his friends, he could not discover any more proper course than the one he had previously decided on adopting. He would, however, endeavour to abstain from any observations which appeared to him not to be absolutely necessary for his defence.— *Colonial Times,* May 13, 1834.

ecutive Councillor, had, in accordance with his oath as
such, faithfully and conscientiously advised the Government to do that very deed, which compelled Mr. Bryan
to have recourse to the laws of his country for redress.
Finding the Executive Government would not investigate
the case; that satisfaction, through the medium of the laws
of the Colony, was denied him, by means of compelling
him to have his case decided by men under Government
influence—he ordered his Counsel to throw up his briefs,
and has since proceeded to the Imperial Parliament, to
seek that reparation of character, which he could not legally, or otherwise, obtain in Van Diemen's Land. Mr.
Bryan is yet proceeding before the Imperial Parliament,
with his cause; but even here, the persecution of his
enemies has not stopped. These men, have, when absent, dared to accuse him of the worst of crimes; a felon,
a convict of Great Britain, without any indulgence whatever, has made a deposition on oath, that Mr. Bryan is
a cattle stealer, and a warrant has been issued against
this gentleman, whom every body in the Colony well
knew to be in England, at the time, and the officers returning the warrant not satisfied, further monstrous process, it is believed is in contemplation. It is the wish of
the friends of the Colony, that Mr. Bryan's case may
be heard and examined—if the conduct of Mr. Bryan
has been such; if he has offended against the laws of
his country, justice should be administered; if he has
not offended, but has been an injured man, no reparation
that can be given in a pecuniary point of view, can compensate him for the odium, the stigma cast upon him by
his enemies.

It was during this year, that the public mind was so
excited by the execution of the unfortunate wretch
Greenwood; and the circumstances connected therewith
were brought under the consideration of the Secretary
for the Colonies. The facts of the case are simply these.
Greenwood, a runaway, was apprehended on the New
Town Race Course, but before this could be accomplished, he had, in self defence, cut and maimed a con-

vict constable. Greenwood was brought to the Police Office, and placed before two magistrates, both of whom sentenced him* to receive a hundred lashes, and one of them, Mr. Mason addressed the prisoner in nearly these words, " You will first receive a hundred lashes, then be handed over to the Supreme Court, where you will be found guilty, and I have no doubt be hung."   The man shortly after, stood his trial in the Supreme Court, and was found guilty of intent to maim the prosecutor—to do him some bodily and grievous harm—and of assaulting him for the purpose of endeavouring to escape. A strong petition was addressed to the Lieutenant Governor, praying that under all circumstances, this man's life might be saved, and one member of the Executive,† it is believed, stoutly protested against the execution, which, however took place shortly after his trial, when the man's back had not healed, from the effect of the lash. In this manner was this poor, wretched creature deprived of life. The execution of this man is looked upon as a disgrace to the Colony, and the writer laments that his duty as an historian, compels him to notice the affair. This transaction did not end here. Orders from home were received to investigate the conduct of Mr. Mason, and exculpatory affidavits were returned to the Secretary of State, denying his having made use of the words said to have been uttered.   One magistrate of the Colony has since openly accused Mr. Mason of perjury, and a civil action has been commenced, and is yet pending against him for the alleged slander. Mr. Mason is still a magistrate of the Colony.

Much feeling was also excited about the Jury question. A Public Meeting was held at the Court House, on the 14th July, when the sheriff took the chair, and after many excellent addresses and observations on this important subject, from numerous speakers, an Address was drawn out to His Excellency, and a Deputation of forty individuals appointed to present the same to the

---

* Mr. Spode and Mr. Mason.

† J. Burnett, Esq.

Governor. This Deputation remained a deliberative body, acknowledged by the Government as such. On presenting the Address* to His Excellency, he read an *evasive* reply, and he expressed himself " That he should

---

* *To His Excellency Colonel George Arthur, Lieutenant Governor of Van Diemen's Land and its Dependencies.*

We, the inhabitants of Van Diemen's Land, in Public Meeting assembled, and duly convened by the Sheriff of the Colony (for the purpose of expressing our consternation at the power vested in the Supreme Court of Van Diemen's Land for refusing Trial by Jury), beg to represent to your Excellency our firm attachment and adherence to the ancient land marks of the British Constitution, of which we considered Trial by a Jury of Twelve to be one of the most important.

We have witnessed with alarm the power of the Supreme Court of refusing Trial by Jury, and of directing the cause to be tried before one of the Judges and two Assessors, appointed by the Crown : and that, too, in a case where the Attorney General openly avowed that the Crown was the real defendant ; this feeling of alarm is much increased from the circumstance of the Chief Justice being one of the Executive Council, from which the proceedings originated, and therefore, that individual would necessarily be to a considerable extent interested in the result, and would unite the two characters of Judge and Jury—a mode of proceeding so repugnant to every principle of British law, so highly calculated to bring the proceedings of the Supreme Court into public odium and contempt, and so injurious to the rights and interests of the people of this Colony, that we feel it our especial duty, to call your Excellency's serious attention thereto, under the hope that a remedy may be forthwith provided.

We beg also to represent our firm conviction, that the mode of trial generally adopted, viz., by one of the Judges and two Assessors, has been unsatisfactory to the community, as repugnant to the English law, more especially the blending of the *two* characters of Judge and Jury in one individual.

We have observed with sincere satisfaction, that the Jury Laws have been extended to New South Wales, and as we are governed by the same Act of Parliament, we are at a loss to understand why the same privilege is withheld from us, more especially as it has been publicly notified by the Attorney General of Van Diemen's Land, that the Local Government has the power to extend the full Trial by Jury to this Colony.

We beg also to represent, that the Public being without any Representatives, there is no barrier between the extraordinary powers of the Crown in the Colony and the People's rights, but a full Jury of twelve persons, fairly and impartially chosen, and with a due regard to a proper qualification, we feel satisfied this measure would tend to strengthen the hands of the Government—produce confidence in,

be happy to hear any gentleman's sentiments on the sub-ject," but so astonished were the whole of the members of the Deputation at the manner in which the requisition had been met, that they gazed upon His Excellency with astonishment! A pause followed, which was inter-rupted by the sheriff and the Deputation bowing to the Governor, and retiring. The Deputation forthwith ad-journed to the Ship Inn, and again called upon the the people to assemble, to petition the British Parlia-ment for redress.* The report of the Deputation was

and respect for, the administration of the laws—and quiet the fears and apprehensions of the public mind ; and we therefore entreat of your Excellency, to introduce as a law, Trial by Jury as it obtains in Great Britain, and more especially without any diminution in number.

* The undersigned having taken into their calm and deliberate consideration, the answer of His Excellency the Lieutenant Gover-nor, to the Address of the People of the 14th instant, cannot sepa-rate without expressing their unfeigned regret that the answer does not afford any reasonable hope, that the wishes of the People, re-garding Trial by Jury, will be carried into full effect by the Local Government ; nor does it afford the information it was anticipated the Local Government would have afforded upon the subject. Con-sidering the answer totally unsatisfactory, they therefore appeal to the People, and call upon them to meet again upon this subject, in which their dearest rights are involved, and do most earnestly recommend that a Public Meeting should be held to make applica-tion to the British Parliament for that redress, which circumstances may require.

Anthony Fenn Kemp	F. Bryant
William Gellibrand	W. Broadribb, sen.
David Lord	G. Stokell
Sholto Douglas	W. M. Orr
Henry Hopkins	W. Kimberly
Thos. Young	Thos. Horne
Robert Kerr	John Jackson
William Hemsley	Askin Morrison
Thos. Hewitt	H. Melville
R. Lewis	John Robertson
John Eddington	D. Barclay
J. Lester	C. Franks
Wm. Bunster	J. G. Briggs
G. Robertson	Hugh Murray
George Cartwright	W. Watchorn
E. Hodgson	H. J. Lloyd

forwarded by Mr. Gellibrand, junior, to the Lieutenant
Governor, who, through the Colonial Secretary, sent
an answer on the following day.*   The answer to
this document being still more extraordinary, the Deputation was called together, and after patiently and calmly
hearing the letter, drew up a second report.†   Public

M. Steele	James Thomson
A. Murray	J. T. Gellibrand
John Dunn	

Members of the Deputation, appointed at the Public Meeting, to
accompany the Sheriff on the presentation of the Address.

* *Government House,* 21*st July,* 1834.

GENTLEMEN—On the occasion of an Address on the Jury Question, being presented to me, during the last month, I gave my assurance, that I should not fail to keep in view the sentiments which
had been expressed, by so numerous and so respectable a Meeting.

Had I not then felt it prudent to avoid exciting expectations, the
fulfilment of which might possibly be delayed, I might then have
added, that it was probable a bill, for the extension of Trial by
Jury, in certain cases, would, at an early day, be brought under
the consideration of the Legislative Council—a measure which
might, indeed, have been anticipated by the public, from my Address to that body at its last Meeting ; and, but for my sincere desire not to provoke further discussion, I might, also, have vindicated
the Attorney General from misrepresentation, by affirming that the
scope of that Officer's report to the Government (in reference to
which the Public Meeting had been convened) had been altogether
misunderstood.

Dissenting, as I do, from the opinion which has recently been
disseminated, that there have been circumstances to justify the alarm
which you have entertained at the continued exercise by the Judges
of the Supreme Court, of the power vested in them by the Imperial
Parliament of awarding or refusing Trial by Jury, as the justice of
the case may seem to require—a power which is still possessed by
the Judges of the province, to the laws of which you have drawn
my attention.   I cannot refrain from expressing my concern, that
the Jury Question should have been again brought forward, before
there had been time to develope the further determination of the
Government.   GEORGE ARTHUR.

To the Gentlemen composing the Deputation
    from the Public Meeting.

† *The undersigned, Members of the Deputation, appointed on the 14th
instant, having re-assembled for the purpose of taking into consideration the letter of the Colonial Secretary, of the 23rd, and addressed
to J. T. Gellibrand, Esq., deem it necessary to record thereon.*

The Deputation most perfectly concur in opinion with His Excel-

opinion, in this instance, gained the victory, and shortly
after, a draft of a Jury Act appeared: this Act resembles but little the Jury laws of Great Britain—in some
instances, it is more adapted to the exigency of the Co-

---

lency " that the Jury question is a subject vitally involving the
interests of every class of the community," and " that it is incum-
bent on all parties interested, to consider well before any measure is
recommended on the one hand, or adopted on the other," and also
" that it is not to be anticipated, that the wishes of the respectable
individuals, who advocate the extension of the Jury Laws, will be
opposed, when such an alternative can be avoided, consistently with
the preservation of the just rights of the Crown, and the peace, welfare, and prosperity of the Colony," and whilst the Deputation concur in these sentiments, they nevertheless feel themselves bound to
express to His Excellency, their regret, that it was impossible for them
to allude to any portion of the answer to the address, as satisfactory to
themselves, or the community at large.

If the question vitally involves " the interests of every class of
the community," it is but natural that the community should feel an
intense interest in the question; that they should be solicitous to
know how, and in what manner, and by what means, their interests
are to be affected ; and above all, that they should have ample opportunity of considering the measure, and of expressing their opinion fully thereupon, before the same is resolved upon by the Executive Government.

The Deputation feel themselves bound to express their unfeigned
regret, that any report upon a subject " vitally involving their interests," should have been ordered or acted upon, without the parties
interested having any voice in the question, or opportunity of expressing their sentiments thereupon ; and although it now appears the measure is so far in progress, as to enable the Government shortly to
announce to the public an abstract of the bill, which is to introduce
Trial by Jury, " in some cases," yet that His Excellency has
not been pleased to afford any detailed information thereupon.

The Deputation express their anxious desire, at all times, to afford
their cordial support, and feel full conviction, that all the free inhabitants of this Colony will at all times support the Local Government, when it can be done with a proper regard to the rights and
privileges of the people.

His Excellency will find, upon reference to the Address,
that the case of the extension of the Jury Laws to New South
Wales, is adverted to, only as an argument, to establish the authority for the extension of the Jury Laws, and it is not even assumed, that full Trial by Jury obtains, as in Great Britain; but the
main objection, pointed at in the Address, is to the Chief Justice
being a Member of the Executive Council, and afterwards sitting in
the character of a Juryman, upon cases previously decided upon by

lony; but in others, it is lamentably deficient, depriving the subject of liberty of fair decision by his peers. The most objectionable part is that which allows Government clerks to act as esquires, or especial Jurymen. In a large community, this is of but trifling importance. but in a small one like ours, it tends to abridge the boasted liberty of Trial by Jury.

Two other Public Meetings took place; one praying for a Legislative Assembly, the other respecting the restriction of grants. The reader has already been informed of the capability of the Colony to govern itself, or in fact, *the absolute necessity of allowing the Colonists some voice in the Representation of the Government:* and as to the land question, it has also been fully discussed.

The Legislative Council was this year most actively employed in framing new laws, and passed nearly a couple of dozen. Among the most conspicuous, was the Abolition of Capital Punishment Act, which indeed, merely adopted the merciful laws now enforced in the Mother Country, " with the exception, that the laws of England decide that death shall not be the penalty for cattle and sheep stealing, whereas the Legislature of Van Diemen's

---

him, in his character as Member of that Council; and the Deputation desire to impress the marked distinction, that in New South Wales, the Chief Justice was removed from the Executive Council. at his own particular request, because that officer considered the office incompatible with his duties as Judge.

The Deputation are compelled to notice the observation made by His Excellency, in his answer to the Address, that " His Excellency might, on a former occasion, have vindicated the Attorney General from misrepresentation," and to state that, until they were informed by His Excellency, in his answer to the address of the 14th instant, that the Attorney General had made a report upon the Jury Question, the Public were in ignorance that any report on the subject had been made, and, consequently, they could not be open to the imputation of having misrepresented that officer.

With respect to that part of His Excellency's letter, which treats of the qualifications of persons—the Deputation feel it their duty to represent to His Excellency, that they cannot, in any way, admit the necessity of adverting to any distinction between the free inhabitants of the Colony, inasmuch as no such distinction does, or ought to exist, to the prejudice of any portion of society.

Land, has decided that death shall be the punishment for such offences." Thus has the Council set aside a British Act of Parliament. Although such a clause was permitted to be enrolled in the Van Diemen's Land Statute Book, not a single protest against such *anti*-British law, was heard of—true, no execution has taken place, in accordance with this truly Colonial law. The Jury Act was also passed, as also the Post Office Act, and others much objected to, by the generality of the community. The Post Office Act was particularly obnoxious, enforcing as it does, a heavy tax upon knowledge, (on newspapers) which is quite unnecessary and uncalled for, in a community composed of twenty-five thousand souls, who already pay upwards of one hundred thousand pounds a year, to support the Colonial Government.

The case of Mr. Lewis has already been referred to; after this gentleman had been incarcerated in jail some six months, a respectable memorial was drawn out, praying His Excellency, " that without any reference to the proceedings on the trial, the sentence pronounced on Mr. Lewis, was one of such unprecedented severity for the offence of which he was convicted, that the memorialists with confidence, respectfully solicited that His Excellency, as an act of justice, would in the exercise of the royal prerogative, order the discharge of Mr. Lewis from prison."* This memorial was signed by nearly two hundred people. It was presented to the Governor, by four of the most influential of the Colonists, and his Excellency's verbal answer to the prayer, was, that " If every man in the Island were to sign the Address, in favour of Mr. Lewis, and my Government were dependent upon it, I would not release him, unless he asked for it."† Suffice that after a voluminous correspondence between Mr. Lewis and the Governor: the former gentleman forwarded his case to the Secretary of State, and neither party exactly compromising, Mr. Lewis was released from jail.

The Colonists complained loudly of the manner in

* The Address to his Excellency.
† Colonel Arthur's own expression.

which the Government had deceived them, with regard
to the supply of wheat in the Island.   In the early part
of the year, the price of that article fluctuated from
about six to eight shillings the bushel. The harvest being
gathered, it was the opinion of many that there was but
a very short crop. The price being yet moderate, and
the Government not requiring any wheat for the stores,
very large shipments were made to New South Wales,
from Launceston and Hobart Town, and some small
quantity was also sent to England.   In the course of a
few months, the real state of the stock became more apparent, and wheat advanced to thirteen shillings the bushel,
when a Commissariat notice* appeared, calling for tenders to supply 5,000 bushels : in consequence of this
advertisement, the price immediately rose to fifteen. The
exportations ceased, and the Colonists became apprehen-
sive that they would be without bread, before the next
harvest.   Some wheat arriving from Calcutta, reduced
the price several shillings, when another Government order was issued, stating that there was a sufficient quantity in the stores to supply the probable wants of the
Government, and also a sufficient quantity in the Colony
to supply the community till next harvest.†   From such

---

* *Commissariat Office, Hobart Town, June* 19, 1834.
    WHEAT.—Required *to complete the supply of* His Majesty's Ma-
gazines, *for the service of the current year*, about 5,000 bushels of
Wheat, of which quantity about 1,000 bushels will be required at
Launceston, and the remainder at Hobart Town.
    Tenders to furnish the same, at so much per 100 pounds, will be
received at the Commissariat Offices at Hobart Town and Launceston respectively, until Monday the 30th instant.
                                    A MOODIE, *A. C. G.*
            † GOVERNMENT NOTICE.
            Colonial Secretary's Office, July 23, 1834.
    The Lieutenant Governor directs it to be notified, that it appears
from reports which have been received, *that there is a sufficient
quantity of Wheat in the Commissariat Store, to supply the probable
wants of the Government ; and, in the Colony, to meet those of the
community generally, until next harvest.*
    The present high price appears, therefore, to be the effect rather
of misapprehension than of any real deficiency ; nevertheless, His
Excellency has acquiesced in settlers and others supplying their

a publication, many of the Colonists naturally believed that the Government had taken the opinion of the best informed on the subject, and fully relying upon the official notification, the price fell considerably, and trifling shipments were made from Launceston to Sydney. Shortly after the appearance of this notification, another was published, stating, that " a board having reported a fall in the price of flour had taken place," the Goverment rescinded a portion of the Government notice, which had allowed convicts under punishment to have a portion of other food, in lieu of wheaten flour.*   Fortunately, some of the Hobart Town merchants did not place implicit confidence on the official notifications, and these gentlemen sent up orders to their agents in New South Wales, to send down flour or wheat, at any cost whatever; and it is a fact that the very wheat which had been shipped from Launceston to Sydney, and there sold at 9s. to 10s. the bushel, was returned to Hobart Town in flour, and sold to the public at upwards of forty pounds the ton. The Government, at the end of the year, appeared in the market, and purchased eagerly, at whatever price the provident merchants thought proper to ask, buying one lot of very inferior flour, impregnated with the flavour of coal tar, as high as £42 the ton.   At the close of the year, the nominal price of wheat was 20s.' the bushel;

---

assigned servants, in lieu of not more than a third of their weekly ration of flour, with an equal weight of rice or oatmeal; and also, in the deduction of 2¾ lbs. of flour from the weekly allowance now issued to each convict in the road parties, for which 1½ lbs. of sugar will be substituted.

By His Excellency's command,

J. BURNETT.

* GOVERNMENT NOTICE.

Colonial Secretary's Office, Aug. 7, 1834.

A Board having reported that a fall in the price of flour has taken place, the Lieutenant Governor has been pleased to rescind such portion of the Government Notice, No. 213, of the 23d ult., as applies to the issue of one and a half pounds of sugar, in lieu of two and three quarter pounds of flour per week, to convicts under punishment in road parties.

By His Excellency's Command,

J. BURNETT.

but none to be had; indeed, had the people depended upon the official notifications, they would have been without bread. The Colonists complained loudly of the manner in which they had been deceived; nor did their complaints tend in any way to relieve them, for the Government sent orders to Sydney, to have a supply sent from thence, as soon as the new crop came in. For this purpose, the Commissariat Officer at Sydney, advertised for tenders; his first advertisement was unavailable, but his second* notification obtained one tender, and a large quantity of Sydney wheat, at a high price, arrived for the stores, at the very time the Van Diemen's Land new crop was coming to market, at a low price. The ignorance manifested by those whose duty it was to be better informed, was highly injurious to the settlement, making the sister Colony drain from us a large sum of money, in the way of profit, upon our own produce. It is to be hoped, that this lesson will serve as a warning for future years, and that the stores will be thrown open for a large stock, whenever the price of wheat may be at a fair average. Whilst on this subject, it may be as well to offer a few words on the situation, in which the farmers are placed, with regard to the Americans —their competitors in the Hobart Town market. During the year 1834, the Americans visited these Colonies, with a view of forming houses of agency, and to their surprise, found that wheat and flour were so much

---

* WHEAT FOR VAN DIEMEN'S LAND.

NOTICE is hereby given, that renewed Tenders will be received at this Office, until 12 o'clock on Wednesday, the 10th instant, from persons willing to supply Six Thousand Bushels of Wheat, of the new crop, for the public service at Van Diemen's Land.

The Wheat is to be delivered, free from all expense to Government, at Hobart Town; Fifteen Hundred Bushels on or before the 10th January next, and the remainder by the 31st of the same month; it must be of good quality and condition, and weigh not less than fifty-eight pounds per bushel. The payment to be made by the Commissariat Officer in charge at Hobart Town, in the same manner that Commissariat Supplies are usually paid for at that station.

JAMES LAIDLEY, Dep. Com. Gen.

Commissariat Office, Sydney, Dec. 3, 1834.

higher in price, than they were in America, that supplies
would always yield a considerable profit. In Great Britain,
the wisdom of past ages has decided that it is necessary
that a protec ing duty should be imposed, so that the
foreigner should not be allowed to ruin the agriculturist,
by inundating the country with cheap grown bread—
here, however, there is no protection, and the celebrated reciprocity law prevents the Colonists from protecting their agricultural interests.   It is generally understood, that wheat at five shillings the bushel, will not
pay the grower, taking one year with the other.   It is
true, that if there were good roads, or indeed any means
of conveyance, Van Diemen's Land, like America, could
sell as cheap all kinds of provisions : but as the Colony
is so deficient in roads, &c., no farmer can afford to send
his wheat for thirty miles to market, and sell it at 5s.
the bushel.   But, by way of argument, suppose that the
farmer could so produce wheat, and bring it to Hobart
Town even at that price, he could not compete with the
American—the latter would undersell him very considerably.   In most of the American ports, the best flour is
only equal to about sixteen to eighteen shillings the barrel, and the American, if he can afford to sell the barrel
in bond in London, at 20s., can afford to sell it here at
a guinea.   Reckoning that it would take four bushels
and a half of Van Diemen's Land wheat to make a quantity of flour equal to an American barrel, it will be seen
that at 5s. the American would have the advantage, and
could undersell the farmers in this Colony.   If however,
a scanty harvest should follow, the Americans could, and
no doubt would, pour in such supplies of flour and wheat,
that the ruin of the farmers must be certain. One of the
Colonial Journals recommended a currency, as a means
whereby foreign goods might be individually taxed, and
the farmer and Colonial manufacturer protected—the
writer supposing that the high rate of exchange, at
which currency would purchase remittable money, would
be at once a protection and a duty !
    Another Government vessel was captured by convicts

A fine new vessel, the *Frederick*, was piratically siezed and carried off from Macquarie Harbour, by ten men, when the place was on the point of being finally abandoned; the whole of the prisoners having been removed to Port Arthur. Neither the vessel nor the pirates have ever been discovered.

The Union Club was this year established, consisting of a number of the most influential gentlemen in the Colony, and partaking in a degree, of the same stamp, as those similar Institutions, so celebrated in the British capital. Its establishment has been highly advantageous, and has served to engender union, and amalgamate interests, by attracting together individuals, who formerly were supposed to move in different spheres.

The present year, 1835, has presented to the Colonists but one continued series of troubles and misfortunes; nothing but Public Meetings, complaining of grievances, and unprecedented distress of every kind—altogether confirming the approach of the often prophesied "crisis." One of the first important public measures was the Meeting of a large body of Colonists, at the Court House, assembled there for the purpose of petitioning His Majesty to remove the degradation and other unspeakable evils, arising from the settlement being of a penal nature. The requisition,* calling the Meeting, was most numerously signed, by the respectable portion of society. Such an attempted blow at the system, which had become obnoxious to the Colonists, was of course, parried by those in authority; but it will be here necessary to offer a few observations, as regards the objects this Meeting had in view. The free population of Van Diemen's Land, in all amounts to about 25,000,

* "We, the undersigned, feeling that the measures adopted by the British Government, of encreasing the penal character of the Colony, by making *the Colonists materials for the punishment of British offenders*, affix a moral degradation upon us, and our children, in the face of the Act of Parliament, which holds out the prospect of restoring to us free institutions—the privileges of our birthright—request you will convene a Public Meeting of the Colonists, for the purpose of addressing the King thereon."—*Signed by the Inhabitants.*

whilst the prisoners are in number, (including the penal settlement, &c.) about 12,000. It has long been manifest, to use Colonel Arthur's own words, that the Colonists have only been considered as *materials for prison discipline*, and finding that nothing but certain ruin to themselves, and their adopted country, must follow the enforcement of such a system, they were determined to strike a blow at the very root of the tree. It has of late become apparent, that there are no benefits arising from the prisoner population. The immense sums levied in the Colony, for the support of a Government, almost entirely occupied with prison discipline, has divided society into two classes, which are not likely ever to agree. There are the Colonists, the industrious and wealthy merchants and settlers—and there are the Government officers. The latter form the aristocracy of the place, and treat with haughtiness, any of a different grade to themselves. At the same time the Colonists are taxed upwards of one hundred thousand a year, the British Government is required to expend nearly double that sum, for the maintenance of certain portions of the prisoner population, and their task masters. It must be evident that a mere tithe of the present Colonial expenditure would suffice to defray the charge of a fitting and proper Government for twenty-five thousand souls: and the Colonists complain, and not without reason, that they are ground down to support the prison discipline of the Mother Country. In addition to being thus compelled to pay for the maintenance of an unwieldy and ill adapted Government, the Colonists discovered that their very bread was taken from their mouths, to feed the British convict, and during the time that one half the free inhabitants of the Colony seldom tasted bread, the assigned servants and convicts in Government works, were luxuriating on their full rations of wheaten flour. The Colonists also, found from the passing of the obnoxious impounding law, that they would shortly be without meat; and had not there been regular weekly importations of live cattle and sheep from Two Fold Bay—salt provisions

2 B

from Ireland, England, America, and New South Wales, the people of Hobart Town would have been in a starving condition. The Colonists, witnessing the distress, and fearing that the Home Government would pour in upon the almost ruined and half starved settlement, more convicts, more mouths, thought it advisable to petition the Home Government, that transports should be no longer sent, or if sent, under a very different arrangement to that which now exists. Those in authority, those living on the vitals of the Colony, and their dependants, are naturally opposed to the Island being relieved from being a Penal Settlement,—because, should such an event occur, many of the salary men must take to the plough ; for the hundred thousand a year levied upon the free Colonists, and divided among a regiment of Government Officers, would be reduced to one fourth of that sum. To any one, that will take the trouble to fairly discuss the subject, it must be apparent that the population of this Colony is too numerous, considering it in its agricultural state. The whole Colony would, years since, have become bankrupt, had it not been for the valuable exports of wool and oil—the Commisariat expenditure—and the increase of capital, by means of fresh emigrants ; but of late the imports have so far exceeded the exports and our income, that a stagnation in pecuniary affairs is now being felt, and hence it is that the lamentable sight is to be witnessed of every other shop in the town being closed, and almost every man that is met in the street, (except Government Officers) being in an almost destitute state. When this Colony produced food sufficient for the Colonists and the prisoner population, *then* indeed, was it prospering, and when the stimulus of *giving* land was held out, and fresh settlers daily arrived, with capital, then indeed, was a foundation laid, perhaps for a mighty empire; but the importation of foreign capital, the pernicious effects of usury, and the Impounding Law, and the vast encrease of pauper and prisoner population, turned the tables. More than the whole of the Commissariat expenditure goes to pay the foreigner for food, for the free and the bond, and the check given to emigration by *selling* land, has left the Colonists with a heavy debt, both to the foreign merchant and the foreign usurer! It is not the intention of the writer to offer one word on the system called Prison Discipline, of which the Home Government and the people of Great Britain are wholly ignorant. The writer may however observe, that he has seen it suggested that it would be more advantageous for both the Colony and the Home Government, to come to a better understanding; by the latter paying a certain fixed price on the landing of each convict. Were the Home Government to do this, and grant the Colonists a Legislative Assembly of its own, there would yet be a chance of success, but to go on as the Colonists have done, for the last few years, is an impossibility.   The system is founded in error, and its continuance will destroy a Colony, which ought to be one of the most thriving of any possessing the British flag.

On the occasion of the Public Meeting, several of the speakers proposed measures so incompatible with the views of the Home Government, that the English reader would be inclined to imagine that transportation was no punishment, but merely banishment; suffice however, that an address was drawn out to His Majesty, praying that the Colony might be relieved from the degradation of being a Penal Settlement.*

To the King's Most Excellent Majesty.

MOST GRACIOUS SOVEREIGN.—We, your Majesty's faithful subjects, the free inhabitants of Van Diemen's Land, in Public Meeting, duly convened by the Sheriff assembled, beg permission to approach your Majesty with every assurance of our loyalty and devotion.

We most respectfully submit to your Majesty, that a very great proportion of your Majesty's subjects, of those who emigrated from their native land, to encounter the difficulties and deprivations necessarily attendant upon their becoming the occupants of a new country, were induced so to do, in the hope and belief, that however necessary the penal character of the Colony might have been to its original formation, yet, that as this Colony increased in independence and importance, that character would have been progressively modified, in order to to its final extinction; instead of which,

Another subject, which created very considerable dis-satisfaction, was the perseverance with which the Government acted, in regard to the enforcing the Impounding Law. It has already been noticed, how exceedingly injurious this Act has been to the Colony; but it was left till the present year to shew the evil effects arising therefrom, in their most glaring light. After nearly the whole of the large herds in the Island, were sold by their proprietors, in consequence of their owners being obliged to keep them from straying on Government land, it was discovered that extensive herds were yet to be found, in what was called the new country—a portion of the Island situated some twenty or thirty miles from the nearest adjacent settler The chief claimant of these cattle was the agent of Sir John Owen, that proprietor, having in former years, had numbers of cattle in that neighbourhood, which had no doubt increased rapidly, no one disturbing them. Other land owners had also stock

your Petitioners humbly submit to your Majesty, that it has lately increased, and is increasing to a fearful extent, thereby violating the feelings of the adult, and barbarizing the habits, and demoralizing the principles of the rising generation, and tending effectually to check future emigration ; and this, while a revenue of one hundred thousand pounds sterling per annum is being drawn from your Majesty's faithful subjects, and the external and internal relations of the Colony being of daily increasing extent and importance, prove to demonstration that the Colonists are fully and fairly entitled to have the land of their adoption placed in its appropriate station amongst your Majesty's free Colonies.

Your Petitioners humbly submit to your Majesty, that while they gratefully acknowledge the restoration to them of that valuable portion of their civil rights—Trial by Jury, yet they consider their dearest interests involved in the reproach that at present attaches to them, that they are the occupants of a large prison, and the materials for the punishment of British offenders—inasmuch, as that thereby, they are effectually deprived of their natural inheritance—the civil institutions of their native land.

Your Majesty's humble Petitioners most respectfully pray of your Majesty, to be pleased in your paternal goodness, to remove from the Colony of Van Diemen's Land, the degradation and other unspeakable evils, to which it is subjected in consequence of its present penal character.

And your Petitioners as in duty bound, will ever pray.

running wild at the same place, but in much smaller
numbers, The Lieutenant Governor was pleased to order a poundkeeper to be appointed at this place, and the
father of the poundkeeper employed himself in collecting
herds, whilst the son sold them to the only bidder present, viz., his father. The Colonists complained loudly of
this disgraceful proceeding, but no notice was taken, and
at the time of the completion of these pages, the poundkeeper demands a considerable sum of the Government,
for his services ; the price at which the cattle sold, approaching to nothing like the amount the Impounding
Law allowed as fees and charges. Why the Government,
and more especially the Lieutenant Governor, insisted on
the destruction of the wild herds, after the certain injury
arising therefrom became evident, must be a secret, but
their destruction, and the effects of the Impounding Law
generally, have made the Colonists importers, instead of
exporters of food.

The Colonists, also held a Public Meeting, for the
purpose of framing an address,* praying the Government

* We, the inhabitants of Hobart Town, beg leave, in Public
Meeting assembled, duly convened by the Sheriff of Van Diemen's
Land, to represent to Your Excellency, that the inhabitants of Hobart Town, are totally dependant upon the Hobart Town Creek, for
the supply of water, and they therefore consider it to be the bounden
duty of the Local Government, to take effective measures to preserve
a constant and sufficient supply of that necessary of life, for the preservation of the health and properties of the inhabitants, and especially of the poor.

An aqueduct having been made at the public expense fully capable of supplying the wants of the public, if properly directed, we
cannot refrain from expressing our astonishment and regret, that the
water supplied by this aqueduct has been most wantonly wasted, and
misapplied, by its being perverted, from its avowed original intention
of the Government—viz. the benefit of the public, the same having
been appropriated chiefly by a few Government Officers.

We have reason to believe, that the Government has been supplied,
at the public expense, for a length of time, with iron pipes, sufficient
to convey the water through the principal streets, but hitherto, a very
small quantity have been used for a public purpose, and some have
been used for the benefit of private individuals, and a considerable
portion has lately been lent by Government to an individual, to convey water to his own mill.

to supply the town with pure water. Nearly in the centre of Hobart Town runs a creek, formed by nature, to
take the drainings of the hills, and, consequently, as the
population increased, this creek became nothing more
than a common sewer, for which purpose it is used.
During the summer months, it can scarcely be termed a
rivulet, frequently not running more than three or four
gallons in the course of a minute. Ten years ago, the
Government had been petitioned that a better supply
should be given, which might be done at a mere trifling
expense. Year after year similar demands were made,
and an aqueduct was talked of and at last constructed ;
but the supply obtained therefrom is trifling, and conducts
the water to a very small portion of the town, where the
greater part of the Government officers reside; and after
doing this, the aqueduct turns from the town, and conducts the surplus water alongside and through the celebrated Cottage Green estate, the property of Colonel Arthur.
Thus summer after summer does the most lamentable
sickness prevail in Hobart Town, and mainly owing to
the impurity of the water, that nine tenths of the inhabitants are compelled to drink.

The editor and proprietor of the *Colonist* became ob-

Your Excellency cannot but recollect, the great misery and disease, which prevailed among the poorer inhabitants of Hobart Town,
during the last summer, in consequence of the putrid state of the
water in the Hobart Town Creek, which they were compelled to
drink, in consequence of the waste and misapplication of the water
in the aqueduct, and that this evil became a general subject of complaint at the time.

The inhabitants were induced to hope, that the Local Government
would long since have adopted means, to prevent a repetition of this
evil ; and we therefore, feel ourselves bound to express, in the
strongest terms, our surprise and regret, that the inhabitants should
still be exposed to this alarming evil, and from which they are now
suffering, without the Government having adopted any measures to
prevent its recurrence.

We therefore, humbly pray, that Your Excellency will be pleased
to cause such measures to be immediately adopted, as will insure a
sufficient supply of water to the town, by the aqueduct, and that the
aqueduct be applied to the purposes for which it was originally intended.

noxious to the ruling powers—that journal had been, ever since its establishment, conducted with a spirit too violent for a Government constituted as is that of this Colony.   It is not intended to uphold the conductor of that journal, in publishing the articles which juries of the Colonists deemed libellous, nor need reference be made to the full particulars of the numerous trials.   The present editor, Mr. Gilbert Robertson, about twelve months since, published, from information he had received, that the Lieutenant Governor had, after enrollment, made an alteration of a clerical error, in a grant, of a Launceston allotment to Mr. R. O'Connor.   The publication of this statement, connected as it was, with certain allusions, was constructed to mean that the writer charged the Governor with forgery.   The prosecution was, of course, criminal, and being found guilty of the libel, Mr. Robertson was sentenced to *four months imprisonment*, and a fine of sixty pounds.   The second prosecution against Mr. Robertson, was also on the part of His Excellency, for a libel, Mr. G. Robertson having accused His Excellency in no very delicate manner, of having appropriated Government hay to his own private use and benefit, which appropriation he indirectly made out to be a felony.   In this instance, Mr. Robertson had incautiously believed statements which it was impossible for him to prove.   The Jury found him guilty of the libel, and the Court sentenced him to *eight* months imprisonment, and a fine of one hundred and twenty pounds. The third prosecution against the same editor, was on the part of an attorney, Mr. T. W. Rowlands, whom it was proved Mr. Robertson had libelled in his character of an attorney of the Supreme Court.   For this offence he was sentenced to one month imprisonment and a fine of twenty pounds.   Nor did the prosecutions against the *Colonist*, or rather its editor, end here; for shortly afterwards Captain Montagu, the nephew of Colonel Arthur, proceeded against Mr. Robertson for another alledged libel! These proceedings were instituted when Mr. Robertson was incarcerated in jail, uuder the first sentence of the

Court.* From certain intelligence received by Mr. Robertson, he had thought proper to accuse Captain Montagu of having built his splendid mansion of Government materials, and that in order to shelter him from the reach of the law, he had obtained an anti-dated letter of license so to do, from his uncle Colonel Arthur. It is to be regretted, that Captain Montagu did not proceed by civil action against the editor of the *Colonist*, for some people were ungenerous enough to say, that so many criminal prosecutions savoured of persecution; and this impression was heightened by the known fact, that the defendant was incarcerated in jail, without any legal advisor, and severed from a large family of grown up daughters. The case came on for trial before Mr. Justice Montagu and a Military Jury, the witnesses in no way proved the truth of the accusations he had unguardedly made, and a verdict was returned of guilty, and for this offence Mr. Robertson received a sentence of *twelve* months imprisonment, and a fine of fifty pounds. The address from the Bench, when the verdict was passed, excited very

---

* " The Editor, suffering incarceration for such libel, is on the ' felons' side ;' he has received, we suppose, more than usual courtesy, for he is allowed to associate with the soldiery, *and* the tried, *and* the twice and thrice convicted felons—happy man, to have such indulgence from a prison discipline Government! This Editor's sitting-room and bed-room are one and the same—it is a lobby, immediately over the gaol guard-room, and has the open staircase leading into it ; its only comfort consists in two glazed iron-barred windows. It has no fire-place, but there is an iron wring fastened into the wall, to which *desperate characters* are, we understand, sometimes chained—we wonder he was not chained there as such! Entrances, from this lobby, lead to—the free women's *coop or den*— the large cell of the twice and thrice convicted felons—the cell or room of the free incarcerated, for non-payment of fines to the King; one door from this lobby leads to the condemned cell, *and*, before the windows, stands the gallows. Such is the abode of a man guilty of libelling in Van Diemen's Land. Whether what he published were truth or otherwise, matters not ; he had published a libel, and had been guilty, according to a criminal prosecution, of having so published it ! What will the upholders of virtue in the Mother Country think of such a punishment for such an offence ?"— *Colonial Times.*

considerable surprise on the part of the thinking portion
of the community.*

* His Honor then proceeded to address Mr. Robertson :—He did
not believe one word of the affidavits ; it gave him much pain to
pass a sentence upon any one, much more upon any one whom he
had known for many years—for more than seven years. He had
known the time when he had seen his talents (which were by no
means common) employed in a very different manner, and he believed, from what he had known of Mr. Robertson, that these were
not the sentiments of his heart, and that, had he followed the dictates and impulses of his own feelings, he never would have acted so
bad—e-pecially towards a person, to whom, he himself had owned,
he had no personal ill-feeling. "No, Mr. Robertson," said His
Honor, " I consider you are the *tool* of a miserable party of agitated
disturbers, by whose directions you have been acting, and sorry am
I to see you prostrating your intellects in so debased, detestable, and
abominable a service. I once knew you to be a respectable member
of society ; but now your writings, or publications—for I do not believe you to be the writer of these articles—are a pest even to Botany
Bay. The crime of which you have been guilty, I consider, in
every respect, to be worse even than those for which I have just sentenced men to transportation. I have no doubt, Mr. Robertson,
but that you are goaded on by these agitators, who are disaffected to
the Government, and that, when they have got you to jump into
the gulf, as the Attorney General expressed himself, (and very properly so) they will, one and all of them, leave you in the lurch,
and not one of them render you any assistance to get you out. You,
Mr. Robertson, I do not consider to be the main spring in these extraordinary proceedings, and sorry I am to see you so forget yourself. The licentious and degraded state of the Press is one of the
worst features in this Colony. It is, I think, impossible, even to
conceive any publication more infamous—more monstrous—more
atrocious, than the libel which you have published upon Captain
Montagu. Good God! in England, what would be thought of a
man, who would openly come forward, and charge the Governor
of a Colony, or the Secretary of State, with a felony ? But is the
society of this Colony so degraded—so depraved—so entirely devoid
of all moral and spiritual feeling, that such abominable publications
are to be tolerated ? The Press—call you this the Press!" (said His
Honor, with indescribable expression in his countenance.) He then
continued—" I doubt not, that many who hear me, will consider
that this is not the language of a good and upright Judge, but that
of a tyrannical and overbearing oppressor, who wished to put down
the Press. I care not what they think, nor what they say—nor
what they may write ; no one could have written such articles with,
out being influenced by the most diabolical motives—for who can-
for one moment, suppose, that either the Governor or Captain Mon-

2 c

The Colonists not only were of themselves, but it appeared also as if the Colony was doomed to be unfortunate.

tagu, could be guilty of such atrocious crimes, as are there charged against them. No one *could* suppose, because there may have been some irregularity on the part of some of the Government overseers, that he was justified in making such assertions as have been adverted to ; and it is clear, that any person who would do so, his object must be to create excitement, and disturb the public peace and tranquality ; and the offence is much aggravated by your coming here, and endeavouring to make it appear that your conduct is that of a good patriot, and your motives praiseworthy—no, I know too well what a good patriot *is*. You never knew a good patriot yet appear in such scenes as this ; his object is to support the Government under which he lives—to promote peace and concord amongst his fellow Colonists or citizens, and *not* to come forward and charge a gentleman with felony, on the mere evidence of seeing a Government overseer at work upon his premises. I say, *not* upon such testimony as this, and *this alone*, to compare such a man as Captain Montagu to those who have been transported for their crime. No, Sir, a good man is very cautious how he publicly asserts anything that may be detrimental to the character or reputation of any man, much more of a man of high standing in life—*he* will act from love, and not from hate ; but you have acted, in my opinion, from the *most inveterate hate*—such hate, as is diabolical, devilish, and wicked in the extreme. instead of love ; and still you had the audacity to come here and state that you were actuated by good and virtuous motives. You have likewise throught proper to throw out your satyrical *cant* concerning the Military Jury ; as if seven gentlemen, because they were military men, had not sense enough to see through the motives of such an attack. I must say, I perfectly coincide with their verdict, and am astonished that you should still persist (as by your affidavits you have done) that your conduct has been that of a zealous patriot, instead of a most malicious demagogue. I would hope, Mr. Robertson, that you are not a wicked man ; but I fear you are a man acting from bad principles—you are a man disaffected to the Government. I happen to know you have had your assigned servants taken from you, and from that time I believe you have become the tool of a Faction. I have heard it said, that I as a Judge, am not fit to pass sentence, because I know the persons upon whom I pass such sentence; but I care not what 10,000 impertinent critics say of me. I have a duty to perform between the public and the Crown, whose servant I am, and that duty I will perform without fear of being entrammelled by the *Press*—this Colony is too much *press ridden*, and I wish all good men—I wish the Clergy—I wish all Christians of all denominations would come forward and oppose it— for my part, I denounce the Press, or the licentiousness of it, altogether. A free an independent Press is what I would support to

Three large British vessels, all bound for Hobart Town,
were wrecked on the coast in the course of a few months,

the utmost of my ability. The Press is a tool of immense power,
and in the hands of good men, one of the greatest blessings--and I
must again repeat, *that* conducted by you (as other licentious portions of it in this Colony) speak worse for it than any thing I know
of. Any sentence the Court may pass upon you can be no reparation to Captain Montagu ; you in your defence stated, that you had
not said half enough, and for my part, I believe all you have said
to be false as *Hell*, and I believe you knew it to be so when you
published it. You have stated in your affidavits, that if you could
have had opportunity to lay your affidavits before the Court when
the rule was applied for, to file the information, that you believe the
Court would not have granted the rule. As far as I am concerned,
I assert, that if the whole of the circumstances that have appeared
on evidence had been laid before the Court, I should not have hesi-
tated one moment in granting the rule. Your conduct towards the
Court from beginning to end, has been calculated to confirm the
impression that you have been acting from some malicious advice ;
you were advised not to come into Court—you were advised not to
return to gaol again voluntarily, but to suffer yourself to be dragged
back. You are not of yourself lawyer enough to know all this without having some ill-advisers to direct you, and after all this, I consider your actions anything but those of a good man. A good man
would at any rate treat the Government and a Court of Justice with
common respect, this is done even in the most uncivilized parts—
even in Turkey. I remember the time when I have admired your
promptitude in the discharge of your duties, but you have forgotten
yourself, and for some time past your conduct has been one continued scene of malice of the very worst description, malice towards
the Government—malice towards its officers—malice towards justice
—malice towards me as its minister. For myself, I can only say, I
perfectly forgive you, Mr. Robertson, as far as I am concerned, and
I lay it more to the charge of those, who, you have been fool
enough to become the tool of. But I expect what I have said will
be treated as a mere nothing, and that when you return to your confinement, you will turn it into ridicule, and make it the subject of
another article of abuse. However, I have the consolation of knowing that I have done my duty to the community. I feel a difficulty
in deciding what sentence to pass upon you, but I shall not mitigate
it in the least, because you complain you have been tried for it before. I feel convinced that those affidavits were got up, merely for
the purpose of creating new excitement, and I hope the writer, be
he whom he may, will pay the fine I shall inflict upon you. If you
have no property, and I am given to understand you have not, you
must from your proceedings be almost reckless of what becomes of
you. Many may wonder why I speak thus to you, but they do not

in the immediate vicinity of the Derwent. The first was
the *George the Third* prison ship,* which vessel struck on a

---

know perhaps so much of you as I do ; but I fear what I say will be
lost upon you. I expect to be held up to derision for it—but I care
not. I care not though your writings were ten thousand times as
vilifying as they have been. Think not that it is from a fear
of what the Press can say of me, (said His Honor, with vehemence)
that I thus speak. No, Mr. Robertson, I have been in Bedlam,
and have seen hundreds of poor creatures grinning and hooting
through the grated windows without fear, and think not I am
to be frighted by such as these, who I can compare to nothing
but a number of dogs baying at me. No, I can walk through the
streets of Hobart Town, and behold them without the least concern.
But I thus address you from the remaining kind feeling I had left
towards you. It is not, Mr. Robertson, every individual who cares
so little for the press as I do. I may perhaps be too independent of
it, but so I am, and I feel confident that you, as an Editor of a
paper, must be convinced, that it is the duty of an Editor to be very
careful how he thus charges *individuals* with such crimes. You
may charge *the system* as far as you please, and to any extent, and
thus far the press will prove a blessing, but when you come not to
charge the system, but to make such personal complaints, and
when such complaints are false to the very letter. If indeed they
were true, the law is such—(I do not say whether it is a good law
or not, but it is the law)—I say, if these statements were true, you
are punishable—if therefore they are proved to be false, how much
is the crime aggravated and reprehensible. Indeed no Government
could be carried on if such articles were allowed to pass unnoticed.
As to your trial, I think you had a very fair legal trial indeed, and
I should have been quite justified if I had not suffered you to go
one half the length I did. The sentence this Court passes on you,
is to pay a fine to the King of £50, and be imprisoned for twelve
calendar months, from the expiration of the term of your present
sentences. (Here Mr. Hone whispered to his Honor, who continued in a hurried manner,)—and to be further imprisoned until the
fine be paid. I am prompted to pass so lenient a sentence upon
you, as the last spark of kindness I have left for you, and as it is
the first time you have been before me ; but depend upon it, if you
come before me again, for any such libel published subsequent to
this time, I will imprison you for three or four years."—*Col. Times.*

* " We made the land about 11 A. M., Sunday, the 12th. (April)
The ship was furnished with the charts published by authority of the
Admiralty. I had not " Bates's Sailing Directions." I was not
aware that there was a book of sailing instructions for navigating the
coast of the Australian Colonies. There are two reefs laid down in
the chart—there is the Actæon, and there are two reefs inside ; ac-

sunken rock in D'Entrecasteaux's channel.   The loss of
life was truly distressing.   The second was about two

cording to the directions, I considered the passage safe.   Horsburgh's Directory says there is no hidden danger, after passing the
reefs.   I adopted the usual precaution of sounding with the deep-
sea lead, and when we got under 20 fathoms, kept the soundings
going with the hand-lead.   We proceeded between the two reefs
laid down, the soundings giving half seven fathoms, right through.
After we had passed the breakers, 1 took the officers and passengers
into the cabin, and showed them the position of the ship, and we were
all satisfied that we were out of danger, and that we might either
proceed on, or come to an anchor.   We proceeded on, under easy
sail, going from a knot and a half to two knots an hour.   The vessel
at that time was under double reefed topsails, and the foresail brailed
up, all ready for coming to an anchor, if it got dark.   After so proceeding for about a quarter of an hour, and whilst I was walking on
the weather side of the poop, the man at the lead sung out a quarter
less four.   I immediately cried out to the man at the helm, to put
the helm "hard port;" before the man sounding could get another
cast of the lead, the ship struck.   She did not strike violently at
first.   I directly ordered the cutter to be lowered, and the third officer, Mr. Field, to go into the cutter to sound round the ship—he did
so, and sounded abreast the starboard gangway first, and found two
and half fathoms ; he then went a-head, and found two fathoms—
and on the larboard quarter, three and a half fathoms ; from thence
he went astern, about four boats' length, and found four and a quarter.   At this time we saw no breakers—a swell soon came on, and
commenced breaking ; the ship then began to strike most violently,
throwing every one off their feet.   After a very short time, about the
fifth shock, the mainmast went over on the starboard side, carrying
the mizen topmast with it—dragging down the weather bulwarks
close to the covering boards.   At this time the boatswain and officers were trying to get the long boat out.   The mainmast being
gone, we were obliged to cut away the lee bulwarks to launch her.
At the same time they were lowering the gig ; the man in the stern
of the gig was lowering the stern tackle, when the rolling of the ship
caused him to leave his hold of the fall ; the gig stove in her quarter,
by striking against the vessel, and was swamped.   I did not know
who were in the gig, with the exception of the steward and one woman and child ; I saw the woman go in ; I desired her to come out,
but she would not ; she persisted, and stowed herself under the stern-
sheets.   When the gig swamped, I immediately ordered the cutter
to come round, and pick up the men that were in the water ; when
this was done, I ordered the third mate to bring the cutter alongside.   The mate said he could not ; he said he could not take in
any more ; the boat was as full as she could hold.   1 then desired
Mr. Field, the officer in the cutter, to look out for the first landing-

months after, it was the *Enchantress*, a fine stately merchant ship, which vessel run on the perpendicular rocky

place, and return immediately with any assistance he might be enabled to get. I then left the poop; the foremost had just gone
over. In consequence of the wreck of the masts on the lee side, the
crew were engaged in trying to launch the long-boat on the weather
side, but a heavy sea struck the ship, and the long-boat floated on
the deck. At this time, all the main deck was completely under ;
this was not a quarter of an hour after the first striking of the ship ;
the vessel struck at about ten minutes after ten. When the long-
boat floated, she was full of people, and washed about from one side
of the deck to the other ; I expected every minute to see her stove.
After great exertion, the people succeeded in floating her outside,
to leeward of the ship, and amongst the spars. I was at this time
sitting on the gallows bits, just above the main hatchway, and encouraging the men in the boat to shove clear of the wreck as fast as
possible; the boat laid there a long time—the people trying to get
her clear of the spars. Finding they could not succeed, I made
towards the boat, endeavouring to assist them, and, in trying to
shove the boat clear of the fore-yard, I got jammed between the
fore-yard and the keel of the boat, and expected to be cut to pieces
every moment ; I was, however, dragged into the boat by some of
the crew. After a long struggle, we got clear, and when we got
clear off, the people remaining on the wreck and spars gave us three
cheers. The long-boat had forty men in her at that time ; we proceeded to land, and could not find any landing place all along the
shore, it was so very rough, and the surf so great. At last we found
the entrance of a bay, several miles off, and proceeded to the bottom
before we could find a landing place. We then landed the prisoners, and the guard that was in the boat, with one woman and
child. The Surgeon Superintendent was in the first boat ; as, also,
my chief and second officer. I left thirty-six in number on shore,
and proceeded to the wreck with four men ; there were about an
equal number of prisoners and guard landed from the boat. It was
about 2 o'clock when we left the shore. In consequence of the
weather, we did not reach the wreck till 6 o'clock next morning ; on
arriving at the ship, the first people I took on board were the women, children, and invalids, and then as many of the prisoners and
guard as the boat would carry. I then considered I had about half
of the number that were on the wreck, and proceeded ashore. I
landed them at 8 o'clock, at the same place as the others ; I considered there were about forty or fifty. This trip Major Ryan,
Captain Minton, and the Doctor of the 50th regiment, were landed.
I then directly proceeded again to the wreck ; before I reached it,
I saw a schooner making towards the vessel, and she reached the
wreck before me. I went and took off all alive from the ship, and
put them on board the schooner, and then proceeded to re-embark

shore of Bruné Island, and went down in deep water,
without any part of the cargo being saved*—the whole of

---

the others from the place were we had landed ; there we took all on
board the schooner, with the exception of the Surgeon of the 50th
regiment, who had strayed. I left there a boat's crew, of eight
men, with provisions, to wait his return.

'· There were 308, including prisoners, crew, and military, embarked at first ; there were two born during the voyage—sixteen
died, leaving two hundred and ninety-four souls on board at the
time of the wreck. On counting them yesterday, there were eighty-
one prisoners, twenty-nine of the guard, three officers, six women,
eleven children, and thirty of the crew—one hundred and sixty in
all saved. *One hundred and thirty-four souls were lost—of which,
one hundred and twenty-eight were prisoners !* the remainder were
three children, one woman, and two of the crew. Scon after the
ship struck, I ordered a gun to be fired, as a signal of distress ; before
it could be done, the mainmast fell, and carried the gun overboard
with it. I heard Major Ryan order to fire as a signal, and I saw
two shots fired in the air. The soldiers were standing over the main
hatchway, endeavouring to prevent the prisoners making a rush to
the boats. For the safety of all hands, it was necessary to keep the
men down. I did not see any firing down the hatchway ; I afterwards heard that a man was shot. The conduct of the prisoners,
throughout the voyage, was remarkably good. From the working of
the ship, after striking, the prison gates fell down, and those prisoners that were saved, escaped that way. Long before we made
the land, we had made up our minds to come up the Channel, if the
wind suited. Before we struck, there was no swell—the sea was as
still as a mill-pond. The weather was not hazy ; the moon shone
brightly between the drifting showers. I am not aware whether any
of the crew had been up that passage ; I could get no information
from any of them—I depended solely on my charts and Horsburgh's
Directions. Nelson, Shaw, and Jones, prisoners, particularly distinguished themselves by their praiseworthy conduct."—*Evidence of
Captain W. H. Moxey, of the Grorge the Third.*

* About 10 o'clock on Friday night, the 17th instant, (July) the
vessel was proceeding up D'Entrecasteaux's Channel, with a foul
wind, Captain Roxborough had just descended from the deck to the
cabin, and was in the act of looking at his chart, the chief officer was
on deck, when the man who was stationed at the head of the vessel,
called out, stating that they were close on the land. The Captain
went immediately on deck ; but before he had reached it, the vessel
struck upon the rocks, in such a manner as to render it altogether impossible to save any thing, except the captain's chronometer, sextant,
and the small box containing the manifest. He immediately ordered
the two boats, a gig and a jolly boat, to be hoisted out, and the pas-

the crew being lost in endeavouring to get out the long
boat.   Within four months from the loss of the *George*

sengers assisted each other to them; the sailors were at the same
time clearing away the long boat to save their own lives.   The captain and chief officer, after seeing the passengers in the boats, with
three boys, one got in each boat, and made the best of their way from
the vessel.   Mr. Anstey, one of the passengers, being on the wreck,
after the boats had left it, jumped into the water, and was picked up
by one of the two boats.   When they left, the long boat they believed was clear, and they expected, that when the vessel went
down, she would have swam with the sailors—whether it was
so or not, appears unknown, as they have not been seen since,
and the vessel went down immediately the boats had left her.   These
two boats proceeded rowing about till next morning—they made several attempts to land, but were unable so to do.   They got the next
morning (Saturday) on Partridge Island, where they landed about 7
o'clock in the morning, and remained during Saturday.   Towards
morning, they saw a sloop on the other side of the water, they immediately dispatched one of the boats to her, which returning with provisions to the island, brought the intelligence that she would come
to them as soon as they could make the island, the wind being contrary.   The sloop *Friends* made the island during Saturday night,
and about 6 clock, on Sunday morning, the passengers from the
wreck embarked on board her, and proceeded towards Hobart Town
Captain Roxborough, with Mr. Bogle and the boys, proceeded in the
gig, and arrived in Hobart Town, about nine on Sunday evening—
and about 11, the *Governor Arthur* steamer, was dispatched with
Captain Moriarty, to meet the *Friends*—she fell in with her between
7 and 8 yesterday morning, and arrived safe in Hobart Town, about
5 o'clock this morning.   From the first striking of the vessel, not more
than fifteen minutes had elapsed before she was a total wreck, and
not a vestige of her to be seen.   The boats, during the night, were
several times near swamping ; and had it not been for one of the females, who sat in the stern of one of them, having a shawl on her
arms, being spread out, a tremendous serf struck her on the back,
which, had it come into the boat, she must have gone down—they
were all, during Friday night, and all day on Sunday, without any
refreshment, save a few muscles, which they cooked in a tureeen, one
of the passengers had saved.   Fortunately, there was plenty of excellent water on the island.   The kindness of Mrs. Moriarty and
others in Hobart Town, who sent many necessaries, such as cloaks,
rugs, &c. proved very acceptable, especially to the ladies on board,
who, during the whole of the time, from when the ship struck, evinced the utmost fortitude and presence of mind.   The lady before mentioned, also had fires and refreshments prepared during the whole of
yesterday, at the Waterloo Tavern.   The cargo of the *Enchantress*
is said to be the most valuable that has come out for some time; and

the Third, news arrived that a third vessel had been wrecked—this was the *Wallace*, a fine, new merchant ship from Leith. These three vessels were all lost within a few miles of each other. Besides these vessels, the *Neva*, bound for New South Wales with female convicts, was wrecked off King's Island, in Bass's Straits, and the *Thomas Munro*, merchant ship, bound for this port, was lost on one of the Cape de Verd Islands.* It is to be regretted, that pilots have not been stationed at the entrance of the channel, where there is dangerous navigation; for where pilots generally board vessels, all danger of every kind is passed. The loss of the three vessels at the entrance of our port, was very nearly followed by that of an American trader. This vessel was crowding all sail, and had not some of the crew noticed some signals made by some whalers, who fortunately were at the station in Recherche Bay, and mentioned the same to the captain, who immediately backed his sails, this vessel also must have been wrecked, and that too on the Actæon Reef, within a stone's throw of the spot where the *Wallace* a few weeks before had gone to pieces.

A strong memorial was presented to the Government, numerously signed, praying for an extension of the jurisdiction of the Court of Requests, to sums amounting to forty pounds. The petition was laid upon the Council

---

Captain Roxborough is the principal owner of the ship. In our next, we hope to present our readers with the full particulars of this melancholy event.

The following is a list of the passengers saved : —

CABIN.—Mr. and Mrs. Butler, Mrs. Yates, Mr. Bogles, Mr. Anstey, Miss Dixon, Miss Smith, Madame Rens, Mr. Rens, and Miss Rens, Mr. M'Arthur, Mr. Lightfoot, Surgeon, Captain Roxborough, and Mr. Toby, chief officer.

STEERAGE.—Mr. and Mrs. Burns, and three sons, and one daughter, Mr. Edwards, the cabin steward, and three boys.

The fate of the rest of the crew and one steerage passenger is yet unknown.—*Colonial Times.*

* It is a singular coincidence, that about two years since, the *Lady Munro*, from India, during the night time, struck upon St. Paul's, when almost every soul on board perished.

table, and a promise made that a bill for that purpose
would be brought forward, but there the affair ended.
Numerous laws, enforcing pains and penalties, as also
others, tending to abridge the liberty of the subject,
have since been passed by the Legislative Council; but
this most desirable law is yet only in embryo, nor is it
likely that the Council will ever sanction its enforcement.
The repeated complaints of all classes, as to the monstrous law charges, induced the Colonists to pray for this
extension of the Court of Requests. Bills of exchange
for small sums, even so low as ten guineas, have been
saddled with costs allowed by the Supreme Court, exceeding upwards of £50; and it is beyond dispute, that
numbers of the Colonists have been ruined by the enormous charges the Supreme Court has allowed to its legal
practitioners. Composed as the Legislative Council is,
relief from such monstrous law charges, is, however,
scarcely to be hoped for. The legal profession is well
supported—well represented—in this Council, of which
both His Honor the Chief Justice and the Attorney General, are members; and whilst the lawyers are so represented, the Colonists generally have no voice whatever in the nomination of the Council, nor is there one
member who is considered by the community as an independent supporter of public rights. The manner in
which the Council is nominated, is sufficient explanation
why the Colonists are reduced to their present distressing
situation. Every member, save those officially appointed, are the personal friends of the Chief Authority,
and if the system on which his administration is grounded
be erroneous, and any member were bold enough to tell
him so, it is natural to suppose the services of such a
member would be dispensed with; and as flattery is more
agreeable than censure, some one more inclined to ap-
plaud, would be chosen in his stead.

Another great objection to the Council is, that the
proceedings are in private, that the doors are hermeti-
cally sealed, the Colonists knowing nothing of what
passes save that which the clerk condescends occasionally

to publish, and which information appears in such an ambiguous and unsatisfactory manner, that the publication of the minutes of the Council is insulting to common sense.

The Legislative Council is at present composed of fifteen members, seven ex-officios, and eight, as before said, personal friends, appointed by the Governor. Of these eight, (which number apparently holds out something like a Colonial representation.) five are country members, who seldom attend, and three residents in Hobart Town. In the Council are two nephews of the Governor, His Excellency's banker ; and the clerk, is his own Private Secretary, It is scarcely necessary to observe, that the ex-officio members are *expected* to attend every sitting, and as these hold their situations entirely dependent upon the Chief Ruler, any opposition to the will and pleasure of the Chief Authority, cannot be expected. It is seldom that above eleven or twelve members are present, and the reader can imagine what little chance any proposed measure would have of being passed, if it did not accord with the wishes of the Chief Ruler. The ex-officios, nineteen times out of twenty, carry every division; but to talk of a division in the Council, will be laughed at in the Colony. The public look upon this body merely as serving as a screen for the Executive Government, passing objectionable laws, should any such that be passed, be so considered by the Home Government. That the Council, constituted as is the present, is totally inadequate to the welfare of the settlement, cannot be doubted. The mere fact, that because a man has sufficient interest in England to obtain the Colonial Treasurership, or the situation of Collector of Customs, does not guarantee that such a man has either the talent or the integrity necessary for a legislator—nor does his appointment to office engraft upon him, as if by magic, the necessary local knowledge for a maker of laws, for a large number of his superiors perhaps, in talent, wealth, and character. Suffice it now to observe,-that so little confidence have the Colonists in either the Council or

the Counsellors, that although their duty as good subjects
to His Majesty compels them to tacitly submit to whatever Acts are enforced, yet it is doubtful if the Colony
had a Legislative Assembly of its own, whether three
fourths of the Acts already passed, would not be repealed,
and it is almost certain, that had the public a voice in the
nomination of the Council, not one of the present members would be chosen.

The despotism too, of the chief authority is superior to
the power of any prince in Christendom.   Scarcely is
there a single settler in the Island, who is not dependent
upon His Excellency's will and pleasure, either for his
grant, or for his decision in some dispute about boundary
lines. Till lately, as it has been stated, the chief authority had the *giving* of land ; but this immense power has
been very properly revoked by the Home Government.
In addition to the depressed state in which numbers are
held by the uncertain tenure of their lands ; others are
dependant for their very bread upon His Excellency s
will and pleasure, in being permitted to have convicts assigned to them, and frequently servants, (as in Mr.
Bryan's case) have been withdrawn from masters, without one single word of explanation, and the Colonists
ruined thereby!   In addition to these powers vested in
him the fact that the chief authority can grant indulgences to convicts, for any services whatever, will bear out the
assertion, that no prince in Christendom possesses equal
despotism; and if the present Governor, or any other
Governor, chose to become a tyrant, the Colonists have
no means of redress.   The Lieutenant Governor can levy,
and does levy, one hundred thousand pounds from the
people, to divide among his friends and relations—he
could appropriate the labour of the whole of the Government hands to his own use and benefit, if he so pleased—
he could, if he so willed it, " *crush*" all those that opposed him.   The Colonists have witnessed Colonel Arthur's Government set aside British Acts of Parliament;*

* For example, Lord Lansdown's Act, passed expressly for these
Colonies, never yet enforced. The Abrogation of the Usury Laws

they have seen positive orders from home, unheeded
by the authorities ;* and men appointed by the Home
Goverment, removed from office, without any apparent
shew of reason†—and witnessing all these things, the
Colonists naturally ask one another whether they are
British subjects, or the subjects of a delegated power,
which holds itself as supreme and responsible to none ?
It is not the intention of the writer to condemn the authorities for their non-compliance with the letter of their
instructions from the Parent State, for the ignorance
oftentimes manifested by the Home Authorities towards
local affairs is truly astonishing, and occasionally the
worst of consequences might result from the strict obey-
ance of the orders of the Secretary of State ; but the
responsibility of judging whether or no such orders are,
or are not advisable, or agreeable to twenty-five thousand
British subjects, ought not to be at the will and pleasure
of one man ! The mere fact that orders from the Secretary of State are often either ill adapted or impossible
to be complied with, shews that the Colonists ought to
have some voice in the management of their affairs, and
the lamentable fact that the Colony is on the very brink
of ruin, ought to convince the Home Government of the
necessity, the *absolute necessity*, of changing a system
which has nigh destroyed a British settlement.

As the present year, 1835, has drawn near to a close,
so have the errors of the system of Government become
more and more conspicuous, and events have lately occurred, which will be remembered by the children of the
present day, when their hair becomes grey with age. The
Colonists, finding their interests so little studied by the
prison discipline Government—finding that their wishes

—the Death Act—the Police Act, nay, almost every Colonial Act
passed.

* The orders respecting the jury question—the reduction of various unnecessary and expensive Colonial appointments—the throwing open to public tender the government printing,—and scores and
of such like.

† Messrs. Rolla O'Ferral—James Gordon—and John Burnett.

were treated with negligence, became determined at all events to *protest* against the unpopular administration. In order to have some open constitutional means of making known the evils of the system, an Association was formed, consisting of nearly the whole of the influential inhabitants that are not directly or indirectly connected with the Government. The members of this Association appointed a Council of twenty-five of its members to represent the grievances under which the Colonists generally were labouring, and to this Council the greatest praise is due.* These gentlemen have enquired into every complaint that has been brought before them ; and after a fair discussion, if it has been considered advisable, letters have been written to the Governor respecting the same. The first communication from this Council to the Chief Authority was on the Felon Police,† the second called upon His Excellency to know whether he had the power to grant Trial by Jury, as it obtained in New South Wales, and to both these letters the Lieutenant Governor was pleased to reply that he could not acknowledge such a constituted body.‡ Occasionally

---

* A. F. Kemp   Thomas Hewitt
  Wm. Gellibrand   Andrew Bent
  George Gatehouse   Alexander Morrison
  W. T. Macmichael   John Lester
  T. Y. Lowes   James Hackett
  J. G. Briggs   Edward Abbott
  D. Lord   G. Stokell
  C. T. Smith   J. T. Gellibrand
  W. A. Brodribb   Thomas Horne
  Francis Smith   Charles Seal
  W. H. Glover   H. Bilton
  Thomas Dutton   H. Melville
  Thomas Lewis

† See page 251.
" ‡ *To His Excellency Colonel George Arthur.*
    " The Council of the Political Association beg leave respectfully to submit to Your Excellency's consideration, the system which now prevails in Van Diemen's Land, of Trial by a Military Jury in criminal cases, composed of seven officers.
    " The policy which originally dictated this system, appears to have been regulated by a necessity, real or fancied, arising from the

General Meetings are convened, and on the last assembly the following Resolutions were carried unanimously ;—

" 1.—That it is expedient for the public welfare, that the Chief Justice of this Colony be restricted from acting as a Member of the Executive Council, and that a letter be addressed on that subject to the Lieutenant Governor."

" 2 —That the office of Public Prosecutor is incompatible in this Colony, with the duties of Private Counsel, and that the Attorney General, whilst performing the functions of Grand Jury, be restricted from acting as Private Counsel."

" 3.—That passive obedience in all cases of obnoxious Colonial Law, be recommended to the Members of the Association."

" 4.—That His Excellency the Lieutenant Governor be requested to pass an Act of Council to confirm as legal titles the old Grants of Land in this Colony, made by former Governors, according to their true intent and meaning."

" 5.—That the power of adding to its number, be given to the present Council."

---

idea, that no other fit persons, either in number or qualifications, could be obtained, to discharge the duties of Jurors. Such a necessity no longer exists, and the Council submit to Your Excellency, whether the anomaly should any longer exist—whether the statute on the one hand, shall dictate, that the laws of England, so far as they can be applied to the circumstances of this Colony, shall be in force, whilst on the other hand, the life and liberty of an Englishman is made dependent upon the verdict of a Military Jury of seven, there being no longer any necessity to select Juries exclusively from the soldiers, nor restrict their constitutional number.

" The Council, in this case, abstain from pointing out particular reasons for a change in this system, not from any want of such reasons, but from causes which they consider not at present necessary to state.

" They desire, however, to impress upon Your Excellency, that in their opinion, the British Government never could have contemplated the continuance of this system beyond the necessity—could never have intended to introduce as fixed law for this Colony, that which is illegal in Great Britain, nor to stamp the Courts of criminal justice in this Colony, with the character and appearance of Courts Martial. In this opinion the Council are confirmed from the practice now prevailing in the Sister Colony, New South Wales, a Colony governed by one and the same statute as this, where, in the Courts of criminal justice, the British right of Trial by a civil Jury is enjoyed at the option of the accused—the Council, therefore, solicit Your Excellency to inform them, whether Your Excellency is authorized to introduce Trial by civil Jury, in criminal, as well as civil cases, and if, as they hope, Your Excellency is thus empow-

It is to be hoped this Council will continue in the same course it has adopted, and the exposures which it has made of the errors in the system of Government must ultimately end in benefitting the Colonists, and shewing the Home Authorities that Van Diemen's Land possesses hundreds of men well capable of performing the duties of legislators—men far superior in intellect to those whom the Chief Authority has thought proper to appoint, and judging from whose laws it would appear they were even lacking the most ordinary sense of school boys.

The proceedings relative to the case of Mr. William Bryan have already been noticed, but the name of "Bryan" will ever remain conspicuous in the history of this administration. It has been shewn that Mr. Lewis was the first victim in this gentleman's cause. In November of this year Mr. R. Bryan, a near relation of Mr. William Bryan, was twice tried at Launceston with his man Stewart, for cattle stealing. It may be necessary to observe, that a faction residing in the neighbour-

---

ered, that your Excellency will be pleased to exercise that power, by at once putting the Colonists of Van Diemen's Land in possession of that great bulwark of their liberty, Trial by civil Jury, in criminal, as well as civil cases, in its fullest extent.

By order of the Council,

T. HORNE, *Hon. Sec.*

November 14, 1835."

"*Government House, November* 21, 1835.

SIR,—I am directed by the Lieutenant Governor, to acknowledge the receipt of two communications, bearing your signature, as Honorary Secretary to certain individuals, styling themselves a Political Association,—and drawing His Excellency's attention to questions, in reference to which, His Excellency is quite confident, the anxiety manifested by the Government, for the public welfare is fully appreciated by the community generally.

" But, I am to add, that the Lieutenant Governor does not feel authorised, without the express sanction of His Majesty, to enter into any correspondence whatever with any such Association.—I have the honor to be, Sir, your obedient humble servant,

ADAM TURNBULL.

" *To T. Horne, Esq.*"

hood of Launceston, possessing considerable influence, had been opposed to Mr. Bryan's family for years past, and the counsel for Mr. R. Bryan being perfectly aware of this, communicated to the Attorney General, (who is also in this Colony Grand Jury,) that his client could not have an impartial trial on the other side of the Island, because the gentlemen likely to sit on the Jury had already discussed his case, and were prejudiced against the family : he therefore requested that his client might be brought over, and tried in Hobart Town, as was frequently the custom. The Attorney General refused this request, and the trials came on before military juries. On the Jury being called on the first trial, three gentlemen were placed in the jury box, when the Solicitor General, who appeared as prosecutor, objected to them, and the names of seven full-pay officers were called over, and these gentlemen took their seats as the Jury. Prior to the foreman being sworn, the prisoner challenged him as a Juryman, on the ground of interest ;* but the Chief Justice, John Lewes Pedder, said that there was no ground of challenge, and the prisoner refused objecting to any of the others. On the first trial there were three convict witnesses for the prosecution, who swore to the guilt of the prisoner, Mr. Bryan. These three witnesses were felon constables, John Boswood, a convict attaint, being a prisoner for life—Richard Gough, also a felon constable and a convict attaint, and George Scandlebury, a man of most infamous character, who in his cross-examination said, " I am a prisoner ; my sentence was seven years—my sentence has been extended three years ; I was at Port Arthur (the penal settlement) until last May twelve months, since which I have been a constable ; I was tried for absconding, and was either dismissed or suspended." The other witnesses for the

* " This is a prosecution against me, by the Government. I object to Major Wellman—he is a Magistrate of the Colony—he has sons holding Government situations, and must therefore be prevented giving an honest unbiassed verdict—and I challenge him on the ground of interest."—*Vide Trial of R. Bryan.*

2 E

prosecution proved nothing whatever. The evidence against Mr. Bryan according to these convict witnesses was, that he had been seen to drive a cow, the property of another person, with other cattle towards his own farm, and that on the evening of the same day a beast had been killed, by whom no one could prove—the next day a warrant was granted to search the premises, and in some fern, at a little distance from the house, the skin of the beast, said to have been driven, was found. It is scarcely necessary to allude to the evidence of the witnesses for the prisoners; a number of most credible witnesses were examined, and flatly contradicted the testimony of the convicts; but the oaths of these three convicts were believed, and Mr. R. Bryan and his servant were found guilty, and for this offence received sentence of death. It is the general belief, that these three convicts themselves killed the beast said to have been stolen, and that in order to gain their indulgences, they had placed the skin in the ferns wherein it was found. As to the evidence against the servant of Mr. Bryan, there was none, save that he had been seen in the stockyard where the beast was hanging, with a bucket in his hand, and that too some time after the beast had been killed; on such evidence, no grand jury in England would have ever placed him on his trial. The second trial was still more extraordinary than the first, and can be considered in no other light than as a dispute as to the rightful owner of two calves; but a military jury of seven found Mr. Bryan guilty of this offence also. It is a matter of regret that the full particulars of these two trials are of such length that they cannot be published in this work, as they appeared in the *Colonial Times* of the 3d and 10th November, 1835—were they so published, they would make the British reader wonder that such verdicts could be returned by any thinking men. The trial, and the circumstances connected therewith, excited but one feeling; several persons of influence, who were present in Court during the trials, signed a document stating that, from the evidence they

heard, they verily believed the prisoner innocent ; and
numbers of persons, after reading an attested report of
the trials, attached their signatures to an almost similar
document. One of the three convict witnesses on the
first trial, has since been sentenced to Port Arthur,
having been found guilty of *stealing his irons*, when in a
chain-gang.

The offence of cattle-stealing is in England a serious
crime, because no man can become possessed of another
man's beast without a *guilty* knowledge ; but in Van
Diemen's Land it is quite the reverse. Large numbers
of wild herds are in the interior, belonging to hundreds
of different proprietors, and it requires the most skilful
knowledge of the bush, and of the habits of the animals,
to distinguish the property of one man from another. Indeed, if all the cattle owners in the Colony were to be put
on their trials, and tried by the strict letter of the English law, there is not one that would escape conviction.
They have each, and every one, over and over again, in
ignorance, branded the cattle of their neighbours ; some
there may be, that have done so intentionally, but happily there are but few of this class in the Colony. Instead of the severe law of England being enforced for
cattle-stealing, much milder laws ought to be in existence here ; but the Colonial Government, when it thought
proper to introduce the British Act of Parliament, doing
away with the punishment of death for the crimes of
forgery—offences against the Crown, cattle and sheep-
stealing—introduced into the Colonial law a clause, by
which the punishment of death *should be awarded* to the
convicted cattle and sheep stealer. The people protested
against such a measure, but the voice of the people was
unheard. The wild cattle of the Colony may be compared to herds of deer in an English forest, to which
herds there are numbers of proprietors of individual
animals ; and because a gentleman might shoot a stag,
or his gamekeeper snare a hind, and kill it through ignorance, should such men be sentenced to die ? This is a
subject for the British Parliament to discuss, and it is

the duty of the historian, only to record facts without comment.

The trial and sentence of death passed upon Mr. R. Bryan, induced the Editor of an independent journal tó comment on such extraordinary proceedings. He believed, as the greater part of the Colonists did, that Mr. R. Bryan was innocent of the crimes imputed to him; and in the journal he conducted of the 3d of November, he commented on the proceedings of the judge—the jury—and the sentence. The publication of these comments caused the Judges of the Supreme Court to order a warrant of attachment to be forthwith issued against the publisher and printer. On his appearance before the Court he was sworn, and ordered to answer before the Master certain illegal interrogatories,* by which he was

---

* 1.—" Are you, or are you not, the Printer, Publisher, and Proprietor of the newspaper, printed and published in this Colony, called the *Colonial Times*—and did you, or did you not, print and publish, or cause to be printed and published, the number of the said newspaper now shewn to you ; to the imprint of which, your name appears as such Printer, Publisher, and Proprietor ?

2.—" If not so printed and published by you, declare and set forth, whether the said newspaper called the *Colonial Times*, bearing date, Tuesday, the third day of November, one thousand eight hundred and thirty-five, was printed, (or if not, whether the same was published) by any and what person or persons, under your directions or in your employ ?"

To these two first interrogatories Mr. Melville answered in the affirmative.

3.—" Look at an article in the said newspaper of the third day of November, now shewn to you, and in the whole, occupying part of the first, the whole of the second, third, and fourth columns of page 349—which article commences with the words—" Mr. Bryan's Prosecution," and terminates with the words—" Nay for a glass of rum"—and declare whether the said article, or some part thereof, and which part was, or not, in fact written and composed, or written or composed by you, or under your directions, or inserted in the said newspaper with your consent and privity ?—Set forth the truth herein fully and at large."

To which Mr. Melville answered—

" In answer to this interrogatory, I declare—protesting against being called upon, to answer whether I wrote or composed the article referred to, because the attachment was issued against me for printing and publishing only, and I protest against being called upon

obliged to criminate himself. He was then admitted to
bail until the next sitting of the Court; but as his sureties were about entering into their recognizances, one of
the gentlemen very properly objected, saying that no
man could undertake that another should answer questions put to him; but that all he could guarantee, was
the appearance of the person of the defendant before the
Court on the day appointed. His Honor the Chief
Justice in reply, asked the gentleman whether he objected
to become bail, and the latter answering in the affirmative, the Chief Justice continued—" then let the defendant be committed to gaol." Subsequently, however,
bail was taken, and the publisher and printer, Mr. Henry
Melville was brought before the Judges for sentence.
At the commencement of the proceedings the Chief
Justice said, that as his name had been made use of in
the objectionable article, he would decline giving an
opinion; but this same individual became his own Judge
and Jury in his own cause—he decided that Mr. Henry
Melville had been guilty of a gross contempt of Court,
and that there were most scandalous insinuations against
him personally. Being thus Judge and Jury in his own
cause, he also passed sentence, and ordered Mr. Melville to be imprisoned in Hobart Town Gaol for twelve
callendar months; to pay a fine of £200; after which
to find sureties for his good behaviour for two years—
himself in £200, and two sureties of £150 each; and

to criminate myself, and of an offence for which the attachment did
not issue; but as I have been compelled to enter into a recognizance with sureties, not only for my appearance before the master,
to answer, but also that I should answer the interrogatories to be
exhibited against me; and therefore to secure that recognizance, but
protesting against the legality of the measure, I do declare, that the
article in the said newspaper of the third day of November, now
shewn to me, and in the whole, occupying parts of the first, the
whole of the second, third, and fourth columns, of page numbered
348, and the whole of the first and second columns of page 349,
(except the space occupied by the note at the bottom of the second
column) which article commences with the words, " Mr. Bryan's
Prosecution," and terminates with the words, " Nay, for a glass of
rum," was in fact written and composed by me."

to remain in gaol till such fine be paid, and such sureties entered into. This unprecedented severe sentence did not astonish the Colonists ; indeed, so accustomed have the people become to unheard of acts of power, that they appeared as if nothing could rouse them. They have found that redress in this Colony is out of the question, and the distance of sixteen thousand miles so great, that redress from the British Government is scarcely to be anticipated—scarcely to be hoped for. And how, let it be asked, can redress be obtained ? The Authorities in the Mother Country will say, impeach the conduct of men whose actions are improper—but where is the man living in this Colony who dare, and who could impeach any in authority—would not such a man be *crushed ?* It is a folly to imagine that British subjects can be protected in this distant settlement by referring to the Home Authorities. The most outrageous —the most oppressive and tyrannical conduct—might be imposed by those in authority, and without any means of obtaining either justice or compensation ; nor will it ever be otherwise, until the people have a power, by means of an Assembly of their own, of redressing their own grievances, and their own wrongs. On concluding these pages, Mr. Melville is yet in the felons gaol of Hobart Town, although he has communicated publicly the sentiments of the British Government to the Chief Justice in a letter, drawing his attention to the censures passed by the Home Government on Mr. Justice Bolton, of Newfoundland, in a case exactly similar to his own.*

---

* NEWFOUNDLAND.—Mr. O'Connell presented a petition, signed by 1,000 persons, complaining of the administration of justice in Newfoundland. The petition also complained of the conduct of Chief Justice Bolton, who, even before he was sworn in, abolished the established rules which had existed for regulating jury process, by which the high-sheriff was enabled to pack juries for party purposes. The petition also complained of the Chief Justice being a violent religious partizan, and of tending, by his conduct and example, to destroy that religious harmony which had previously existed among the inhabitants. The hon. and learned member said he had good evidence to prove this part of the case. The petition

These pages must now be concluded—the end of the
year is fast approaching—and the Colony of Van Diemen's Land is in a truly lamentable condition ; commerce is almost at an end—and unless the system be

next complained of the conduct of the Chief Justice, with respect to
the press. *A case had been tried and decided, and was reported in a
paper called the " Patriot," with some comments on it by the Editor.
The Judge, instead of having this libel, if libel it were, prosecuted
by the Attorney General of the Colony, called the Editor before him,
and for this alleged contempt of Court, sentenced him to three months
imprisonment in a most unhealthy prison, and to a fine of £50.* The
Petitioners complained of the conduct of this individual generally,
as having given dissatisfaction to the inhabitants.

Sir G. Grey regretted that petitions containing general allegations
should be brought forward, but he was glad that the good sense of
the hon. and learned gentleman did not dwell on them. The only
charge on which the hon. and learned gentlemen did rest, and said
he had evidence to prove, was one of which the Government would
feel bound to take notice, if the circumstances were such as were
described, and the Colonial Department would make enquiry into
it, for certainly there was nothing which should be more regretted
than any attempt to foment religious disputes. As to any attempt
of the kind, he must say, on the part of Mr. Bolton, that he stoutly
denied it. With respect to the change in the Jury process, it was
done to prevent the inconvenience which was found to result from
the practice of taking names in alphabetical order, by which sometimes all the same family were taken on a Jury. *As to the conduct
of Mr. Bolton towards the individual who had commented on his conduct as Judge, he (Sir G. Grey) admitted that Mr. Bolton was in
error, for though the libel was one which no Jury would acquit him
of, yet to take on himself the punishment of an offence against himself
(though it might be strictly legal) was going back to the practices of
other days, which the Government was not disposed to renew ; and
he would add, that so much did the Government disapprove of that
course, that they would accede to the petition of the party condemned,
by remitting the remaining portion of the sentence.*

Mr. Shaw defended the conduct of Mr. Bolton *in all but the case
of the sentence on the Editor of the newspaper.* So far from his having
taken any steps hostile to the Catholics, it was stated by many in the
colony that he was on the best terms with persons of all religious
denomiuations in the colony—that his lady was, and still continued
a Roman Catholic. As to the opinions of the press in the colony,
it was a fact that the greatest excitement prevailed there, and as a
proof of it he might mention that the Editor of one paper was met on
the high road, and assaulted, and had his ears cut off.

Mr. O'Connell expressed *his satisfaction at the manner in which*

changed from the very foundation, the total ruin of this settlement, before long, is most certain. Blessed as Van Diemen's Land is with the finest climate—ordained by Nature to be the gem of the Southern Ocean—with the means of procuring every comfort that man can wish to enjoy, it is lamentable to see that a system of Government has so reduced the Settlement to misery, and brought five-and-twenty thousand free British and loyal subjects to so low an ebb of poverty. Immediate relief from present difficulties is out of the question, and were it to please His Majesty to grant this Colony the boon which all are praying for—an enlightened genrous Governor—it would take five years before simimilar prosperity could be obtained, as that which existed in the year 1830, from which period the Colony has been gradually sinking into the present disastrous difficulties. That the historian who may next have to record the events of this Colony, may have a more pleasant task, is the sincere wish of the writer, and that the change in the unfavourable aspect of affairs may be soon, is his wish as much as it can be the wish of the most fervent of the friends of this their adopted land.

Hobart Town, December 18, 1835.

---

this case had been taken up by the Government, and he was sure it would give very great satisfaction to the colonists. At the same time he must say, that the charge of religious partizanship was not disproved. As to Mr. Bolton's conduct towards the press, it had been very properly treated by the Government, and he would add nothing to what must be considered the severe reprehension of his proceeding in that case.—The petition was ordered to lie on the table.—*House of Commons, August* 18, 1835.

A FEW WORDS

ON

PRISON DISCIPLINE.

F

PREFACE.

PRISON DISCIPLINE *having engrossed much attention, and numerous writers having been found to oppose, and others to support the system adopted by the Mother Country towards her criminals, it may not be out of place to occupy a few pages of this Annual, to the discussion of a subject of such vast importance.*

Before proceeding, we might observe, that all public writers that have hitherto supported the system as it exists, have invariably been parties deeply interested in its continuance ; *whilst those of the opposite opinion, have had no interest whatever, save that of benefitting mankind by the recommendation of other systems, thought by the writers likely to effect the great end contemplated. As this little Essay has been written in the Colony of Van Diemen's*

Land, and as the writer has resided therein nearly eight years, and is well versed in all the routine of what is generally understood by the term Prison Discipline, the publication, it is presumed, will have some little influence ; and therefore the utmost care has been taken to avoid giving publicity to any statement which may not be strictly relied on.

PRISON DISCIPLINE.

I᷂ commencing our short Essay, it is desirable to trace the cause of crime to the fountain head, and consider what constitutes the crime, and what the punishment! Poverty may be fairly considered the mother of crime— at all events, Poverty is the cause of the commitment of four fifths of all offences. There are most certainly exceptions, for instance, the feelings of Jealousy, Revenge, or Disappointment, may prompt men to outrage the laws of their country ; but such cases are of rare occurrence, and if the whole of the convictions in Great Britain for one twelve months, were taken as an example, it would be found that the majority of offences, in some way or other, are instigated by Poverty. It should, however, be admitted, that were justice administered in that impartial manner which theory might describe, but practice cannot enforce, that numerous would be the convictions for offences which now pass unpunished. The law of England does not, nor indeed, can any law be made to bear with equal justice both towards the rich and the poor ; justice may be blind, but the balance will be influenced by the magnetism of wealth. If a rich man is to be tried for an offence supposed to have been committed by him against the laws, money, the god which all men more or less adore, procures an acquittal—tact and talent is at his command, and the prosecutor for the Crown has most frequently opposed to him men of superior learning in the law, whose duty it is to carp and cavil at every word of the proceedings, and to dispute inch by inch the evidence brought forward. We have seen the rich man's fee command the most splendid talents, abilities that have almost proved to the satisfaction of an ignorant Jury, that black was white, and that the offence for which a client was upon trial, was no offence whatsoever, or if perpetrated, the prisoner was yet not guilty. But how is it with the poor man?—he is sacrificed to the laws of his country; and ten poor men suffer innocently to every ten guilty rich men that escape. Poverty makes the criminal— that which the rich man can do with impunity, is an offence with the poorer, and crimes which the rich are daily committing, are passed over as offences not tangible by the law. If example were wanting, let us imagine an orchard, on the one side of which is a gentleman's boarding school, and on the other side a peasant's cottage. The cottager's child and the gentleman's son are found robbing the orchard, both are punished for the offence—the poor lad is transported, and the rich lad is flogged by his master with a rod—is this justice? The rich little offender's crime is soon forgiven and forgotten, but the Judge, on passing sentence on the poor lad, tells him transportation is worse than death. Again, what can be more horrid than the thought, that hundreds of families yearly have their peace and happiness destroyed by the seduction of those dear and cherished, by some of the more fortunate of their fellow-creatures? Is the inflicting such misery not virtually criminal, and yet not legally so? Can pounds, shillings, and pence compensate the father for the destruction of a beloved daughter, or the husband for the loss of a cherished wife? But these are *no crimes* in civilized society, whilst the poor starving wretch, who has not bread to put into his mouth wherewith to stop the cravings of hunger, *if he* deprives a fellow creature of but a small crust, that is a crime, and the horrid criminal, for such offence, by law is scouted from society. What therefore constitutes crime? Is it criminal for the poor starving wretch to steal a portion of the food or clothing of his wealthy fellow creature, or is it criminal for the wholesale robber to deprive whole families of their happiness ?—the English law has settled this point, but yet is not what English feeling calls justice.

That punishment by way of example, for the diminution of crime, is absolutely necessary, is beyond dispute, and without such punishment the good order of society would be overthrown, and nothing but a system of universal spoliation would ensue ; the strong arm would be the only safety, and not as is now the case—riches. The grand difficulty is, to enforce laws which shall inflict suitable punishment, in proportion to the crime committed, but as yet, no laws have been discovered by which an equality of punishment can be administered. Even suppose two men are convicted of a similar offence, and their sentences of punishment the same, would the severity of the punishment be equally felt by the father of a large and hitherto happy family, as it would be by the giddy youth who has neither friends nor kindred for which he cares ? and should two culprits be sentenced to corporal punishment, one man might receive the whole number of lashes, with only trifling bodily harm, whilst the mental sufferings of the other might far exceed those inflicted by the torture. Instances have been known in this theatre of crime,* where convicts who have behaved themselves tolerably well, have turned out the worst of offenders after the lash has been inflicted : such men have undergone the sentence of transportation, and they have still had a respect for themselves, but once make the man equal to the brute beast—once inflict the scourge as the whip to the bullock, and it is a chance if he has courage to recover his own self-respect. And again, the uncertainty of punishment is so varied, and so undetermined ! According to law, it is a nice point for an offender, or even his counsel, made as he is, fully acquainted with the circumstances of the case, to know what sentence will be passed, should conviction be the result of the trial—all is chance—all hazard. In the courts of this Colony, as

* Van Diemen's Land.

also in those of the Mother Country, law plays sad freaks. The culprit at the bar, whom every one firmly believes to be guilty of the offence with which he is charged, is acquitted by the law, by a quibble, or by the word of a witness: why? no man of common sense can comprehend—whilst the prisoner whom most persons may consider innocent, and at least consider his case as doubtfull, is found guilty, because the law assumes guilt in certain cases; but it is needless to dive further into the chance work of the administration of law.

It is notorious that the father that commits crime to obtain food for his starving children, and the felon who commits crime, actuated by the worst of motives, suffer alike the same punishment, although it may be the first offence of the former, and the latter be a hardened, thorough-bred villain—character too, is of no avail, the written law does not appreciate the former good conduct of the culprit, it is not weighed in the uncertain scale of justice.

What is expected from punishment—is not the murderer's life forfeited, as an example to others? But to follow the next grade of crime, is the convicted felon transported for an example to others, or to rid the community of a villian, or to reform the offender himself, and instigate him to become a useful member of society? Here is the difficulty—if the convicted felon is transported as an example to others, how can that example be of service, when those to whom it is to serve as a lesson are ignorant of the consequences of such punishment, and perhaps taught to consider it no punishment whatever? If the convicted felon is transported to rid society of a worthless member, then does the expatriation of the offender serve the end required; but does it hold out any example of punishment to others? None! The march of intellect has been such, that men now think little or nothing of a voyage round the world, the curiosity of many would be excited, and some would *chance** every thing to be transported, if all that is required by the law

---

* A Colonial expression of considerable force.

is the banishment of the offender. If the convicted felon
is transported for the purpose of reformation, how is that
reformation to be effected? Unless some stimulus, some
encouragement be held out for good conduct, the mind
is crushed, and human nature sinks, the more merciful
sentence would be death instead of transportation, under
a system without encouragement; but if encouragement
be given, does it not act as a stimulus to crime—does it
not encourage the starving to commit offences against
the laws, for the purpose of obtaining transportation,
and a possibility of prosperity? Upon these points hinges
the difficulties of penal coercion. Punish a man so as to
render him truly miserable, and it will be merciful to give
him a razor to cut his throat—nay, he will steal one to
do so; offer him a stimulus for good conduct, and you
encourage crime—a middle course is impossible.

The vast increase of crime of late in Great Britain,
plainly shews that Prison Discipline is anything but perfect, that it does not answer the desired end. Leaving
out of the question for the present the effect of transportation to these Colonies, and regarding the consequent effect of crime in Great Britain, we find that many
offences are committed merely for the purpose of obtaining the comforts, the luxuries of the jails—indeed, how
can it be otherwise, when the food, the lodging, and the
clothing of the offender are cause of envy on the part
of the honest and industrious poor? Much has been
urged about the value of a clear conscience, and the
happiness and virtue planted in the breast of the poor
yet honest man; but Poverty, we repeat, is the mother
of crime; and although a man may one day congratulate
himself that he never committed an offence against the
laws of his country, let that man be starving—let his
children be wanting nourishment—let him be told of th.
comforts of the jail, of the good wholesome food, and the
warm clothing—and let him decide within his breast
what *is* and what is *not* crime; and will there be many
men so situated who can resist the temptation—will not
the feeling of upright honest pride give way to the cra-

2 G

ving of nature, and will not advantage be taken of the prize held forth for crime—will he risk nothing for food for his children and himself? So long, therefore, that the criminal is treated better than the hard working classes, so long as idleness, good food, and good clothing are the rewards for the offender, it cannot be wondered that increase of crime should be so rapid—indeed, it is rather matter of surprise that so few offenders are to be found, and that the force of honest, industrious, and virtuous principles, have the effect they have over a half starved population. The Schoolmaster is abroad, he has already taught the poor that the jails are palaces of comparative comfort to the huts which they inhabit; and before long, if the imperfect system now carried on is not remedied, Great Britain may abolish her poor-houses, and build fresh jails for her starving population!

Having thus offered a few brief observations on crime generally, it is the intention now to proceed with the discipline carried on after the transported felons arrive in the settlement of Van Diemen's Land. During the whole voyage to these Colonies, the convicts are invariably treated with kindness, and enjoy many comforts—indeed, it has often been remarked by individuals that have tried both, that the comforts of the prisoners on board transport ships far exceed those of ordinary steerage passengers on board the free traders; and although this may appear impolitic, still, to treat such men otherwise would be cruel, and might be dangerous. The convicts, for the greater part, are ignorant of the fate which awaits them—some have been led to consider transportation worse than death, because the Judge who sentenced them so explained; others look forward to it as a pleasure, as a change from the poverty and misery to which they have been accustomed, to a life of ease and comfort. To make the former more wretched would be cruel, for mental agony and bodily suffering are too much at one and the same time; therefore, to make such unhappy men suffer by privations, would, we repeat, be most cruel; and as to the danger spoken of, the worm

will turn when trampled on, and man driven to despera-
tion is a dangerous animal ; therefore is it the impe-
rative duty of the Government that convicts on board
transports should be treated as they are—and although
such treatment may serve to give encouragement to
others to commit offences, still it is only of a piece with
the whole penal system of Great Britain.

On the arrival of a convict ship in the harbour, one
or two officers of the Government go on board the vessel
to take the description of the prisoners, and when this
is completed, the men are landed early in the morning,
and conveyed to the Prisoners' Barracks—and it is here
the fate of thousands is decided. Settlers, merchants,
and tradesmen apply in a formal manner for various
kinds of servants, and officers * are appointed to select as
near as possible, the description of servant each applicant
may require—this is the hazardous cast of the die for
the convict ! If he be fortunate, he will pass into the service of a good master, with whom, if he behaves himself, he will be well off, and lead a comfortable life ;
occasionally he will be obliged to muster, to shew the
Authorities that his master clothes and feeds him properly, and so forth, but even this muster is evaded by
a large majority of the prisoner population. If the convict be placed in the service of an ordinary settler, he
invariably becomes one of the family, takes his meals
with his master, and enjoys all the little comforts the
master can purchase. If he falls into the service of a
person more exalted in society, he takes his meals in the
kitchen, and is treated like a servant in the Mother
Country ; but if he falls into the hands of some of our large
overbearing tyrannical Colonists, then does he live a life
of coercion. The crime for which each offender is transported, is purposely kept secret from the master, and the
convict becomes a new man, enjoying all, or nearly all
the same privileges as an articled free working emigrant.

* The most inefficient department in the Colony is that of the As-
signment Board, it allows jobbing of the worst description, and no
one is responsible.

It is proverbial in most parts of the world, that a good master makes a good servant, and so is it, even in Van Diemen's Land. Convicts whose characters one would have been led to imagine would have turned out badly have, by being placed in comfortable situations, completely reformed, obtained their indulgences, and become wealthy and respected members of society ; whilst the convict from whom much might be expected, if fallen into the service of a bad master, has terminated his existence at a penal settlement—of course this does not always follow, but may be taken as a general rule. It might be here observed, that convicts arriving here, from whose standing in life, and from the great interest excited on their behalf in England much might be expected, invariably deceive the expectations of those who might be willing to assist them ; and so generally is this believed, that documentary proof of good conduct at home, is always disbelieved by the masters, who wish their servants to prove themselves what they *ought to be* in Van Diemen's Land, rather than what they *were* in Europe.

From this shewing it would appear, that the convict is as well off as the house and farming servant in Great Britain, and that he enjoys the comforts of life, which the pauper population cannot obtain in the Mother Country—of this there cannot be a question. In former years the punishment of transportation was in the banishment of the offender ; at first, such banishment only expatriated either from a county or the dominion, but when fresh settlements were established, the banished offender became instrumental in founding young Colonies. At first, the offenders were landed and left mainly to their own industry to supply themselves with the necessaries of life, but as foreign shores became more known to the generality of the people, and sea voyages less dreaded, free emigration began, and it was then necessary that the offender and the free emigrant should migrate under different expectations. The last material change in the system is that which has long since prevailed—

that of allowing the free emigrant and the colonists the services of the bond.

We have shewn the manner in which a prisoner arrives in this Colony, and that he is in every sense of the word a new man, and on himself depends his future happiness or misery. The prisoner in assigned service is the same as the working class of Great Britain ; if he behaves himself for a term of years, as well as common workmen generally do in the Mother Country, he obtains what is termed a ticket-of-leave, viz. a permission to work for himself, and for his own emolument ; and if his conduct is such whilst holding this ticket—if there are no material offences entered in the police books against him—after serving a few additional years, he obtains his conditional pardon, which confirms his freedom in every sense of the word in the Colony. A free pardon shortly follows, and the man may then return to the place from whence he was transported, if it so please him.

The term, prison discipline, cannot and does not in any way apply to the government of the British prisoner of good conduct. Prison discipline, or the severity of the system which these words would imply, consists in the punishment of the colonial offenders, and, strange as it may appear, the free emigrant and the transported British felon are punished for a similar offence, alike and together ! The convict on his first arrival may be compared to an indented servant, and offences which the police can alone take cognizance of among free men, are considered as necessary to delay the indulgence every prisoner naturally wishes to enjoy. We shall now offer a few observations on the abuses the system presents ; in doing so, we shall assert the truth fearlessly, daring refutation, even from the pen of the best paid writer.

The first great objection to the present system of prison discipline is, the expense it incurs ; the second, the evil resulting therefrom, causing the increase of crime. The free population of Van Diemen s Land amount to about

twenty-five thousand souls, and the Government expen‧
diture suitable to a proper administration of the affairs of
such a body of British subjects, even allowing an unnecessary degree of patronage, ought not to exceed twenty-
five thousand pounds per annum : whereas the Colonial
expenditure alone, by taxes levied on the Colonists for
this year (1835) exceeds one hundred thousand pounds.
Nor is this nearly the total of the amount required ! In
addition to this large sum, the Commissariat will this
year draw upon His Majesty's Treasury, for more than
two hundred thousand pounds. Thus the real expenditure is upwards of three hundred thousand pounds—a
monstrous sum of money, when all things are taken into
consideration. How it is the British Parliament can be so
totally ignorant of the expenditure of their money in this
settlement, is a matter of astonishment. The last Parliamentary grant for the support of the convicts was somewhat about seventy thousand pounds, for the two Colonies : and yet it comes to our knowledge, that the demand
of our Commissariat alone amounts to upwards three
times that sum. Before proceeding further it may be well
to observe, that the secret manner in which the finances
of the Colony are transacted—indeed we might say, the
secret manner in which every thing connected with expenditure is managed—precludes us from laying before
our readers official information thereupon.   Prior to the
publication of this work, the printer was requested to
apply to the authorities for such information, in order
that the truth might be elicited, but the applicant being
the printer also of an independent journal, it was
thought expedient to deny him such information ; and
thus this work is offered to the British Public without
any other assistance as to returns, than those which are
taken from last year's demi-official publication.*

---

* *Colonial Secretary's Office,* 14th *July,* 1835.
   Sir—Having submitted to the Lieutenant Governor your letters
of the 3rd and 8th instant, requesting that you may be furnished
with certain returns, from several Departments of the Public Service; I am directed to acquaint you, that, although it has always

In looking over the returns of convicts for December, 1834, (see the Annual published by Dr. Ross, the Go-

been the desire of the Government that the utmost publicity should be given to every species of statistical information, more especially when it could be afforded in aid of individual enterprise, His Excellency regrets that your present application cannot be acceded to, as a compliance therewith, when considered in connection with the very detrimental publications, emanating from the portion of the Press of this Colony over which it is understood you exercise an undivided control, might be construed to indicate an inattention to, or disregard of, those moral distinctions which cannot be overlooked by the Government of any country, without inflicting an injury of the most serious description upon the best interests of society.

I remain, Sir, your obedient Servant,

JOHN MONTAGU.

Mr. Henry Melville.

Hobart Town, 14th July, 1835.

SIR—I have just received a letter, bearing your signature, dated Colonial Secretary's Office, 14th July, 1835, in answer to my two applications for permission to obtain at my own expense, certain returns from several departments. I learn therefore, what I was before ignorant of, viz., that " it has always been the desire of the Government that the utmost publicity should be given to every species of statistical information, more especially when it could be afforded in aid of individual enterprise ;" but beyond this, I candidly acknowledge my ignorance as to the meaning of the letter, excepting that of a refusal to my request.

Am I to understand, that because " detrimental publications emanate from the portion of the Press of this Colony over which it is *understood* I exercise an undivided control," that the information wished for is to be denied—or am I to understand that the granting my request " might be construed to indicate an inattention to, or disregard of, those moral distinctions which cannot be overlooked by the Government of any Colony without inflicting an injury of the most serious description upon the best interests of society ?"

What I asked for was, simply the permission to obtain at my own cost from the different departments certain authentic returns, by which *truth* might be elicited ; and the Colonists and the British Public made acquainted with the true state of the Colony—its Commissariat and its Colonial Expenditure. Whether the information be granted or not, will make no difference as to the sale of the work now in progress ; but I should have thought it advisable for all parties that truth should go to the world in preference to statements which are not to be relied upon—perhaps there are other good reasons why the information required should be with-held.

With reference to the observation respecting publications issuing

vernment Printer), we find the total number to be 12,819.* Deducting seventy-five thousand pounds, which the Colonists are taxed for their share of the expences of paying for the system, and adding to that sum the two hundred thousand pounds paid by the Home Government, it becomes very apparent that the annual expenditure for the prisoners is *two hundred and seventy-five thousand pounds*, or upwards of twenty-one pounds for each convict. Carrying these calculations a little further we find that out of the total number of prisoners, there are 9,696† in assigned service, or living without one iota of expense to the local or British Government, so that the number in Government employ, only amounts to 3,123 ; and it is for the maintenance and control of these, that the enormous expenditure of two hundred and seventy five thousand pounds is required—or, calculating the average expense for each convict, the sum will be found to be *up-*

from my Press of a detrimental nature, I beg leave to say, that I have invariably endeavoured to protect and further the interests of the Colonists on all occasions ; but I feel perfectly satisfied *truth* must oftentimes give offence to those individuals placed near His Excellency's person ; and even supposing the letter alluded to implies that immoral publications have emanated from my Press, (of which I am totally ignorant) still I have the satisfaction of saying, that I never did publish or print such an immoral and blasphemous work as lately issued from a press supported by the Government— the proprietor of which no doubt could obtain, without any trouble, the information now refused.

I have the honor to be, with all due respect,
Your humble servant,
HENRY MELVILLE.
J. Montagu, Esq., Colonial Secretary.

* Convicts	-	-	-	-	-	11,938
Ditto at Port Arthur	-	-	-	-	-	881
			Total	-	-	12,819
† In assigned service	-	-	-	-	-	6,046
Tickets-of-leave	-	-	-	-	-	1,887
Artificers on loan	-	-	-	-	-	245
Females assigned to settlers	-	-	-	-	1,518
			Total	-	-	9,696

wards of eighty pounds. We often read of members of Parliament discussing the expences of the jails and penitentiaries in England, and the cheap rate at which convicts can be transported is urged as a reason why transportation is preferable to the penitentiary system; but how extremely absurd is this argument. The expense of transporting the convict, it is true, is but trifling; but it is the subsequent expense of maintaining the expensive management of the *offending convicts,* which is so great—the *direct* expense we say, is but trifling, whilst the *indirect* expense is, as already shewn, enormous, and amounts to upwards of eighty pounds for each and every *twice* convicted felon.

The British reader will probably say, if so large a sum is expended by the British and the Colonial Governments, that surely the labour of these men is equal in value, or nearly so, to the cost of their keep and other expences; but how little is the English Public aware of the system—how truly ignorant is the British Parliament of every thing connected with the management of the convicts !

The first penal settlement, formed for the worst offenders of Van Diemen's Land, was Macquarie Harbour, where convicts, and free Colonists who committed crimes of a grave nature, were transported; offences punishable by transportation in the Mother Country, banished such offenders in Van Diemen's Land to this distant port on the western coast. Macquarie Harbour has been well termed a very " Hell upon earth ;" and it is the terrible severity practised at this as well as other penal settlements, which has served the authorities to write home to the British Government respecting the terrors of the system. The British convict, as before said, on his arrival, if he behaves himself well, is *better off than are millions of his fellow countrymen at home ;* but if he once offend the laws in the Colony, misery follows ! One of the most remarkable features of the manner in which prison discipline is enforced, (and as if it were to prove that there is no punishment in transportation in

2 H

the first instance,) is the fact that the free emigrant is
tried and punished in the same manner as is a British
convict. The felon, for a second felony committed by
him in the Colony, is transported to the penal settlement, and the free emigrant, if he commits an offence,
he also is sent down to the settlement along with the
twice or thrice convicted. Of late years however, it
is understood some distinction has been ordered by the
Secretary of State, regarding the punishing differently
the once and twice convicted; but the power vested in
the rulers is so extensive, that no remonstrance or request of the Colonists is allowed to interfere with their
will and pleasure—and thus it is, free emigrants are yet
sent to convict chain-gangs, and other places for the
punishment of convicts. After Macquarie Harbour had
been established about *ten* years, and after scores of
thousands of pounds had been expended on the settlement and the prisoners, all of a sudden the place was
abandoned, and the whole expenditure thus wasted—
not any advantage worth naming having been derived
by the labour of the number of men constantly undergoing punishment. Previously to the abdication of
Macquarie Harbour, another settlement was selected,
viz., that of Maria Island : this latter place engulphed
large sums of money, and after a few years this also
was abandoned, and another site chosen for *experimental discipline*. Port Arthur is at present the penal
settlement, and thousands of pounds are there annually
expended, without any advantage to the Colony—this
settlement, in all human probability, will also be abandoned before long. The paid supporters of the present
system, or those otherwise interested in its continuance,
will no doubt lay great stress on the advantages derived
from this settlement—that Hobart Town is at present
partially supplied with coals from thence, and that the
sum thus levied should be adduced in favor of the establishment—but, although the coals are denominated
"Port Arthur coals," the pits from whence they are produced are at least twenty miles distant from the penal

settlement; and did the Government not possess the monopoly, the pits could be worked at a less expense by private capitalists, and the coal obtained at a cheaper rate in Hobart Town.

The money hitherto expended on the penal settlements may fairly be called a total loss to the Mother Country, without any benefit arising to the Colony. If, however, these settlements have been a sink of money, the next consideration is, whether or no they have assisted in either reforming the offenders, or rendered a service to the community by deterring others from the commission of crime. With regard to the reformation of offenders, experience has proved that the penal settlements in nine times out of ten, are ineffectual, and that a sojourn therein only hardens the feelings, and renders callous the breasts of men in whom, perhaps, some spark of remorse or shame might yet be lingering—indeed, were it necessary to give proof thereof, the fact of murders· having frequently been committed for the purpose of allowing the offenders to be brought to Hobart Town for a change, and for trial, and for execution, would suffice. At these settlements the desperate hardened villian, and the less offending, are compelled to work together; the latter soon becomes as experienced in crime as his asso‐ ciate; or if he stands aloof and regards his companions with horror and disgust, he is taunted and made to feel the desperate situation in which he is placed—death in such cases is far preferable.

When the mind of man has become lost·to all feeling of shame—when man has lost all self-respect, and be‐ come as a brute beast, he is callous of what may happen; he looks upon life as a burthen, and becomes reckless of what follows—such are the majority of the characters to be found at the penal settlement. These men, we re‐ peat, inculcate into the less hardened a feeling of despe‐ ration, which nothing but the lash or a prospect of im‐ mediate reward, can set aside. Huddled together, the scenes of vice and infamy which are likely to occur, among such a class, work an evil instead of good, and almost every man that returns from Port Arthur is a proficient in vice and wickedness. In such a place there can be no classification—to talk of such classification is to make use of deceit, and were any one to enquire of those who have been transported to such settlements, such men would tell it to be a place of horror, a sink of immorality, but no place for reformation. The secret manner in which every thing connected with this settlement is conducted, is no doubt advisable; but whilst such secrecy prevents the exposure of an impolitic and expensive system of punishment, at the same time it prevents the punishment of the place—the horrors of the settlement being held out to others as a warning—and thus, both for deterring others from the commission of crime, as also as serving as a place of reformation, the penal settlements are complete and total failures, and only serve to encrease the already monstrous overgrown power and patronage of the local authorities. Again, the number of men now undergoing punishment at Port Arthur is sufficient to prove that transportation to that settlement does not deter offenders—indeed, the uncertainty of punishment is such, that when a man commits a crime there are always chances in his favor—perhaps he will not be found guilty—and perhaps he will receive a mild sentence to a chain-gang. The uncertainty of the punishment which follows the crime is like a lottery, with few blanks and many prizes.

Another difficulty in the punishment of offenders occurs! A man arrives in the Colony a convict for life: we have seen such men put on their trial, both before the Supreme Court and the Court of Quarter Sessions; men of this description have again been sentenced to transportation for life, they have visited a penal settlement, and a few years good behaviour has caused their return to the settled districts, and again have they offended against the laws, and *again* have they received a third and fourth sentence of transportation for life. About two years since we were present at the trial of an old man, a prisoner for life; he was tried for two offences, found guilty, and sentenced for the first offence seven years, and for the second fourteen years transportation, after the expiration of the first sentence ! Thus the time of servitude was, firstly, by the British sentence, for his natural life, after which a seven years probation, and at the end of that, fourteen years additional ! ! It will, perhaps, be considered that cases similar to these are of rare occurrence, but the contrary is the fact ; nearly the whole of the prisoners brought up for trial before the Supreme Court and the Quarter Sessions are British convicts with home sentences, varying from seven years transportation to that of life.

If, however, the penal settlements are objectionable on account of the great expense incurred, and the complete failure of the work of reformation, the next subject for consideration is, whether or no the chain-gangs and road-parties serve as places of punishment, and at the same time as a means of reformation.   Men whose offences are of a minor grade are sent either to road-parties or chain-gangs ; and in these parties are to *be found free emigrants and twice and thrice convicted felons*. These men are, generally speaking, employed advantageously to the Colonists ; although it might be here as well to observe, that high influentials profit by the labour more than the community generally.   Among the great undertakings where gangs are stationary, the most conspicuous are the New Wharf, and the grand Bridgewater Work.   The former consists in moving a large portion of a hill into the Derwent at Hobart Town, so that a space may be made alongside of which vessels of burthen can discharge—this undertaking is highly beneficial to the commercial interests, as also to His Excellency Colonel Arthur and his nephews, who have large and valuable properties in the immediate vicinity.   Great expense, and perhaps very unnecessary expense, has been occasioned by this work, which might have been spared had the harbour been made into a dock by a mole running from the Battery towards the end of the old Wharf. The second grand undertaking is that of Bridgewater, where for five years a large number of men have been employed in forming a causeway across the Derwent—many people consider this undertaking as a complete waste of money. It is computed that upwards of one hundred thousand pounds have been expended in filling up an almost bottomless mud bank of some half mile, and when the undertaking is completed, it will even then be necessary that a punt should be placed there to answer the purpose of a ferry. Had one half the money, uselessly thrown away on this undertaking, been expended on roads and bridges in the interior, farming produce might have been brought to market, and food might have been obtained at less than one half the present expense. Next to these two grand undertakings, the roads employ the men subject to a less severe discipline; and although, considering the few men employed, much has been done, yet no country perhaps in the world is so deficient in roads as is Van Diemen's Land. The main road between Hobart Town and Launceston can scarcely be termed a line of road: in many parts the art of man has rendered it excellent, but a great portion is as nature made it, being but a tract formed by the vehicles that pass over. For several years past many hundreds of men have been employed cutting a new line of road, called after the property of Colonel Arthur, " Carrington Cut." The formation of this road for the first ten miles from the Derwent or to Richmond—to which place there is already a far preferable line, through a populous country—only serves to encrease the value of four estates, the proprietor of the most extensive of which protested against the formation of the road, (although his own property would be encreased several thousand pounds by its formation,) as a most " useless waste and misapplication of money." The general opinion is, that this line is formed for the purpose of encreasing the value of the Governor's property at the Coal River, but this cannot be the case, inasmuch as the old road is a far preferable line to his numerous estates in that district.

Had the whole strength of the offending British convicts been properly employed in the Colony, Van Diemen's Land would have been in a very different condition to the present. With respect to the discipline of the chain-gangs and road-parties, it is beneficial : the labour of the men is of service, and the controul under which they are kept, serves also as a punishment. Of course there are occasional exceptions, but in speaking of the discipline of the road-parties, it may be said very little alteration could be made for the better.

The British Judges, when passing sentences upon offenders, frequently express themselves, " that transportation is *worse than death.*" How little are they acquainted with the working of the system—how little do they imagine that men whom they consider their sentence is dooming to almost utter destruction, ought to fall on their knees, and would fall on their knees and thank the country and the judges for transporting them from misery and wretchedness to a life of ease and prosperity. In discussing the direct abuses of the system it will be necessary to offer some observations on different heads. We shall commence with a comparison between the convicts and the soldiery—we shall proceed to the felon constabulary and the free people—and then offer a few words on the advantage the convicts possess over the poor free people in general ; and lastly, we shall offer a few specimens of prison discipline, shewing the effect of the system on the prisoner population.

In discussing the relative situation in which the soldiery and the convicts are placed, we purposely abstain from commenting at too great a length on this head, for reasons which must be obvious. It is a lamentable fact that the British felons, on arrival, are much better off than are the soldiery ; their food is better, their clothing is better, their dwellings are better, and their duties far less severe. In a late Parliamentary enquiry, the following table of the rations of the several classes was brought forward, and ordered to be printed :—

I. The Honest Agricultural Labourer

According to the returns of Labourers' Expenditure, they are un‑ able to get, in the shape of solid food, more than an average allow‑ ance of,

	oz. solid food.	
Bread (daily) 17 oz.=per week	119	
Bacon	3	
		—— 122

II. The Soldier—

Bread (daily) 16 oz.=per week	112	
Meat ...... 8 cooked	56	
		—— 168

III. The Able bodied Pauper..

Bread ....per week	98	
Meat	21	
Cheese	16	
Pudding	16	
		—— 151

In addition to the above, which is an average allowance, the in‑ mates of most workhouses have—

Vegetables	48 oz.
Soup	3 qts.
Milk Porridge	3
Table Beer	7

IV. The Suspected Thief—
(Lancaster.)

Bread ....per week	112	
Meat	18	
Oatmeal	40	
Rice	5	
Peas	4	
Cheese	2	
Onions	2	
		—— 185

and 160 oz. potatoes.
(Winchester.)

Bread ....per week	192	
Meat	12	
		—— 204

V. The Convicted Thief—

Scotch Barley ......per week	28	
Oatmeal	21	
Bread	140	
Meat	56	
Cheese	12	
		—— 257

and 72 oz. potatoes

VI. The Transported Thief—

10¼lbs. meat ... .= 168
10¼lbs. flour, which will encrease, when made into } 218
    bread, to about ....

—— 386

By this it appears, the transported thief is better fed than any of the poorer classes; but the above table is not quite correct, it should be—

DAILY RATIONS OF FOOD.

The Soldier.	The Transported Thief.
One pound of meat	One and half pound meat
One pound of bread	One and half pound bread
About one gill of rum	One ounce sugar
	Half an ounce of soap
Besides the above, the pay of a soldier is 6d. per diem	And about half an ounce of salt
	Any further quantity of these articles, or any tea or tobacco, are to be supplied at the discretion of the master.
	Government Order.
The Soldier on duty over a chain gang.	*The twice convicted Felon working in the chain gang.*
One pound of meat	One and half pound meat
One pound of bread	One and half pound bread
About one gill of rum	Two pints flour soup
&c. &c.	Half pound vegetables

SUPPLY OF CLOTHING, &c. PER ANNUM.

The Soldier.	The Transported Thief.
One coat	Two suits woollen clothing
One pair trowsers	Three pair stock-keepers' boots
One pair boots	Four shirts
One great coat in three years	One cap or hat
One mattress, two blankets, and one rug	A palliass stuffed with wool, two blankets, and a rug

The dwellings of the men in Government employ is as far superior to those of the soldier as are their rations. A prisoner of the Crown, for a serious offence, if found guilty, is sentenced to a chain-gang or a penal settlement, where by good conduct the term of his sentence is invariably remitted—not so the soldier, if he commits a crime and is found guilty, he is transported to Norfolk Island, the penal settlement of the Sister Colony, at which place he remains till the very day his sentence expires—the best of conduct cannot alleviate

his punishment.   From this shewing the reader must
draw his own conclusions—he must decide which is
most to be envied in this British settlement.

Our next point for consideration is the constabulary.
Has any of our English readers ever attended at a court
of justice the day on which sentences are passed ? Has any
one of them witnessed the trials of men whose offences
against the laws have been such, that they trembled
for their lives ? Has any one of them heard the awful doom
passed, that a culprit shall be transported for life—and
heard the Judge say, transportation is worse than death ?
If such a man peruse this work, let him imagine the unfortunate victim of the offended laws arrived in the Derwent, and let him imagine the day he lands he is nominated as a peace officer, and vested with the same power
that the Bow street officers are in England ! Yes, of
such men is the constabulary of this Colony composed—
nor is this the worst part of the system ; the twice and
thrice convicted felons are appointed as constables ; men
that have escaped the gallows in England, and are sent
out here, and again have narrowly escaped with their
lives to a penal settlement—from thence have they been
drafted to be appointed as peace officers of the territory.*
Men stationed as these men are, openly set at nought

---

* The English reader will scarcely credit this assertion, but it is
nevertheless, strictly true.   A few days since, on the trial of a respectable settler, named R. Bryan, three convicts were the only evidence as to the guilt of the prisoner—one was a ticket-of-leave constable, the second a dismisssed convict constable, without indulgence, and the third a convict named Scandl bury, who in his cross-
examination said, " I am a prisoner, my sentence was seven years, my
sentence has been extended three years. I was at Port Arthur till
last May twelve months, since which I have been a constable, I
was tried for absconding, and am either dismissed or suspended."
On such evidence was Mr. Bryan found guilty and sentenced death.
Men of this description are stationed in the towns, and to this oppression are the free Colonists subjected, without any means of obtaining redress.   The convicts appointed to act as constables in the
interior are armed, and under scarcely any controul whatever—the
English reader will be surprised that such a system could prevail, but
however astonishing this may be, it is a fact which cannot be disputed.

the British Acts of Parliament. By the English law a
convict attaint is not allowed to possess either property
or money ; but the daily cases which are brought before
the Police Office prove that such persons are allowed to
sue and recover fines and penalties to large amounts,
which are thus levied on the free portion of the community. And again, the British law will not allow a convict attaint to give evidence in a court of justice, but the
greater part of the evidence adduced before the courts in
the Colony is that brought forward by convicts ; and
from such evidence numbers of both convicts and free
emigrants have suffered death. The most monstrous
part of the system is the stimulus held out for perjury ;
tickets-of-leave and free pardons are given for convictions, and when such a bonus is held out for the conviction of offenders, what man's life is safe in the hands,
or rather on the oaths, of such a set of wretches. The
Association, which the unsettled state of society rendered necessary for the safety of the free Colonists, communicated with the Government relative to the monstrous system, but in this penal settlement it appears as
if no complaint of the free people would be attended to
by the local authorities, composed as they are, of men
appointed from home, to be, as it were, only head jailors
over the convicts of this large jail.*

* *To His Excellency the Lieutenant Governor.*
The Members of the Political Association, who have been noimina-
ted as a Council, for the purpose of protecting the interests of the Colonists, desire to express to His Excellency the Lieutenant Governor their
most anxious desire, at all times, to draw the attention of the Local
Government to those existing evils, which, in their judgment, may
tend to retard the moral, political, or commercial prosperity of the
Colony ; they trust that the Local Government will give them credit
in being actuated by the best motives, and a sincere desire of producing union and concord between the Government and the people
—in doing which, the Members of the Council will be giving full
effect to the principles of the Association.
The Members of the Political Council desire to present to the serious consideration of the Lieutenant Governor, the demoralizing,
degrading, and dangerous practice, of employing felons in the execution of the responsible office of constables, and permitting them

Not only are convicts of the description we have named appointed by the Government to act as constables, but the hosts of messengers belonging to the various Government departments, and many of the clerks in

---

to traverse the country, not only with arms, but without controul, and in too many instances selecting them, even from penal settlements and the chain gangs, to which they have been sentenced for improper conduct.

It must be quite apparent, that to such men, the sanctity of an oath can be but little, if at all regarded, and the experience of various trials in the Courts of this Colony, fully establishes the fact, that men thus placed in those responsible situations, expect by their diligence in proving the commission of crime, that they will obtain indulgencies, varying from a ticket-of-leave to that of a free pardon. It must be therefore, evident that to prove crime, whether committed or not, is, and in the nature of things, must be a temptation to which such men ought not to be exposed; and that the lives, characters, and property of innocent men, not only may be, but are endangered, and it is to be feared, in some instances, have been sacrificed.

The Council cannot believe that the British Government ever intended to invest a felon with the power and office of a constable, to give him the power of apprehending a free subject upon his own authority, and without warrant; to invest him with the situation of a conservator of the peace, to apprehend a free subject, and place him in a watch-house, upon suspicion of a breach of a Colonial Act; to appear as an informer, and sue for a moiety of a penalty, and in order to obtain that penalty, to be a witness in his own cause! Still less can the Council conceive it possible, that the British Government ever could have intended, that a felon should sue for a penalty on behalf of the King, and after share that penalty with the King!

It may, perhaps, be expected, that to justify such observations, the Council should refer to cases which have arisen, bearing upon these points, and the Council therefore refer His Excellency to the case of constables Lamph, (who had thus recently obtained his pardon) and Bolter, who were committed by His Honor Mr. Justice Montagu, for perjury in the Supreme Court, in trying, by their evidence, to convict four men of a capital offence; also, to the case of James M'Pherson, recently ried at Launceston before the Chief Justice, and who was convicted of sheep stealing, upon the testimony of two convict constables, named Griffiths and Collins. Upon the trial of this case, it was proved that constable Collins was a convict, and was afterwards apprehended as a prisoner at large; but instead of being punished, he was then made a constable, and placed in the Field Police, in the neighbourhood of Avoca; he denied that

those departments, are also convicts without indulgences.
The jails too, are guarded partially by the military and
partially by prisoners—indeed the very avenues to the
courts of justice are defended by British felons. Whilst

he ever stated that he would hang twenty men, to save his punishment in the chain-gang, or anything like it ; and yet this fact was
clearly established by the testimony of three or four soldiers, who
deposed to that effect.

The other witness, Griffiths, was also a convict holding a situation of constable ; and His Excellency will find, upon examining
the police records, that this man was tried about four years ago,
with seven or eight others, as bushrangers, and having committed
various felonies—that the whole party had sentence of death passed
upon them, and that, with the exception of Griffiths, they were executed ; and that this man Griffiths was shortly afterwards appointed
to the important situation of constable in the interior, and which
office he has held ever since.

It is considered material to state shortly, the outlines of this case
as an illustration of a system, against which no man's life or property can be secure. The prisoner had been an assigned servant of
Captain Grey, and in whose service he obtained his ticket-of-leave
for good conduct, and after he obtained his ticket, he was retained
in his master's service, in the capacity of shepherd : a strong proof
of the opinion that his master had of him.

The two felon constables swore that they were watching the prisoner's hut, and that at night, they saw a man coming towards the
hut with a sheep upon his back, that he dropped the sheep about a
hundred yards from the hut, and then killed it, and upon some noise
being made, the man ran away—they shortly afterwards went to the
prisoner's hut, knocked at the door, and apprehended him—that a
sheep had been killed, was proved beyond dispute, but the material
question was by whom ? The Council do not for one moment presume to decide that point, but they confidently ask, whether the
temptation in such a case is not too great, whether men so circum-
stanced ought, with a due regard to the safety and liberties of a Free
People, to be invested with such power, and whether a charge of
such a similar nature, might not, with the greatest ease, be established against any man.

The Council also desire to draw His Excellency's attention to the
case of Mr. Robert Bryan, convicted at the same Sessions, and
mainly upon the testimony of three felon constables, and upon evidence in principle similar to the last. It is well known to be the
constant practice of settlers to kill their own cattle and sheep, and
the facility with which a hide may be placed near a stock-yard, or
amongst others kept by the settlers, is self-evident, and, in such a
case where the hope of reward is so great, and the instruments by

speaking of the jails in the Colony, it may be as well to remark the manner in which they are conducted. The building of Hobart Town, contained in a square of about 40 yards, is encircled by a wall, and was built when there were only about six hundred inhabitants in the Colony. At that period it was a splendid edifice ; but now the population amounts to more than *thirty five thousand* souls, it is quite inadequate for the purpose. The jail is divided into two parts, the one portioned for the debtors, and the other termed the " felons' side." In the latter are to be found the free emigrants waiting for trial, mixed up with the twice and thrice convicted felons, who are also waiting again to undergo the usual routine of being sent to a penal settlement, and from thence to return for a repetition of crime and punishment. On the felons' side there are four rooms, in which prisoners are usually

---

whom the facts can be proved, so demoralized and base, it appears to the Council, that unless an immediate check is put upon the present system, that no man can with security live upon his estate, or consider his liberty safe for one instant.

The Council are enabled to adduce numerous other instances, fully establishing the dangerous principles of employing felon constabulary, but they feel satisfied, the present recent instances will sufficiently warrant their drawing the attention of the Government to the system, and procure an immediate alteration—they have no desire in any manner to interfere w th the management or other arrangements of the convicts, or of prison discipline, but they consider it high time that the Free Colonists of Van Diemen's Land should record their solemn protest against the employment of felons, from penal settlements and chain-gangs, and others, who have not acquired a goood character, as constables, and in the execution of the important duties attached to that office, exercise a control over the lives, liberties, and properties of " Free Englishmen."

In conclusion the Council feel it their duty honestl y to state to His Excellency, that in consequence of the operation of this system alarm prevails widely through the Colony—men's minds are irritated and unsettled, and in some instances the most respectable settler-have offered their estates for sale, and expressed their fixed determis nation to leave a Colony, where under such a system they have no guarantee for the security of life, reputation, or property.

By order of the Council,

T. HORNE, *Hon. Sec.*

Hobart Town, Nov. 14, 1835.

confined ; there is also one apartment for the women, besides five small condemned cells.   In the four rooms and
condemned cells allotted for male prisoners, which rooms
are of ordinary dimensions, no less than 250 of them
have been confined at one time.*   The prisoners are allowed to exercise in a small confined court yard, where
the stench is occasionally enough to bring on disease.
As to the women, the apartment in which both the free
and the convicts are incarcerated before trial, consists
of what formerly were two condemned cells, the two
measuring about six feet in width, and about twelve feet
in length.   No sooner is a woman once committed to
jail, than she remains locked up till the day of trial—
she is not allowed exercise, and the light of heaven is
scarcely permitted to enter into the cell. We have known
a score of women incarcerated in this confined space—we
have known women to be incarcerated therein for three,
six, nine, and twelve months—we have seen women,
accused of murder, locked up therein with the unfortunate free female emigrants, who were kidnapped on
board the *Princess Royal* and *Strathfieldsay*, and whose
crimes consisted in not being able to pay a fine of five
shillings (half to the King, and the other half to a convict constable)—for drunkenness. In this same unwholesome dungeon, in which there is no fire-place, nor till
lately any window to shut out the boisterous weather,
(which the wooden and iron bars allowed to enter) are not
only incarcerated the free and the convict women, but a
large number of unoffending children, whose mothers have
taken them to this den, having no place, no connexions,
to whom they could intrust them, or rather there being
none who would take charge of them.   In this school of
vice, and in this unwholesome dungeon, are the weak and
sickly offsprings brought up—this is the school of morality !   Were one tithe of the tales of misery which could
be told of this " *Bastile*," recorded, it would make the hair
stand on an end !   Out of the very cell in which the

* Two of the rooms are seventeen feet by eleven feet six inches,
and the other two about twenty-five feet by fifteen.

latter portion of these pages are written, twenty-five
human beings were marched to the scaffold in three suc-
cessive days ; and in many instances the death of these
men procured free pardons and other indulgences for
British felons, who were thus interested witnesses in the
destruction of their fellow-creatures.   In such a jail, in
a space so confined, it is not to be wondered that sickness is very prevalent ; many and many a poor creature
is removed from thence to the hospital, from which
place he is borne to the burial ground.   Lest the
British reader may be inclined to disbelieve the assertions which the writer has already offered to his notice—
lest he should imagine the writer some poor, miserable,
offending creature, whose crimes have brought him to
justice, it will be necessary to remark, that the writer
is incarcerated for the political offence of committing
what the Judges of the Supreme Court were pleased to
construct into a contempt of Court.   The particulars of
the case are of importance, inasmuch as they will explain the terrors of the Colonial system.   The Council
of fifteen passed an Act of Council contrary to British
law, and in direct opposition to the wishes of the people,
whose only hope is, that they may be governed by British law till such times as they can make laws for themselves, through a representative body of the people, by
whom their interests will be studied.   This law, so obnoxious, was one which made the crime of cattle stealing
punishable by death ! A Mr. Robert Bryan, the nephew
of Mr. William Bryan, a gentleman of known integrity,
and fortune, was charged with cattle stealing, under
circumstances which excited great suspicion.   He was
accused by three convicts, and on the oaths of such
men was found guilty ; scarcely was the sentence passed
before the three British felons were accused of wilful
and corrupt perjuy—Mr. Bryan was, nevertheless, sentenced to die.   It was in consequence of a thorough
conviction of the innocence of Mr. Bryan, that the
writer commented on certain facts connected with the
trial—the Jury, the Judges, and the sentence ; and al-

though the Attorney General acknowledged it was no case to go to a Jury, the Judges were called upon to defend the dignity of the Court—to be Prosecutors, Jury, and Judges, in a case wherein their own conduct had been censured. Their Honors decided that the article was a contempt of Court, and a sentence, equal to imprisonment for life, was passed upon the Printer and Publisher.*

Before closing our observations on this terrible *Bas-*

---

* The greatest praise is due to the visiting Magistrates, for their late attention to the inmates of the gaol. On Mr. Melville being first incarcerated, he was locked up with Mr. Robertson in a condemned cell, from whence the man-eater Pearce—the aborigines—and some score of malefactors were taken to execution—nor was this all, the virmin and the confined space, rendered the imprisonment the description of torture, the Christian, the merciful authorities, had no doubt intended. Complaint was first made to the Judge, but he treated the applicant " *with contempt.*" Application was made to the Governor—he promised Mrs. Melville a great deal for the accommodation of her husband, but of course his promises are like pie crusts. The Sheriff was applied to, but he shielded himself under the 67th clause of the Consolidation Act. As to the gaoler, he appeared to be all civility, ready in words to accommodate as much as the confined state of the prison would allow, but his civility was no more than the Governor's promises. At last the visiting Magistrates being applied to, they came, but these gentlemen knew not their power : however they have also promised much. All that Mr. Melville requires, is a room or cell to himself, and that his wife may be allowed to remain with him—not a great deal to ask, when a man is illegally incarcerated, for an offence, which he was ignorant of having committed ; and convicted too by a man who was his own Judge, his own Jury, and his own Prosecutor, and that man too one of the most prejudiced and hottest tempered in the Colony. There is however a time for all things!—*Colonial Times.*

On Monday last, during divine service at St. David's, we exercised our cramped limbs in this miserable gaol. As a matter of great favor, we are allowed to walk with the felons ; our two companions during divine worship, were, on our right, a man in chains— we did not dare ask him why he had the ornaments, because he might have considered it a " *contempt* ;" on our left, was a man in a yellow jacket, the very picture of death—both were at least twice convicted. Reader, these are the companions for two men who dare offend the authorities by telling the truth. Editors and such like are considered by Colonel Arthur, as fit companions for the twice and thrice convicted felons !—*Ibid, Dec* 1, 1835.

2 K

tile, it may be as well to remark that this Government is generally termed a religious administration—that the rulers attend churches and chapels, and gospel and bible meetings—that they are loud in offering up their prayers, and put on the cloak of meekness and self-devotion; but whilst this outward show—this over righteousness is so conspicuous—this place of wretchedness—this place, wherein the strayed sheep are penned, is considered by them a worldly hell, wherein, those suffering, are not worthy to advance to the same heaven with themselves. Yes, British reader, the word of God is debarred to the greater part of the unfortunates within these walls, and a man must be a felon before be can be allowed to attend divine worship, which is held but once a fortnight in one of the apartments on the felon's side, when the Colonial Chaplain officiates.   True, when a man is sentenced to die, and left for execution, he is then surfeited with religion—but not till then.   We must not omit to mention, that the greatest praise is due to the Reverend William Bedford, whose praiseworthy exertions in preparing men to meet their awful doom, denote a good man and a devout Christian.   The debtors in this gaol, and the females, never by any chance hear divine service, and it is a true type of the system, that felons only are allowed to hear the gospel—and those of a worse grade—those condemned to die, are more blessed even in that respect, than are any others.

The facility with which indulgences can be obtained by some persons, and the difficulty others of good character find in procuring what their term of servitude ought to procure for them, is an evil which is much complained of.   There is no rule, for a man with influence; he can obtain indulgences for his servants, as also for the servants of others, without the least trouble ; whilst the master who has no influence, uselessly wastes his time in seeking to procure any indulgence for his assigned servant of good character!   Another great evil complained of loudly by the Colonists is, the manner in which the mechanics are employed.   There is what is termed "the loan gang," consisting of a parcel of men, the best workmen in the Colony ; these men it is understood, are lent on loan to the settlers generally, but this is not the case, these men are for the greater part employed by Government Officers, or men friendly with the chief authorities—such individuals, by the aid of this loan gang, are enabled to build fine palaces, and make fine improvements, with scarcely any cost to themselves; whilst the settler who dares have an opinion of his own, if that opinion chimes not with the wishes of the authorities, he may in vain ask for such assistance ! It is a notorious fact, that brick-makers, bricklayers, stone masons, carpenters, sawyers, &c., &c., are lent on loan from this gang to the Government Officers and Government Clerks; and these officials demand a certain portion of weekly work from the men, and the remainder of the time is allotted them to provide themselves with food and clothing—thus it is that Government Officers can, and do build houses, without one farthing cost to themselves for their erection. In addition to this glaring evil, every Government Officer of any note has his own tailor and shoemaker assigned to him—these men have also to perform a certain task of work, and when that is done, they employ themselves for master tradesmen. The British Government, in giving such enormous Colonial salaries to the authorities, little imagine that scarcely one penny of the same would be expended by them in the Colony ; these gentry, from the very highest, (not even excepting the Governor himself,) import almost every article they require, and the money saved by their miserable parsimony is laid out at usurious interest.

With regard to the advantages the convicts have over the poor free emigrants, those advantages must have been abundantly apparent, It must be evident that both classes land on these shores under very different circumstances. The convict on his arrival is forwarded to a comfortable barracks, far, far preferable to those of the military, he is well taken care of, has cleanly lodging and clothing and plenty of excellent food—and whoever starves he is certain to be well fed! It matters not from whence the bread or the meat comes, the infant of the duped emigrant will have it taken from its grasp to feed the over fed convict. Contrast with this the poor emigrant! He arrives with perhaps a large family; on his landing does he proceed for advice to the Chief Authority? Oh no! in former years such was the case, but of late the Government and the people appear completely distinct. The poor emigrant, on his first setting foot on shore, walks about the streets seeking a lodging; he has none to advise, none to befriend him. He is as desolate as if he were in a wilderness! With considerable loss of time he finds a shed wherein to creep with his children, and in a hovel does he spend the last farthing the most parsimonious frugality allowed him to scrape together in the Mother Country. What is to be done?—work he cannot procure, and to beg he is ashamed. *He has no penitentiary* wherein he and those dear to him can find shelter—oh no! *he is not a convict.* He cannot call upon a master for food, for rations for himself and starving children—*oh no, he is not a transported thief, he is not a felon, and has no right to partake of the indulgences such men enjoy!* If he calls upon the Chief Authority the door is shut against him—such as he are not worthy of notice, he has no money to let out on usury, and he must commit some crime before he can be indulged as convicts are, with good food and good clothing. Reader, this is too true a picture, as hundreds, nay thousands of poor creatures can prove; and whilst such men are destitute— are thus without bread, they see felons acting as peace-officers—they see felons privileged plunderers, who can obtain wealth by oppressing the free population. It is enough to sicken the heart to hear the tales of misery, the tales of wretchedness the honest industrious people now tell, whilst the British felon lavishly wastes the food, and the poor free emigrant willingly picks up the crumbs that fall from his table.

It is not our intention to point out the numerous respectable individuals now enjoying comfortable situations

in life, and who formerly have been prisoners ; such allusion would be uncalled for, and uncharitable. Men
that have undergone probation—men that have obtained
their free pardons, or even their emancipations—are in
this Colony entitled to possess the full privileges of the
free emigrants.   We fancy we can hear the scrupulous
British reader express—" what! is there to be no distinction made between men who have never offended,
and those who have been convicted ?" and to this we
reply, that *no difference ought to be made in this Colony !*
The British law, written as it may be said to be in blood,
punishes too severely ; but even suppose the transported
convict is not too severely punished, at all events he is
sufficiently punished, or the law is insufficient to deter
from crime.   The convict having undergone the sentence, may be said to have settled his account with his
country, and ought to be stationed in the same rank
of life, to which his good conduct in this settlement
entitles him.   If a British convict can pass through
the narrow path which leads to the enjoyment of a free or
conditional pardon—if he can escape the difficulties with
which he is surrounded in this Colony, his good character for a certain number of years ought to be held in
his favour, and he has a right to be a member of society.
Because a man may commit an offence in England, he is
not, nor ought he to be doomed to perpetual servitude—
if such were the case, it would be far better at once to
deprive him of life.   No, we maintain that if a convict,
conducting himself properly in this Colony, *is* entitled to
the indulgence of his pardon—he should have that indulgence in the fullest sense of the word ; and if the free
emigrants objected to this, we would say, they knew to
what place they were coming—they knew that the settlement was partly penal.   The free emigrants of Van
Diemen's Land however, happily wish to make no distinction between the emancipist and themselves, and on
all occasions have shewn their determination not to allow
the Government, or any of those in authority, to sow
those seeds of distinction, which have been so often at-

tempted; and this feeling speaks loudly in their favor.
But if the colonists are wishing to go hand in hand
with the emancipists, one and all agree that the encouragement held out to convicts who have not undergone
probation, is detrimental to discipline, and is but an encouragement of crime.   Hence it is, that the Colonists
complain loudly of felons being employed as constables—
hence it is, that they complain of their holding situations
under Government, and thus robbing the poor free emigrants of honest livelihoods.   What will the British
reader think, when we tell him, that felons without any
indulgences whatever, are allowed to keep wholesale and
retail stores ?   Is this what the Home Government contemplated, when they transported such men for offences
committed against the laws ?   What would the English
reader think, were we to tell him, that men without indulgences are allowed to become sub-editors of newspapers which advocate the Government cause and the
prison discipline system—yet such is the case ;* and
although such men are openly allowed to be connected
with the Government press, a man, a prisoner of the
Crown of good character, was lately transported to
the settlement of Port Arthur, under *suspicion* of having
given certain information to a reverend gentleman, who
is on unfriendly terms with the chief authorities ; and
which reverend gentlemen was *suspected* of having held
a correspondence with the editor of an independent
newspaper.   Thus it would appear that convicts are
allowed to write in favor of prison discipline, and not in
furtherance of the interests of the people.   To comment
on such proceedings, is quite unnecessary.

The publication of any individual case, shewing the
impolicy of the present prison discipline system, may
have an injurious effect on that individual ; but it is necessary that reference should be made, in order to de-

* A prisoner of the Crown (who has lately obtained a ticket-of-
leave,) is generally considered as sub-editor of the *Courier*, (a Government paper,) and has been so ever since his arrival in the
Colony.

monstrate the working of the system—we cannot do better than offer an extract from a letter addressed to the Recorder of London, which was inserted in the *True Colonist* of the 6th November, 1835 :—

" I will use the freedom to relate for your information a case which was brought under my notice last week. I could select some hundreds of a similar tendency, in confirmation of the truths which I would impress on your mind. I select the present case, not more on account of some peculiar circumstances connected with it, than on account of the notoriety which some of the parties named had attained in England, rendering it easy for you to trace the history of the principal characters in the narrative, and thereby obtain an illustration of the grounds of qualification on which the " Prison Discipline" Authorities here select convicts to be vested with civil authority over the free inhabitants, without undergoing one hour of coercion or probation in the Colony. The convict, whose history I beg to introduce to your notice, is a man named George Madden, who was transported to this Colony for robbing the betting-room at Doncaster. This man was appointed a constable immediately upon his arrival, and soon afterwards was selected as a proper person to watch in the Treasury, where an extensive robbery was said to have been committed. I presume the authorities must have selected this Madden for this duty, in consequence of the recommendation from the Judge and Jury who sent him hither, *for his experience in matters of that description.* The robbers of the Treasury were never detected ; and poor Mr. Joscelyn Thomas, the Treasurer, had to bear the blame and the loss. I will not venture to insinuate that Madden had anything to do with the original robbery, the suspicion of which induced Mr. Thomas to apply to the Police for a watch ; but the selection of the robber of the Doncaster betting-room, and known only to the authorities in that character, to watch in the Colonial Treasury, for the purpose of detecting suspected purloiners, must appear to you a very strange specimen both of the Colonial police and prison discipline. Madden was next stationed with another convict constable at Roseneath Ferry, a very important pass on the great road between the two principal ports, about eight miles from Hobart Town, their principal duty being to examine all suspected persons, for the purpose of detecting runaways, and other improper characters. You will observe, that here were two convicts without immediate control, and trusted with this most important and responsible duty. Here Madden became acquainted with an old woman between seventy and eighty years of age, who had lived as house-keeper with an old settler named Austin, who on his death bequeathed her a life-interest upon certain pro-perty to the value of about £600 a-year. Madden being still a convict, without any remission of sentence, per-suaded the old woman to marry him ; and, incredible as it may appear, the Lieutenant Governor gave his sanction to this preposterous union.

" It may occur to you, that this sanction was given as a matter of course ; but I can assure you that such is not the case, for I have seen many instances where the Go-vernor has refused his sanction to the marriage of con-victs, where there was no desparity of years ; and it is a general rule that no female convict is allowed to marry before undergoing a certain period of probation in the Colony, besides being subject to other restrictions—many of which, with great moral benefit, could be dispensed with in most instances—but here, the Government al-lowed of this marriage, contrary to every principle of moral decency, and surely in direct violation of every in-tention of Government as regards transportation. It is evident that the object of Madden in marrying this old woman, was to obtain possession of her annuity, and thus place himself above the influence of prison disci-pline ; which the possession of money always will do in some way in this Colony. By this marriage, Madden became possessed of a beautiful residence, which any of His Majesty's Judges (who talk to convicts in England of the terrors of transportation) would consider a delightful and valuable acquisition ; besides an income sufficient to support him in the style of an English Squire. Some time after his marriage, he had the additional good luck of obtaining the farther indulgence of a ticket-of-leave, from the following cause :—A soldier, conveying Govern-ment dispatches, dropped his bag near to Madden's re-sidence ; Madden, who was travelling on the road behind him, picked it up, and proceeded with it to its destina-tion, pressing the horses of the respectable settlers on the road to expedite him on his journey. One very re-spectable emigrant settler (not being ready at a moment to comply with the requisition of the self-constituted convict courier,) Mr. Madden was pleased to complain to his friend, the Chief Police Magistrate, and I, from my own knowledge, can state, that it cost Mr. Armytage a good deal of trouble, and some journies to town, to save himself and his family from the ruinous conse-quences of being set down as a man obnoxious to the Government, because he had not *instantly* respected the commands of this privileged convict. And from what I know of this Government, I am convinced that nothing could have averted from Mr. Armytage and his family the certain destruction of all his prospects, as far as that could be effected by the act of a despotic Government, had it not been the previous good opinion which the Lieutenant Governor, from his own knowledge, had formed of Mr. Armytage.

" To you, Sir, it may appear strange that a convict should be allowed to exercise the power of locomotion so extensively as was done by Madden in this case. His exercising such authority, as demanding relays of horses *on his own requisition,* must appear incredible to you. And finding that such power in this Colony is vested in convicts, it may also appear strange to you, that the con-veying of the mail bag, under such circumstances, by a person placed in such a responsible situation, should be considered by the Authorities so decided a mark of re-formed character, as to entitle the individual to a remis-sion of sentence, contrary to what you have stated from

the Bench, to be the express provisions of an Act of
Parliament. If you were acquainted with the ways of
this Colony, it would occur to you, as it has done to
many respectable Colonists who have spoken to me on
the subject, to ask—' Did not Madden bribe the courier
to drop the bag, that he, Madden, might have the opportunity of performing this highly valued and richly
rewarded service ?' I would not myself venture to de-
tract from Madden's merit, by giving an opinion that
he did ; but I will relate to you a similar circumstance,
which came under my own observation; About eight
or nine years ago, when the Colonial Treasury was
robbed, the Government amongst other rewards, offered
a free pardon to any prisoner of the Crown, who would
discover where a certain sum of money, I think about
£1,000, was concealed. There was then a person in
Hobart Town, holding a ticket-of-leave, possessed of
very large property, who was very willing to pay almost
any price for a free pardon. It was suggested to this
individual by persons holding subordinate situations connected with the police, that he should hide the amount
of money for the discovery of which the reward was offered, near to a place where it had been represented that
certain persons on whom a suspicion was attempted to
be fixed, were represented to have been seen, under
questionable circumstances. From some cause, with
which it is not necessary to trouble you, this arrangement was discovered, and never put in execution. I
merely mention it here, to shew you what money may do
in defeating the law in this Colony. I will now return
to Madden's history.

" I left him in the second year of his transportation,
an influential conservator of the peace, somewhere about
his 30th year, with a wife about 80 ! a beautiful villa to
reside in, riding in his stanhope, with an income of £600
a year ! ! ! Still his fashionable character was not complete until he got a mistress, on the approved aristocratic
principle of crim. con. with his friend's wife. I presume
the name of Ikey Solomon has not yet been forgotten in

London. I believe it was some of the learned judges who preceded you in office, by whom Ikey Solomon and his wife were, at different times, sentenced to transportation. After a little time, Ikey and his wife were permitted to live together, with their family; and, as I am informed, lived very happily, until Ikey, for some common place breach of prison discipline, was removed for a time to the penal settlement at Port Arthur. He left his wife in possession of property to the amount of £360, and in the receipt of rents amounting to £3 or £4 per week. His wife, being assigned to her family during his absence, Mrs. Solomons became acquainted with Madden, who, in the Colonial phrase, openly keeps her as his mistress; and makes it his boast, that when he becomes free, which will be in the course of two years, he will take her home with him to England! These circumstances are all notorious, and I have no doubt well known to the Chief Police Magistrate. Indeed, while writing this letter, I have received intimation that some of the parties have been judicially before him *on matters connected with this case;* and I am also informed, that Ikey Solomons (who, since his return from Port Arthur has been removed into the interior, his wife remaining in Hobart Town) has, through two Magistrates, presented a petition and complaint to the Governor. I am in justice bound to state that I do not believe His Excellency has been at all acquainted with the true circumstances of the case which I have just related. Other circumstances have been related to me on what I consider unquestionable authority, to shew the influence which this man, Madden, possesses over the Chief Police Magistrate; but having been once before deceived by persons who gave me information relating to existing abuses, I am unwilling to incur the responsibility of repeating the whole of what has been stated to me on the subject. I will endeavour to get the facts authenticated, and then I will take the liberty of communicating them to you in another letter, or of publishing them in a newspaper article, which I will take care shall be forwarded to you. In the meantime I conceive that the specimen which I have brought under your notice (and it forms but one of many hundreds, which I could communicate) will be sufficient to convince yon of the truth of my motto, ' *Prison Discipline is all a lie.*' Now, Sir, when this man, Madden, returns to Doncaster, Newmarket, or Tattersal's—himself a living evidence of the truth of his statement—is it not evident, that the numerous candidates for transportation, who frequent these haunts of iniquity, will believe his account of transportation, and laugh at the Judge who attempts to describe it in terrific colours, when he awards them their sentence ? It is an invariable characteristic of the human mind, particularly amonst persons who are engaged in vicious pursuits, to set before them only the bright instances of success, which occur in a similar career. One such example as Madden's, will incite the emulation of a thousand juvenile candidates for transportation or the gallows—while the fate of hundreds of poor wretches, who are suffering misery under colonial sentences at Port Arthur, will be unheard of, or unheeded. In addition to the other circumstances, which I have above related, I have just been informed that Madden has got a wife in England! You may probably think it worth while, as an illustration of Prison Discipline, under transportation, to make some enquiry into this fact, among the others, which I have related for your information.—I have the honor to be, with great respect, your most obedient servant,

" GILBERT ROBERTSON.
" *Editor of the True Colonist.*"

We will give only one other example of the system. It is taken from the *Colonial Times* of the 22d December, 1835, and will serve to shew the villainy practised by the felon constabulary :—

" *To the Editor of the Colonial Times.*

" SIR.—I beg to forward the following statement for your perusal, I can vouch for its correctness, as I received it from Reardon himself before witnesses : should

you think proper to publish it of course you will make
what remarks you think proper :—

" CONFESSION OF REARDON.—*Wednesday Morning,
Dec.* 2, Constable Drinkwater, (a convict constable)
came to me, Daniel Reardon, (also a convict constable)
as I was standing at the Police Office door. He asked
me if I would go with him, I said where ? He answered
to bring Lanky Taylor down on a charge of murder.'
I asked him what murder he had committed, he told me
for shooting Capt. Sergeantson, and added ' we shall get
our free pardons for it.' I told him I was ordered to go
to Ross by Mr. Gray, he said, ' I can get you off going
there ;' accordingly he went to Mr. Gray and asked him
if I (Reardon) could go with him, which Mr. Gray consented to. Drinkwater afterwards came to me, and said
he had a scheme in his head by which we should
get our liberty, I said, what is that ? he said he would
tell me as he went along the road, as he should have a
better opportunity of talking. As we were going towards Mr. Willis's, he said ' Dan, if you will stick up
for me, I will do the same for you, and we shall be sure
to get our pardon ;' he said, ' I was the first person that
discovered a shot in Captain Sergeantson ; I lifted up the
corner of his waistcoat, and picked a piece of flesh off,
and squeezed it between my fingers, and a shot came
from it. I was up at Mr. Willis's house this morning,
I was talking to young Mr. Willis in his bed room. I
told him I was the first person who discovered a shot in
Captain Sergeantson. Mr. Willis said, the shot that
were found in him should be saved, and now our main
point is, after we take Lanky Taylor in charge and bring
him to Campbell Town, I will get some small shot which
will correspond with the shot that I have taken out of
Captain Sergeantson ; I know the sized shot I want, as
I took particular notice of what I had taken out of the
body.' I (Reardon) made answer, let us see Lanky
Taylor first, then we shall see what we can do. Before
we reached Lanky Taylor's hut he was in charge of two
constables, Duxberry and Edmonds ; he (Drinkwater)

stepped on one side and said, he had the main point—
the shot was the main point, and, using a vulgar oath,
said he would stick to him. We then went to Lanky
Taylor's hut, which was locked, and therefore did not
go in; we went into another hut (Innes's) about forty
yards distant, and had a drink of water, and from there
we returned to Campbell Town. All the way we went
along, Drinkwater was very pressing in getting me
(Reardon) to back his evidence; but of course I made
no promise, feeling,at the same time much hurt at his
supposing for a moment that I should be guilty of such
fiendish intentions. After arriving in Campbell Town,
Drinkwater said, ' are you willing to back my evidence?
If we get some small shot and swear we found it in
Lanky Taylor's hut, it is sure to hang him, and we
shall get our liberty.' I (Reardon) told him it is a foolish
thing altogether, as any person could see we had never
been in the hut; he remarked, ' *it was no d—d odds, as
Mr. Whitefoord would take his word for anything he said.*'
With that he wanted me to go into the constables' hut
and get a shot belt which was hanging on a nail; there
was some small shot in it, which would answer our purpose. I told him I did not like then, as there were so
many constables in the hut; he then went himself, and
when I found he could not be persuaded off, I went and
told Mr. Hughes, the gaoler of this place, the whole
circumstance, as the Chief Constable was away from
home. Mr. Hughes immediately recommended me to
keep in with him, as that would be the most likely way
of finding out his real intentions, so as they might be
brought to a bearing. A few minutes afterwards I saw
Drinkwater return from the constables' hut; he told me
he could not get the shot belt without being seen, at the
same time giving me a shilling to go to Mr. Emmett's
store, to get two pounds of the smallest shot he had;
I accordingly went, while I was there he stood on the
outside of the shop, and before I came out he had gone
away with Mr. Emmett's female servant; I'then went
and took the shot to Mr. Hughes, and told him these

are the shot I have just bought, and at the same time
gave him a part of them ; the remainder I gave to Drinkwater, which he said were very much like the shot
he had picked out of the body. Opposite the Caledonian
Inn I assisted in putting the shot into a small bag, he
said, ' d—n my eyes if we have not got our liberty now,
he can't get over us if you stick up for me ;' with that he
said, ' come along with me to Mr. Whitefoord, the Police
Magistrate : I did so ; he sent the cook into Mr. Whitefoord to say constables Drinkwater and Reardon wished
to speak to him.   Mr. Whitefoord came out, Drinkwater
told him we had been up after Lanky Taylor, and as
two constables had previously taken him in charge, we
did not think it necessary for us to come with him, so
we thought it advisable to search his hut, and in search-
ing his hut, myself and Reardon found this bag of shot,
planted on the top of the wall plate, which corresponds
with the shot I found in Captain Sergeantson's body.
He also said, Lanky Taylor* was sure to deny the shot,
and of course it will tend to confirm the suspicion.

" I at the same time beg to forward you another case
of a similar nature, I am renting a small farm within a
short distance of Mr. Willis, and I believe my reputation
has remained unimpeached at present ; but still, if
the present proceedings are suffered to continue, God
only knows how soon I may be placed at the bar of the
Supreme Court, and my life sacrificed by the system.

" CONFESSION OF REARDON.—In the month of October,
last, constable Drinkwater asked me (Reardon) whether
I would go with him, (as he was determined to obtain
his liberty) and get a sheep out of Mr. Willis's paddock,
and plant it on James Smith's premises, (he mentioned
either stable or stock-yard,) and afterwards lay an information at the Police Office, and get a search-warrant
and have his place searched, and then ' we will find this
sheep ; as there is a h— of a down on Smith, there is no

* The man's name is John Taylor, but is better known about
here as Lanky Taylor.

doubt but we shall get something for it.' I told him to go and do it himself.

" It was his intention to have got the sheep the night before, and have tied his legs and then to have hid it under some straw, and his excuse for absence would have been to the Chief Constable, that he had been in search of a runaway.

" I can assure you it is really awful to contemplate the state of the Police in this district, no person's life or property is safe under its present protection.

" Your obedient humble servant,

JAMES SMITH."

" *Campbell Town, Dec. 7th,* 1835."

It would, however, take whole volumes to record cases almost similar to the above, proving what is well known in the Colony, that prison discipline is *really nothing but a lie from the beginning to the end;* but we trust the above specimens will suffice to shew why it is *that crime is on the encrease in the Mother Country.*

With a knowledge of the vast fortunes prisoners have amassed—with a knowledge of the system maintained towards the transported thief, can it be wondered, that transportation is not regarded as a system of punishment? We frequently see by the English papers, that men commit crime purposely to be transported, nor can it be a matter of astonishment that such should be the case, when the convict can write to his friends in England and shew to them the advantages of being convicted and transported. With what exultation, with what feeling of ridicule must a man so acquainted with what transportation really is, appear before an English judge who is about to sentence him for banishment for life to a penal settlement; the man laughs in his sleeve when he hears the judge say, that transportation is worse than death, for probably just prior to his committing the offence for which he has been tried and found guilty, his own friend or relation has returned from transportation a man of wealth !

The grand difficulty then, is to discover a punishment

that can serve as a means of reformation, and as a means of punishment—*under the present system, it is impossible.* The Authorities may well laud themselves for their prison discipline system; hitherto none have been opposed to them, and for why ?—the truth must at length come out !. —because it has been the interest of the Colony to deceive the British Government. In these few words has hitherto consisted the secret of prison discipline. The Colonists' were in favor of the system, because they profitted by the labour of the men, and by the large Commissariat expenditure—which expenditure formerly remained in the Colony ; but a change has taken place—the labour of the convicts can be superceded by free emigrants, and as to the Commissariat expenditure, more than the whole of such expenditure is sent elsewhere for food, for the convicts and the free people. These are the reasons why people wish now to do away prison discipline, and transportation to this Colony. Nothing whatever is gained by the prisoners—on the contrary, the people are monstrously taxed for salaries for gaolers ; and they see the well fed convict take the food out of the mouth of the starving free emigrant. At the time of the completion of these pages, nearly the whole of the Colonists are of opinion, that prison discipline is but a mill-stone round the neck of this infant settlement ; and that the sooner the system is broken up, the better will it be for the British Government—for the people in England—for the Colonists—and for their rising generation. The few miserable exceptions to this opinion, are the paid scribes of the chief organizers of the system, and for want of argument in favor of their profitable and pet system, these men maliciously slander those opposed to them.

By one of the latest received English papers, we find that even the Chief Ruler of this Colony condescends to write in support of prison discipline ; but Colonel Arthur knew better than to publish his effusions in this Colony. In the *Weekly Despatch*, of the 2d of August last, we find an advertisement to the following effect :—

2 M

" COLONEL ARTHUR ON TRANSPORTATION.—Just received from Hobart Town, price 6s. boards—' *Defence of Transportation, in reply to the remarks of the Archbishop of Dublin, in his second Letter to Earl Grey—by Colonel George Arthur, Lieutenant Governor of Van Diemen's Land.*' Also, price 5s. by the same Author— ' *Observations upon Secondary Punishments, to which is added, a Letter upon the same subject—By the Archdeacon of New South Wales.*' Sold by George Cowie & Co., 31, Poultry.''

It was well known in Hobart Town some time since, that such a work was being printed by the Government printer, and that it was to be sent for publication to England, and with the utmost exertions we ourselves have made, we have not been able to obtain the sight of a single copy—every number being forwarded to England. We repeat, his Excellency knew better than to publish anything in this Colony, in favor of the system, because here it could be refuted, disproved, and easily shewn that prison discipline is, to use the words of a public speaker, " *but a lie, from the beginning to the end.*"*

Transportation, as far as the interests of this settlement are in consideration, is an evil in every sense of the word. We have shewn that in a pecuniary point of view nothing is to be gained, and every man must be aware that the system must be highly injurious to the rising generation. The child is educated in a gaol; its nurse takes it to witness the working of the twice convicted felons in the chain gangs, the same as that nurse in England would take the child to see a military parade. The infant is educated among convicts, and the clanking of the chains is a music to the ear—the cry of the unfortunate, suffering under the lash of the flagellator, it becomes accustomed to—in fact, its education is commenced, continued, and finished in a gaol ; all feelings of humanity, all those finer feelings, the

* James Hackett, Esq. made use of this expression at a public meeting, convened for the purpose of petitioning His Majesty to do away with transportation to this Colony.

foundation of intellectual society, are precluded from the
breast; the native youths are taught to have no feelings
save those natural to human nature, and the term friend-
ship is scarcely understood. This publication, however,
is intended as an exposure of prison discipline as it is,
nor shall we presume to point out to the Mother Country
what is most expedient to be done in order to punish and
diminish crime. We might, however, give our opinion
that there are several ways by which effectual discipline
might be maintained. The most profitable to the British
Government would be the management of the labour of
the men in the collieries, or in the mines, or in the cultivation of waste land—this plan would, we deem it,
be most profitable; but then the difficulty occurs, that men
so employed must be fed and clothed *as well, or better*,
than the soldier—then such a system would encrease
crime, for the *unwilling* agent (the convict,) must be provided for better than the *free agent*, (the soldier) you *must
drive* the one, whilst you *can lead* the other. If the penitentiary system were adopted on a similar plan to that of
Ohio, punishment then would be severe. Solitary punishment in cells has proved to be in this Colony the most effectual that can be inflicted on an offender. The naturally
bad character will undergo the first transportation from
England, and laugh at it; when here, he may be sent to
the chain-gangs, but he is there well fed and lightly
worked—it is no punishment to many; the first makes
him a confirmed villain, and the repetition of corporal
punishment but hardens the skin, and the lash in time
becomes but the torture of a few minutes; yet, put such
a man in a solitary cell—let his mind be unoccupied with
villainy and worldly affairs—the memory of the past becomes his punishment; place a Bible in the hands of a
man so situated, and if any thing will tend to reform
him, it is solitary confinement, with such a companion
as the Bible. If the British Government should adopt,
as it must do at no distant period, the penitentiary system,
the terms of the punishment will require an alteration,
and no better plan in our opinion can be adopted than

that of the American state, which has been found to work so beneficially. Should, however, the Home Government still persist in continuing the system of transportation to their infant British settlements, justice to the free Colonists demands that they should have some voice in the management of these outcasts ; and had the people of this Colony any control over the management of the prisoner population, Van Diemen's Land would not have been as it now is, well nigh a ruined impoverished country, with not food sufficient to feed the inhabitants, or exports adequate to the value of its importations.

We close these observations on prison discipline, fully trusting that they may be useful in furthering the grand end of decreasing crime, and that the exposures contained in these pages must have that effect there can be no doubt, that is, provided the British rulers place confidence in the assertions made. We defy, we boldly defy, any one to refute any thing that we have brought forward. Let any man that ever visited Van Diemen's Land within the last few years, who may be in England when this book arrives, be asked whether the whole of these assertions are not true, and we dare him to point out one line which is incorrect, scarcely to the very letter. We will conclude by repeating what we have over and over again said, that under the present system of transportation *millions of the poor of Great Britain would benefit themselves by transportation, for on arrival they have only to conduct themselves as men of good character do at home, and competence and happiness may be safely relied on ! It is the secondary punishment only that is severe—and that is terribly severe—but it is the same for the free as the bond.*

EDITOR OF THE COLONIAL TIMES.

Felons' Gaol, Hobart Town, Dec. 21, 1835.

Printed by H. Melville, Hobart Town, Van Diemen's Land.

For EU product safety concerns, contact us at Calle de José Abascal, 56–1°, 28003 Madrid, Spain or eugpsr@cambridge.org.